Practice Book

mheducation.com/prek-12

Send all inquiries to:
McGraw Hill
1325 Avenue of the Americas
New York, NY 10121

ISBN: 978-1-26-581298-0
MHID: 1-26-581298-5

Printed in the United States of America.

7 8 9 SMN 26 25 24 23 B

Contents

UNIT 1

Week 1

Week 2

Week 3

Week 4

Week 5

UNIT 2

Week 1

Week 2

Week 3

Week 4

Week 5

UNIT 3

Week 1

Week 2

Week 3

Week 4

Week 5

UNIT 4

Week 1

Week 2

Week 3

Week 4

Week 5

UNIT 5

Week 1

Week 2

Week 3

Week 4

Week 5

UNIT 6

Week 1

Week 2

Week 3

Week 4

Week 5

Name ____

- A **sentence** is a group of words that expresses a complete thought. It begins with a capital letter and ends with a punctuation mark.
- A **sentence fragment** is a group of words that does not express a complete thought: *Went to the store.*
- A **statement** is a sentence that tells something. It ends with a **period**.

  The playground is under construction.
- A **question** is a sentence that asks something. It ends with a **question mark**: *Have you visited the new zoo?*
- You can use **interrogatives** such as ***how, what, when, where, why,*** and ***who*** to ask questions.

Read each group of words. If it is a sentence, add the proper punctuation mark. If it is not a complete sentence, write *fragment*.

1. My mother walked into the kitchen ____________________

2. Looked out the window ____________________

3. One of my sisters ____________________

4. What were they looking at ____________________

5. A deer stood in the yard ____________________

6. Underneath the apple tree ____________________

7. We watched quietly ____________________

8. The deer looked up ____________________

9. Did it see us ____________________

In your writer's notebook, write about a time you saw an unusual animal. Check your work to make sure each sentence expresses a complete thought and ends with a period or question mark.

Name ______________________________

- A **command** is a sentence that tells or asks someone to do something. It ends with a **period** or an **exclamation point**: *Be careful.*
- An **exclamation** expresses strong feeling. It ends with an **exclamation point**: *Carrots are my favorite vegetable, too!*

Add the proper punctuation mark to the end of each sentence. Then write whether the sentence is a *statement, question, command,* or *exclamation*.

Walden Pond

Massachusetts

Boston

1. Where are the maps ____________
2. I had them in my backpack ____________
3. Help me look for them ____________
4. I'm so angry about losing them ____________

Reading/Writing Connection

Read this paragraph from "A Life in the Woods." Underline the exclamation. Then explain why you think the author used an exclamation in the paragraph.

Thoreau's move to the woods indicated that he liked to be alone. But Thoreau did not feel that way. "I have a great deal of company in my house," he wrote. Red squirrels awoke him by running up and down the sheer sides of his cabin. A snowshoe hare lived in the debris under his cabin, thumping against the floorboards. A sparrow once perched on his shoulder. Thoreau recorded these experiences in his journal. How easily writing came to him with the beauty of nature!

____

____

____

Name ______________________________

- A **sentence** is a group of words that expresses a complete thought. It begins with a capital letter and ends with a punctuation mark.
- A **statement** ends with a **period**. A **question** ends with a **question mark**. A **command** can end with a **period** or an **exclamation point**. An **exclamation** ends with an **exclamation point**.
- An **interjection** is a word or a phrase used to express strong emotion. It is followed by an exclamation point. *Wow! You won the race!*
- Use a comma in **direct address** with the name of the person. *Ali, thanks for the book. That's great, Susan!*

Rewrite each sentence by putting capital letters and punctuation marks where they belong.

1. did you hear about the elephants outside

____

2. they are coming to town for the fair

____

3. go over to the window to see them

____

4. this year's fair will be the best ever

____

5. where are you going Amir

____

6. hey don't touch that

____

Think of an exciting time in your life. Write a paragraph about this experience in your writer's notebook. Include one exclamation and one question in your paragraph. Edit and proofread your work.

Name ______________________________

- A **sentence** is a group of words that expresses a complete thought. A sentence begins with a capital letter and ends with a punctuation mark.
- A **statement** ends with a **period**. A **question** ends with a **question mark**. A **command** can end with a **period** or an **exclamation point**. An **exclamation** ends with an **exclamation point**.

Proofread the paragraph. On the lines below, correct any fragments or mistakes in sentence capitalization and punctuation.

last night my sister wanted to go to the movies? I wanted to go with her. what was stopping us. I had to finish my math homework first. The hardest problems ever. I asked my sister to wait for me? what do you think she did. She helped me figure out the answers. made it to the show just in time

HANDWRITING CONNECTION

Be sure to write legibly. Use proper cursive and remember to leave spaces between words.

____

____

____

____

____

____

____

____

____

____

____

Name ____

Read the student draft and look for any corrections that need to be made. Then choose the best answer to each question.

(1) My friends and I decide to race over by the new sports field. (2) How long will it take to run a mile (3) I take off my watch and give it to Amber. (4) She doesn't want to race. (5) "Use this watch to record our time."

(6) My new sneakers. (7) I cross the finish line first. (8) Angela calls out my time. (9) That is my best time ever!

(10) My heart is pounding like crazy. (11) But I think I can do even better. (12) decide to race again (13) Is everybody ready?

1. Which of the following is a fragment?

A Sentence 1

B Sentence 3

C Sentence 6

D Sentence 13

2. What change, if any, should be made in sentence 2?

F Insert a period after ***mile***

G Insert a question mark after ***mile***

H Insert an exclamation point after ***mile***

J Make no change

3. Which of the following is a command?

A Sentence 4

B Sentence 5

C Sentence 7

D Sentence 12

4. Which of the following is an exclamation?

F Sentence 8

G Sentence 9

H Sentence 10

J Sentence 11

5. What is the **BEST** way to write sentence 12?

A Decide to race again.

B Decide to race again!

C We decide to race again?

D We decide to race again.

Name ______________________________

Fold back the paper along the dotted line. Use the blanks to write each word as it is read aloud. When you finish the test, unfold the paper. Use the list at the right to correct any spelling mistakes.

1. ________	**1.** jut
2. ________	**2.** nick
3. ________	**3.** tenth
4. ________	**4.** shrug
5. ________	**5.** stuff
6. ________	**6.** sense
7. ________	**7.** damp
8. ________	**8.** cot
9. ________	**9.** fling
10. ________	**10.** notch
11. ________	**11.** gush
12. ________	**12.** scan
13. ________	**13.** batch
14. ________	**14.** rough
15. ________	**15.** stump
16. ________	**16.** tough
17. ________	**17.** laugh
18. ________	**18.** guess
19. ________	**19.** lead
20. ________	**20.** dove
Review Words	**21.** ________	**21.** past
	22. ________	**22.** dock
	23. ________	**23.** plum
Challenge Words	**24.** ________	**24.** cinch
	25. ________	**25.** blond

Name ____

Short vowel sounds can be spelled in different ways.

- ***Shrug*** and ***tough*** each have the short *u* sound.
- ***Tense*** and ***head*** each have the short *e* sound.
- ***Scan*** and ***laugh*** each have the short *a* sound.

Read each spelling word out loud. Listen carefully to each short vowel sound.

SPELLING TIP

The short *i* sound is usually spelled using the vowel *i* (*skin, fin, twin*). Similarly, the short *o* sound is usually spelled using the vowel *o* (*lot, stop, plot*).

Read the words in the box. Place each word in the column that describes its short vowel sound. Underline the letter or letters that make the sound.

jut	stuff	fling	batch	laugh
nick	sense	notch	rough	guess
tenth	damp	gush	stump	lead
shrug	cot	scan	tough	dove

short *a* as in *plan*	**short *e* as in *hen***	**short *i* as in *spin***	**short *o* as in *lot***	**short *u* as in *fun***

Look through this week's readings for more words to sort. Create a word sort for a partner in your writer's notebook.

Name ______________________________

Short vowel sounds can be spelled in different ways.

- ***Shrug*** and ***tough*** each have the short *u* sound.
- ***Tense*** and ***head*** each have the short *e* sound.
- ***Scan*** and ***laugh*** each have the short *a* sound.

Read each spelling word out loud. Listen carefully to each short vowel sound.

SPELLING TIP

The short *i* sound is usually spelled using the vowel *i* (*skin, fin, twin*). Similarly, the short *o* sound is usually spelled using the vowel *o* (*lot, stop, plot*).

Read the words in the box. Place each word in the column that describes its short vowel sound. Underline the letter or letters that make the sound.

jut	stuff	fling	track	lamp
nick	bend	sock	rough	pest
tent	damp	gush	stump	lead
sung	cot	scan	rust	dove

short *a* as in *plan*	short *e* as in *hen*	short *i* as in *spin*	short *o* as in *lot*	short *u* as in *fun*

Look through this week's readings for more words to sort. Create a word sort for a partner in your writer's notebook.

Name ____

A. Read the words in the box. Place each word in the column that describes its short vowel sound. Underline the letter or letters that make the sound. If a word has two different short vowel sounds, include it in both columns and underline the appropriate vowel sound.

credit	slumped	fling	batches	blond
summit	sense	notch	roughly	guess
tenth	stranded	gushing	stump	lead
shrugged	orally	scanned	tougher	dove

short *a*	short *e*	short *i*	short *o*	short *u*

B. Circle the word with the short vowel sound to complete the sentence.

1. My brother is the ______________ chef at the restaurant.

worst head only

2. Do you enjoy going to ______________ each year?

school work camp

3. Please ______________ the door before you leave for the day.

close lock seal

Look through this week's readings for more words to sort. Create a word sort for a partner in your writer's notebook.

Name ______________________________

jut	stuff	fling	batch	laugh
nick	sense	notch	rough	guess
tenth	damp	gush	stump	lead
shrug	cot	scan	tough	dove

A. Write the spelling word that matches each definition below.

1. throw with force ______________
2. slightly wet ______________
3. stick out ______________
4. material in pencils ______________
5. pour out ______________
6. cooing bird ______________
7. raise one's shoulders ______________
8. v-shaped cut ______________
9. small, narrow bed ______________
10. look through quickly ______________
11. estimate or prediction ______________
12. next after ninth ______________

B. Write the spelling word that best completes each analogy.

13. *Quiet* is to *noisy* as *gentle* is to ______________.
14. *Scratch* is to *scrape* as *cut* is to ______________.
15. *Cry* is to *weep* as ______________ is to *chuckle*.
16. *Fill* is to *empty* as ______________ is to *unpack*.
17. *Bunch* is to ______________ as *couple* is to pair.
18. *Foolishness* is to ______________ as *weak* is to *strong*.
19. ______________ is to *tree* as *part* is to *whole*.
20. ______________ is to *easy* as *puzzling* is to *simple*.

Name ____

Underline the six misspelled words in the paragraphs below. Write the words correctly on the lines.

This morning Mrs. Clark said that our class would be part of a school spelling bee. Then she gave us a list of practice spelling words to scane. All the words were hard, but the teenth word was really tugh. "I'm going to need some help!" I cried.

After class, Mario came up to me. "Don't worry," he said. "I'll give you some tips. First, if a word doesn't make sens, ask to hear it again. Then if you're still not sure, take a gess. You just might be right. And don't worry if your hands feel dampe. Everyone gets a little nervous at these things!"

1. ____________________ **4.** ____________________

2. ____________________ **5.** ____________________

3. ____________________ **6.** ____________________

Writing Connection

Write a passage for a story about another school contest. Use at least four spelling words in your writing. As you check your work, remember the different spelling patterns for the short vowel sounds.

____

____

____

____

____

____

____

____

____

____

____

Name ______________________________

Remember

Words with the same short vowel sound are not always spelled the same way. The short *a* sound, **/a/**, can be spelled with the letters *a* or *au*. The short *e* sound, **/e/**, can be spelled with *e*, *ea*, or *ue*. The short *u* sound, **/u/**, can be spelled with *u*, *ou*, or *o* (as in *love*).

A. Underline the spelling word in each row that rhymes with the word in bold type. Write the spelling word on the line.

1. **lamp**	limp	damp	long	________
2. **snug**	brag	snip	shrug	________
3. **hatch**	head	which	batch	________
4. **spring**	fling	sprang	song	________
5. **shut**	shun	jut	chat	________
6. **plan**	land	plot	scan	________
7. **bread**	lead	brim	rest	________
8. **tense**	test	sense	tans	________
9. **rush**	trash	gush	rind	________
10. **clump**	stamp	clang	stump	________
11. **gruff**	stuff	grand	off	________
12. **love**	land	have	dove	________
13. **slot**	flat	cot	slam	________
14. **brick**	nick	rack	brim	________
15. **blotch**	notch	black	match	________

B. Write these spelling words on the lines in reverse alphabetical order: ***tenth, rough, tough, laugh, guess.***

16. ________________ **19.** ________________

17. ________________ **20.** ________________

18. ________________

Name ______________________________

Expand your vocabulary by adding or removing inflectional endings, prefixes, or suffixes to a base word to create different forms of a word.

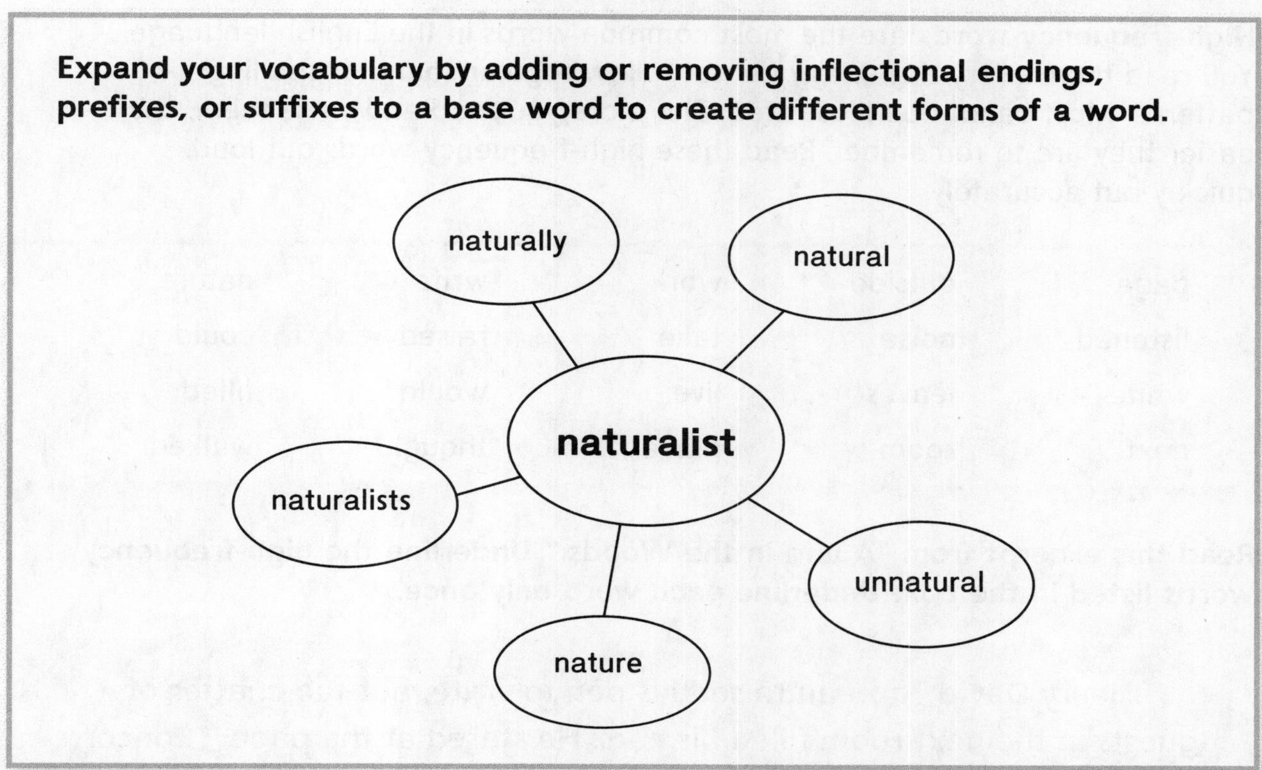

Write as many related words in the web as you can. Use a dictionary to help you.

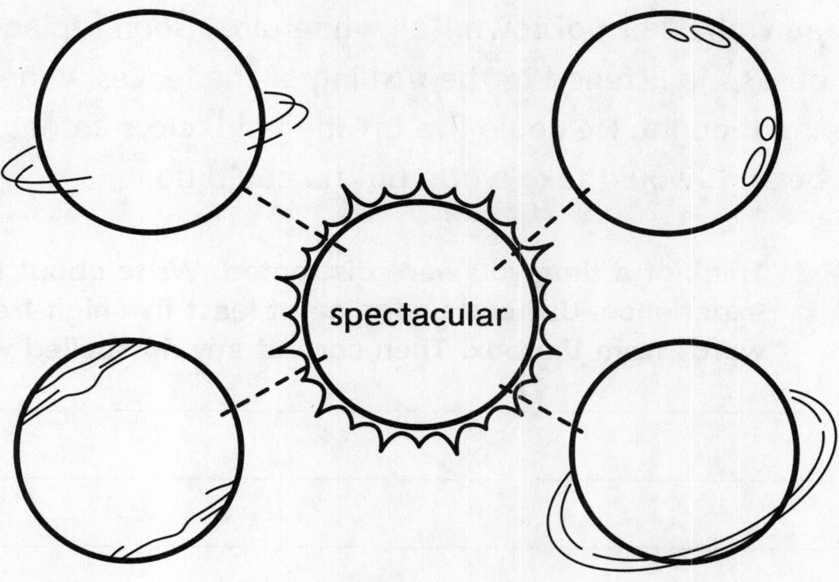

Name ____

High-frequency words are the most common words in the English language. You read them every day. Many do not follow regular sound or spelling patterns. Most cannot be illustrated. The more you read and write them, the easier they are to remember. Read these high-frequency words out loud, quickly but accurately.

page	outside	work	write	nature
listened	noise	take	raised	could
white	leaves	live	would	filled
next	room	place	thought	walked

Read this excerpt from "A Life in the Woods." Underline the high-frequency words listed in the box. Underline each word only once.

Henry David Thoreau raised his pen to write, but the chatter of guests in the next room filled his ears. He stared at the page. "Concord, 1841" was all that he had written. How would he write a book with such noise in his family's house? Thoreau headed outside, shutting the door with emphasis. He would have to find a place of his own.

Thoreau walked out of town. Tall white pines soon replaced the painted houses. He listened to the rustling of the leaves. What if I could stay here, he thought. He could live off the land, close to nature, and begin his book. It would take work, but he could do it.

Reading/Writing Connection

Think of a time you were distracted. Write about this experience. Use and underline at least five high-frequency words from the box. Then correct any misspelled words.

____

____

____

____

____

Name ____

- The **simple subject** is the main noun or pronoun that names the subject of the sentence: *The friendly dog waited for her owner.*
- The **complete subject** includes all of the words that tell whom or what the sentence is about: *The friendly dog waited for her owner.*
- The **simple predicate** is the verb that tells exactly what the subject does or is: *The friendly dog waited for her owner.*
- The **complete predicate** is the verb and all of the words that tell what the subject does or is: *The friendly dog waited for her owner.*

After each sentence, write whether the underlined word or words are the *simple subject, complete subject, simple predicate,* or *complete predicate*.

1. My grandparents live on an island. ____________________
2. A small boat travels there every hour. ____________________
3. The entire ride takes about twenty minutes. ____________________
4. My family visits them every summer. ____________________
5. We stay for about a week. ____________________

Talk to a parent or another trusted adult about somewhere you would like to visit. Then write a paragraph about why you want to visit there. Underline two simple subjects and two simple predicates in your writing.

____

____

____

____

____

____

____

Name ______________________________

- A **compound subject** is two or more subjects that share the same verb. The subjects are usually joined by a conjunction such as *and* or *or.*

  My brother and sister are still asleep.

- A **compound predicate** contains two or more predicates that have the same subject.

  The journalist reads and writes a lot.

- Compound subjects and predicates can use **coordinating conjunctions** (*and, or*) or **correlative conjunctions** (*either/or, neither/nor*).

  Neither Julia nor her friend participated.

  Can you either clear the table or do the dishes?

After each sentence, write whether the underlined words are a *compound subject* or *compound predicate*. Circle each conjunction.

1. The students arrive and sit down. ______________
2. The teacher and the students open their books. ______________
3. The boy or the girl will read first. ______________
4. The class listens and takes notes. ______________
5. Either the teacher or the principal will speak. ______________
6. The cafeteria opens and serves lunch. ______________
7. The students neither rush nor hurry. ______________
8. The pizza and the pasta are the favorite meals. ______________

Use the sentences as a model. In your writer's notebook, write about your favorite or least favorite cafeteria food. Use at least one compound subject and one compound predicate in your writing. Underline each one. Check to make sure that you use conjunctions correctly.

Name ____

- Use **commas** to separate three or more words or phrases in a series: *We packed water, trail mix, and a map.*
- **Appositives** are words or groups of words that identify and usually follow a noun. They are often set off by commas:

  Iggy, our lizard, sat still all day. I will visit Chicago, my hometown.
- Commas set off introductory words, such as *yes, no,* and *thank you.*

Write each sentence correctly by putting commas where they belong.

1. The school's sports teams include baseball soccer and football.

   ____
2. Mr. Tompkins our coach will lead the team onto the field.

   ____
3. Yes we love it when people sing the school song!

   ____
4. Our team got the ball raced down the field and scored a goal.

   ____

Reading/Writing Connection

Read this excerpt from "At Home in the Desert." Underline the appositive. Then write two sentences about a place you want to see in person. Include one appositive. If necessary, set it off using commas.

The desert landscape enchanted O'Keeffe, the daughter of dairy farmers.

____

____

____

Name ____

- Compound subjects and predicates can use **coordinating conjunctions** (*and, or*) or **correlative conjunctions** (*either/or, neither/nor*).
- Use **commas** to separate three or more words or phrases in a series.
- Use commas to set off **introductory words** in sentences.
- **Appositives** are often set off by commas.

Proofread the paragraph. On the lines below, correct mistakes in the use of conjunctions and commas.

My parents have hired a tutor to help me with my reading writing and spelling. I also need help with science my hardest subject. The tutor, and I work together most afternoons. We meet almost every Monday, Tuesday, and, Thursday. She and I either read together, or work on my homework problems. No she doesn't give me the answers. My teachers parents and tutor are all proud of my progress.

HANDWRITING CONNECTION

As you write in cursive, make sure that your letters are slanted in the same way and joined with the correct stroke.

____

____

____

____

____

____

____

____

____

____

____

Name ____

Read the paragraph and choose the best answer to each question.

(1) The squirrels and the chipmunks are gathering acorns. (2) The daylight hours grow shorter every day. (3) Leaves fall and cover the ground. (4) Our town's farmers harvest their crops. (5) Many of them pick and sell corn in town.

1. Which sentence has a compound subject?
   - **A** Sentence 1
   - **B** Sentence 2
   - **C** Sentence 3
   - **D** Sentence 4

2. Which sentences have a compound predicate?
   - **F** Sentences 1 and 3
   - **G** Sentences 1 and 4
   - **H** Sentences 3 and 5
   - **J** Sentences 4 and 5

3. What is the simple predicate in sentence 2?
   - **A** The daylight hours
   - **B** hours
   - **C** grow
   - **D** grow shorter every day

4. What is the simple subject in sentence 4?
   - **F** Our town's farmers
   - **G** farmers
   - **H** harvest
   - **J** harvest their crops

Read the student draft and look for any corrections that need to be made. Then choose the best answer to each question.

(1) My father prepares a salad soup, and main dish for dinner. (2) My aunt, uncle, and cousins will join us this evening. (3) Yes, the house will be filled with all kinds of activity! (4) My mother, a trained musician will play the piano. (5) Should I sing along?

5. What change, if any, should be made to sentence 1?
   - **A** Insert a comma after ***father***
   - **B** Insert a comma after ***salad***
   - **C** Insert a comma after ***dish***
   - **D** Make no change

6. What change, if any, should be made to sentence 4?
   - **F** Delete the comma after ***mother***
   - **G** Insert a comma after ***trained***
   - **H** Insert a comma after ***musician***
   - **J** Make no change

Name ____________________

Fold back the paper along the dotted line. Use the blanks to write each word as it is read aloud. When you finish the test, unfold the paper. Use the list at the right to correct any spelling mistakes.

	1. ________	**1.** paste
	2. ________	**2.** bride
	3. ________	**3.** shave
	4. ________	**4.** spice
	5. ________	**5.** greed
	6. ________	**6.** plead
	7. ________	**7.** greet
	8. ________	**8.** heap
	9. ________	**9.** paid
	10. ________	**10.** coach
	11. ________	**11.** theme
	12. ________	**12.** type
	13. ________	**13.** oak
	14. ________	**14.** growth
	15. ________	**15.** yolk
	16. ________	**16.** folks
	17. ________	**17.** aim
	18. ________	**18.** prey
	19. ________	**19.** tow
	20. ________	**20.** grind
Review Words	**21.** ________	**21.** tenth
	22. ________	**22.** damp
	23. ________	**23.** stuff
Challenge Words	**24.** ________	**24.** decay
	25. ________	**25.** lifetime

Name ______________________________

Long vowel sounds can have different spellings.

- Long *a*, or **/ā/**: ***they, stain, steak, cake***
- Long *e*, or **/ē/**: ***see, clean, shield, compete, neither***
- Long *i*, or **/ī/**: ***five, kind, fry, invite, sight***
- Long *o*, or **/ō/**: ***pole, throw, soak***

When a word ends with a silent *e*, as in *compete*, the vowel before the consonant will have a long sound. This is called a **vowel-consonant-*e* (VC*e*)** pattern. The VC*e* pattern must stay in the same syllable: *com/pete*.

DECODING WORDS

Divide the word *invite* into syllables: *in/vite*. Blend the sounds of the first syllable, *in-*. Use what you know about syllable types. Blend the sounds of the next syllable, *-vite*. Now say the syllables together to decode the word.

Read the words in the box. Place each word in the column that describes its long vowel sound. Underline the letter or letters that make the sound.

paste	greed	paid	oak	aim
bride	plead	coach	growth	prey
shave	greet	theme	yolk	tow
spice	heap	type	folks	grind

long ***a*** as in ***table***	long ***e*** as in ***seen***	long ***i*** as in ***find***	long ***o*** as in ***snow***

Look through this week's readings for more words to sort. Create a word sort in your writer's notebook. Some of the words you find will have more than one syllable. Try to include at least one VC*e* syllable in each column. Then read each word out loud to a partner.

Name ______________________________

Long vowel sounds can have different spellings.

- Long *a*, or **/ā/**: ***they, stain, steak, cake***
- Long *e*, or **/ē/**: ***see, clean, shield, compete, neither***
- Long *i*, or **/ī/**: ***five, kind, fry, invite, sight***
- Long *o*, or **/ō/**: ***pole, throw, soak***

When a word ends with a silent *e*, as in *compete*, the vowel before the consonant will have a long sound. This is called a **vowel-consonant-*e* (VC*e*)** pattern. The VC*e* pattern must stay in the same syllable: *com/pete*.

DECODING WORDS

Divide the word *invite* into syllables: *in/vite*. Blend the sounds of the first syllable, *in-*. Use what you know about syllable types. Blend the sounds of the next syllable, *-vite*. Now say the syllables together to decode the word.

Read the words in the box. Place each word in the column that describes its long vowel sound. Underline the letter or letters that make the sound.

paste	leash	paid	oak	gain
bride	heat	coach	grow	gray
shave	greet	theme	spoke	tow
spine	see	pride	folks	grind

long *a* as in *table*	long *e* as in *seen*	long *i* as in *find*	long *o* as in *snow*

Look through this week's readings for more words to sort. Create a word sort in your writer's notebook. Some of the words you find have more than one syllable. Try to include at least one VC*e* syllable in each column. Then say each word out loud to a partner.

Name ____

A. Read the words in the box. Place each word in the column that describes its long vowel sound. Underline the letter or letters that make the sound. If a word has two different long vowel sounds, include it in both columns and underline the appropriate vowel sound.

paste	greedy	tornado	crowing	claimed
wildcats	pleaded	coach	growth	prey
parade	succeed	theme	yolk	tow
spices	heap	lifetime	upbeat	grinding

long *a* as in *table*	long *e* as in *clean*	long *i* as in *find*	long *o* as in *snow*

B. Compare the words *great* and *pleaded*. How are the words similar? How are they different?

____

____

____

____

____

Look through this week's readings for more words to sort. Create a word sort in your writer's notebook. Some of the words you find will be multisyllabic words. Try to include at least one VC*e* syllable in each column. Then read each word out loud to a partner.

Name ______________________________

paste	greed	paid	oak	aim
bride	plead	coach	growth	prey
shave	greet	theme	yolk	tow
spice	heap	type	folks	grind

A. Write the spelling word that matches each definition below.

1. part of an egg ______________

2. to stick down ______________

3. pull something ______________

4. to beg ______________

5. a kind of tree ______________

6. to crush ______________

7. to say hello ______________

8. an overall idea ______________

9. a kind or sort ______________

10. people ______________

11. a mound or pile ______________

12. to cut off hair ______________

B. Write the spelling word that best completes each sentence.

13. He was not ______________ for his work at the food bank.

14. My friend's dad is our soccer ______________.

15. Owls hunt their ______________ at night.

16. The cook added lots of ______________ to the chili.

17. She did not ______________, so she missed the basket.

18. The ______________ carried a bunch of white flowers.

19. I saw lots of ______________ on the new plants.

20. His ______________ made him a selfish person.

Name ______________________________

Underline the six misspelled words in the paragraphs below. Write the words correctly on the lines.

Each year the students in Kendra's class raised money for a class trip. This year they came up with a new theem: "Breakfast at School." The students decided they would cook breakfast for friends and family, and they would grete their guests wearing funny pajamas! Any money that foaks gave them would go for the trip.

Kendra helped cook the eggs. She made sure each yowk was just right. Her friend Sam walked around to grinde fresh pepper for the guests. Other kids helped serve and clean up. They made a good team, and they were payed enough to go on the trip.

1. ______________________ 4. ______________________

2. ______________________ 5. ______________________

3. ______________________ 6. ______________________

Writing Connection

Write a passage for a story about another fundraising event. Use at least four spelling words in your writing. As you check your work, remember the different spelling patterns for the long vowel sounds.

____

____

____

____

____

____

____

____

____

Name ______________________________

Remember

- Long *a*, or **/ā/**, can be spelled *a_e, ai,* or *ay* (***parade, laid, stay***).
- Long *e*, or **/ē/**, can be spelled *ee, ea,* or *e_e* (***seed, read, these***).
- Long *i*, or **/ī/**, can be spelled *i, y,* or *i_e* (***find, try, ripe***).
- Long *o*, or **/ō/**, can be spelled *o, oa, ow,* or *o_e* (***so, road, row, stone***).
- **VC*e* syllables** have a long vowel, a consonant, and a silent final *e* (***divide***). Blend the sounds of the word *divide* together: /di/ /vīd/.

A. Read each bold word out loud. Then underline the spelling word in each row that rhymes with the bold word. Write the spelling word on the line.

1. **tide**	bride	raid	pipe	________
2. **seat**	met	greet	hedge	________
3. **wave**	shave	dive	have	________
4. **go**	too	tow	good	________
5. **game**	gram	aim	room	________
6. **need**	plead	head	beam	________
7. **mind**	grin	mice	grind	________
8. **joke**	oat	lake	oak	________
9. **nice**	spice	speck	nose	________
10. **ripe**	twine	type	rope	________
11. **dream**	them	keep	theme	________
12. **trade**	pail	paid	mad	________
13. **taste**	paste	tank	stall	________
14. **deep**	damp	heap	step	________
15. **bead**	great	grand	greed	________

B. Write the words in alphabetical order: *coach, yolk, folks, prey, growth*.

16. ________________ 19. ________________

17. ________________ 20. ________________

18. ________________

Name ____

A **prefix** is a word part that is added to the beginning of a word. It changes the root's meaning. Knowing the prefix of an unfamiliar word can help you figure out its meaning.

- The prefix ***super-*** means **over** or **above**. The word ***supervise*** means **watch over** or **oversee**.
- The prefix ***trans-*** means **across** or **move between**. The word ***transport*** means **carry or move from one place to another**.

Use your knowledge of the prefixes *super-* and *trans-* to determine the definition of each word.

Prefix	Word	Definition
super-	superstar	
	superstore	
trans-	transfer	
	transatlantic	

COLLABORATE **How many more words can you and a partner make with the prefixes *super-* and *trans-*? Write your words and a brief definition on the lines below. Use a dictionary to help you.**

____

____

____

____

____

____

Name ______________________________

Like **homonyms, homographs** are words that are spelled the same but have different meanings. Unlike homonyms, homographs sometimes have different pronunciations. For example, *bear* can mean "a large, heavy mammal." *Bear* can also mean "to carry."

Read each passage from "At Home in the Desert." Underline context clues that help you figure out the meaning of each word in bold. Write the word's meaning and then your own sentence using the word in the same way.

1. Georgia O'Keeffe always thought of herself as an artist. By 1928, the **rest** of the world did, too.

____

____

2. New York City and her family's summer home had been the source of ideas for almost ten years, but now those ideas were drying up. O'Keeffe felt like she needed a **change** of scenery.

____

____

3. She had visited New Mexico in 1917 with her sister, and the wide open **space** had thrilled her.

____

____

4. She spent hours just watching the sky change. The clear **light** made her feel as if she could see for the first time.

____

____

5. It was the start of a pattern she would keep up for almost twenty years. Each **spring**, she traveled to New Mexico to paint.

____

____

Name ____

- A **simple sentence** expresses one complete thought.
  The family went out to celebrate.
- A **compound sentence** contains two simple sentences joined by a comma and a conjunction.
  The streets were empty, and the sun was setting.
- A **conjunction** joins words or groups of words. The words *and, but,* and *or* are conjunctions.

Write whether each sentence below is *simple* or *compound*. Circle each conjunction.

1. The dog barked, and I woke up instantly. ____________
2. Something was tapping on my window. ____________
3. Was the noise real, or was I still dreaming? ____________
4. A bright light flashed, and I ducked under the covers. ____________
5. The dog ran down into the basement. ____________
6. I called the dog, but he wouldn't come back. ____________
7. My parents heard me and came into my room. ____________
8. They both seemed calm, or I would have kept hiding. ____________
9. There were strong winds, and a power line had snapped. ____________
10. That explained both the tapping and the bright light. ____________

In your writer's notebook, write a short passage about a strange noise you hear. Make sure to include simple and compound sentences. Underline the conjunctions. After you finish, check your work. Did you use commas correctly in the compound sentences?

Name ______________________________

- A **run-on sentence** joins together two or more sentences without the proper conjunctions and punctuation.

  I went to the store it was closed. (incorrect)

- You can correct a run-on sentence by rewriting it as a compound sentence.

  I went to the store, but it was closed.

- A **comma splice** joins together two sentences with only a comma: *We ran a race, I won first place.* To avoid this error, make sure the compound sentence has a conjunction: *We ran a race, and I won first place.*

Correct each run-on sentence or comma splice by writing it as a compound sentence.

1. The official waves the flag the race begins!

____

2. The driver pushes the gas pedal the car zooms forward.

____

3. She speeds around the curve she doesn't lose control.

____

4. The race is soon over, she wins another trophy.

____

Writing Connection

Think about a competition you would like to enter. Write three compound sentences about why you want to enter the competition. As you edit and proofread your work, make sure to avoid run-on sentences, comma splices, and fragments.

____

____

____

____

____

Name ______________________________

- When you correct a run-on sentence, use a **comma** before *and, but,* or *or* if the subject in each independent clause is different.
- To coordinate two closely related sentences without using a conjunction, use a **semicolon** (;).

Correct each run-on sentence. Use commas and semicolons where needed.

1. There is a concert this weekend we want to go.

____

2. It's our favorite band we have to see them!

____

3. Will you buy the tickets should I pick them up?

____

4. We want seats in the front row they are sold out.

____

5. Our seats are in the back we'll have a great time anyway.

____

Reading/Writing Connection

Read this excerpt from "A Fresh Idea." Underline the compound sentences and circle the conjunctions. Then explain whether or not you think the author could have used semicolons instead of conjunctions.

This was the first spring since his wife had died, and Mali saw the sadness on his face. Then she had an idea.

Mali cleared her throat, and Mr. Taylor looked up. Mali decided to walk over to the fence.

____

____

____

Name ____

- Rewrite a run-on sentence as two separate sentences or as a **compound sentence**. To coordinate two closely related sentences without using a **conjunction**, use a **semicolon** (;).
- When you correct a run-on sentence, use a **comma** before *and, but,* and *or* if the subject in each independent clause is different.

Proofread the paragraph. On the lines below, correct any run-on sentences or mistakes in punctuation.

My father drove up to the theater I stepped out of the car. Would it be a great show? Or would I forget all my lines? I had rehearsed every night, my sister had even helped with the hardest scenes. Would all that hard work pay off? Some people waited at the ticket booth others were going inside. My stomach felt like it was full of frogs but I headed to the stage door anyway. The cast was counting on me I couldn't let them down.

COMMON ERRORS

Connecting two sentences using a comma is an error called a **comma splice**. Either add a conjunction after the comma or replace the comma with a semicolon. If the two ideas are not closely related, split the ideas into two **simple sentences**.

____

____

____

____

____

____

____

____

Name ________________________________

Read the paragraph and choose the best answer to each question.

(1) The volunteers arrived at the shelter after the storm. (2) People brought food and passed out bottled water. (3) I wanted to help, but my parents had other plans. (4) They wanted to check on our grandparents first. (5) Should I join them, or should they go on their own?

1. Which sentence is a compound sentence?

A Sentence 1

B Sentence 2

C Sentence 3

D Sentence 4

2. What word in sentence 5 is a conjunction?

F them

G or

H they

J on

Read the student draft and look for any corrections that need to be made. Then choose the best answer to each question.

(1) The mayor told us his plan we listened very carefully. (2) We all wanted to help, but some of us were needed elsewhere. (3) A news van arrived. (4) Soon after, a camera crew came into the shelter. (5) They took many pictures, and a reporter spoke to the mayor. (6) We were in good shape, there was still much to do.

3. What is the **BEST** way to revise sentence 1?

A The mayor told us his plan, we listened very carefully.

B The mayor told us his plan, but we listened very carefully.

C The mayor told us his plan, and we listened very carefully.

D No revision is needed.

4. Sentence 6 contains a comma splice. What is the **BEST** way to write this sentence?

F We were in good shape but there was still much to do.

G We were in good shape, but there was still much to do.

H We were in good shape and there was still much to do.

J We were in good shape, and there was still much to do.

Name ____________________

Fold back the paper along the dotted line. Use the blanks to write each word as it is read aloud. When you finish the test, unfold the paper. Use the list at the right to correct any spelling mistakes.

	1. ____________	1. tuna
	2. ____________	2. duty
	3. ____________	3. lose
	4. ____________	4. few
	5. ____________	5. doom
	6. ____________	6. bamboo
	7. ____________	7. soothe
	8. ____________	8. crooks
	9. ____________	9. hoof
	10. ____________	10. hooks
	11. ____________	11. booth
	12. ____________	12. handbook
	13. ____________	13. prove
	14. ____________	14. mute
	15. ____________	15. amuse
	16. ____________	16. plume
	17. ____________	17. hue
	18. ____________	18. view
	19. ____________	19. bruise
	20. ____________	20. union
Review Words	21. ____________	21. theme
	22. ____________	22. coach
	23. ____________	23. bride
Challenge Words	24. ____________	24. strewn
	25. ____________	25. accuse

Name ______________________________

The spelling words in the box have three different *u* sounds. Each of these sounds can have different spellings.

- **/ū/: *cute, unit, argue, review***
- **/u̇/: *shook, could***
- **/ü/: *tune, flu, move, tooth, suit***

SPELLING TIP

The same spelling pattern can have different sounds. For example, the patterns *u* and *u_e* can have either the sound /ū/ (*human, huge*) or the sound /ü/ (*tuba, tube*).

Write the words that contain the matching sound and spelling pattern.

tuna	doom	hoof	prove	hue
duty	bamboo	hooks	mute	view
lose	soothe	booth	amuse	bruise
few	crooks	handbook	plume	union

/ū/ spelled *u_e*
1. ____________
2. ____________

/ū/ spelled *ue*
3. ____________

/ū/ spelled *u*
4. ____________

/ū/ spelled *ew*
5. ____________
6. ____________

/u̇/ spelled *oo*
7. ____________
8. ____________
9. ____________
10. ____________

/ü/ spelled *u*
11. ____________
12. ____________

/ü/ spelled *o_e*
13. ____________
14. ____________

/ü/ spelled *u_e*
15. ____________

/ü/ spelled *oo*
16. ____________
17. ____________
18. ____________
19. ____________

/ü/ spelled *ui*
20. ____________

Look through this week's readings for more words to sort. Read the words aloud. Then create a word sort for a partner in your writer's notebook.

Name ____________________

The spelling words in the box have three different *u* sounds. Each of these sounds can have different spellings.

- **/ū/**: ***cute, unit, review, argue***
- **/u̇/**: ***shook, could***
- **/ü/**: ***tune, flu, move, tooth, suit***

SPELLING TIP

The same spelling pattern can have different sounds. For example, the pattern *u* can have either the sound /ū/ (*human*) or the sound /ü/ (*tuba*). The pattern *oo* can have either the sound /u̇/ (*book*) or the sound /ü/ (*room*).

Write the words that contain the matching sound and spelling pattern.

tuna	choose	hood	prove	due
duty	soon	hooks	mute	view
lose	troop	booth	amuse	bruise
few	look	handbook	cartoon	music

/ū/ spelled *u_e*

1. ____________________
2. ____________________

/ū/ spelled *u*

3. ____________________

/ū/ spelled *ew*

4. ____________________
5. ____________________

/u̇/ spelled *oo*

6. ____________________
7. ____________________
8. ____________________
9. ____________________

/ü/ spelled *u*

10. ____________________
11. ____________________

/ü/ spelled *ue*

12. ____________________

/ü/ spelled *o_e*

13. ____________________
14. ____________________

/ü/ spelled *oo*

15. ____________________
16. ____________________
17. ____________________
18. ____________________
19. ____________________

/ü/ spelled *ui*

20. ____________________

Look through this week's readings for more words to sort. Read the words aloud. Then create a word sort for a partner in your writer's notebook.

Name ______________________________

A. Write the words that contain the matching sound and spelling pattern.

spruce	soothe	statue	proved	hue
reduce	bamboo	woodpeckers	recruit	viewpoint
toucan	accuse	deciduous	raccoon	bruise
chewy	crooks	handbook	plume	union

/ū/ spelled *u_e*

1. ______________

/ū/ spelled *ue*

2. ______________

3. ______________

/ū/ spelled *u*

4. ______________

/ū/ spelled *ew*

5. ______________

/ù/ spelled *oo*

6. ______________

7. ______________

8. ______________

/ü/ spelled *u*

9. ______________

/ü/ spelled *o_e*

10. ______________

/ü/ spelled *ou*

11. ______________

/ü/ spelled *ew*

12. ______________

/ü/ spelled *u_e*

13. ______________

14. ______________

15. ______________

/ü/ spelled *oo*

16. ______________

17. ______________

18. ______________

/ü/ spelled *ui*

19. ______________

20. ______________

B. Compare the words *union* and *deciduous*. How are the words similar? How are they different?

____

____

____

____

Look through this week's readings for more words to sort. Read the words aloud. Then create a word sort for a partner in your writer's notebook.

Name ______________________________

tuna	doom	hoof	prove	hue
duty	bamboo	hooks	mute	view
lose	soothe	booth	amuse	bruise
few	crooks	handbook	plume	union

A. Write the spelling word that has the same, or almost the same, meaning.

1. tint ____________________

2. job ____________________

3. to misplace ____________________

4. entertain ____________________

5. a guide ____________________

6. hangers ____________________

7. to show ____________________

8. robbers ____________________

B. Write the spelling word that best completes each sentence.

9. Do you know ____________________ can grow as tall as a tree?

10. Gentle rocking may ____________________ a crying baby.

11. The horse raised a ____________________ and began to prance.

12. The new building will block our ____________________ of the park.

13. A ____________________ of smoke rose from the chimney.

14. For a special treat, Dad cooked ____________________ on the grill.

15. I have a dark blue ____________________ on my arm.

16. A ____________________ of pet owners called for a new dog park.

17. The old, broken piano has been ____________________ for years.

18. Only a ____________________ people showed up for the meeting.

19. I got a stuffed toy from a ____________________ at the fair.

20. An injury will ____________________ his hopes of winning the race.

Name ____

Underline the six misspelled words in the paragraphs below. Write the words correctly on the lines.

Our yard has only a fue trees. The big maple tree in back is my favorite. I have a good vyoo of it from my room. In the fall, the maple leaves change color. They turn a beautiful red huwe.

Before long, the tree begins to loos its colorful leaves. I often amews myself by collecting maple leaves to display in my room. It is also my dooty to rake the leaves. I don't mind. Spending time under my tree is not a problem.

1. ____________________ **4.** ____________________

2. ____________________ **5.** ____________________

3. ____________________ **6.** ____________________

Writing Connection

Write about something that you've seen or done in nature. Use at least four spelling words in your writing.

____

____

____

____

____

____

____

____

____

____

____

____

Name ______________________________

Remember

Words with the same *u* sound can be spelled in different ways.

- **/ū/** as in ***menu, nephew, value, use***
- **/u̇/** as in ***took, should***
- **/ü/** as in ***rule, truth, remove, mood, fruit***

A. Read each word in bold type aloud. Then underline the spelling word in each row that rhymes with the bold word. Write the spelling word on the line.

1. **choose**	close	lost	lose	______
2. **tooth**	booth	both	cloth	______
3. **cue**	would	hue	plug	______
4. **cute**	cut	clung	mute	______
5. **fruity**	duty	funny	dusty	______
6. **few**	foot	view	fudge	______
7. **gloom**	plume	glum	put	______
8. **smooth**	root	soothe	should	______
9. **brooks**	bunks	moods	hooks	______
10. **cruise**	bruise	bush	crunch	______
11. **move**	dove	prove	moose	______
12. **room**	rush	dome	doom	______
13. **woof**	won	hoof	half	______
14. **pew**	pool	flow	few	______
15. **confuse**	among	amuse	compare	______

B. Write these spelling words in reverse alphabetical order: *tuna, bamboo, handbook, union, crooks.*

16. ______________________ 19. ______________________

17. ______________________ 20. ______________________

18. ______________________

Name ______________________________

Expand your vocabulary by adding or removing inflectional endings, prefixes, or suffixes to a base word to create different forms of a word.

profit

profits

profitability

profitable

nonprofit

unprofitable

Write as many related words on the flower petals as you can. Use a dictionary to help you.

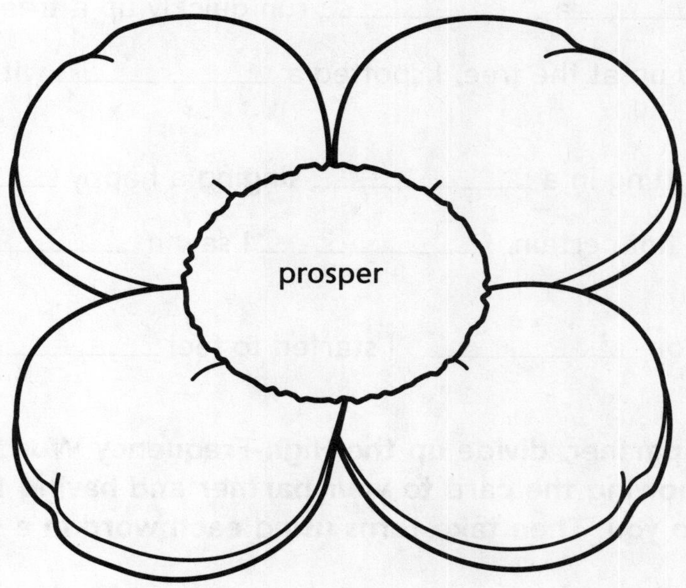

Name ____

High-frequency words are the most common words in the English language. Many of these words do not follow regular sound or spelling patterns. The more you read and write them, the easier they are to remember. Read these high-frequency words aloud.

different	nest	noticed	believe
brown	approached	squirrel	temperature
narrow	rabbit	beautiful	song
exhausted	families	robin	amount

Complete the sentences using the high-frequency words listed in the box. Make sure to check your answers for spelling. Then read the sentences aloud.

1. The ______________ was warm, so I took a walk along a ______________ path in the forest.
2. Other ______________ were there enjoying the ______________ weather, too.
3. I saw many ______________ animals during a short ______________ of time.
4. First I ______________ a ______________ run quickly up a tree.
5. When I looked up at the tree, I spotted a ______________ with ______________ feathers.
6. The bird was sitting in a ______________ singing a happy ______________.
7. Although I am not certain, I ______________ I saw a ______________ hop into a bush.
8. As the afternoon ______________, I started to feel ______________.

With a partner, divide up the High-Frequency Word Cards. Take turns showing the card to your partner and having them read it aloud to you. Then take turns using each word in a sentence.

Name ____

- **Coordinating conjunctions** join two words or word groups of the same grammatical rank or importance (e.g., two nouns, two independent clauses). The coordinating conjunctions *and, but,* and *or* can be used to create a **compound sentence.**
- **Subordinating conjunctions** tell where, when, why, or how. Some common subordinating conjunctions are *after, although, as, because, before, if, since, so that, until, when,* and *while.*

Circle the conjunction in each sentence below. Then write whether it is a *coordinating* or *subordinating* conjunction.

1. My dad looks great when he wears a suit. ____________________
2. I gave him a tie, and he wears it all the time. ____________________
3. It's his favorite because it reminds him of home. ____________________
4. He took me to work one day, and I sat at his desk. ____________________
5. I wanted to attend a meeting, but he wouldn't let me. ____________________
6. I stayed in his office until he returned. ____________________
7. After we ate lunch, we went on a sales call. ____________________
8. He gave me some advice before we went inside. ____________________
9. I had to be polite, or he would send me to the car. ____________________
10. We both laughed since I'm always polite to everyone. ____________________

In your writer's notebook, write about a favorite piece of clothing. Include at least four different coordinating or subordinating conjunctions. Circle the coordinating conjunctions and underline the subordinating conjunctions. Edit and proofread your work.

Name ______________________________

- A **complex sentence** is a sentence that contains two related clauses joined by a conjunction other than *and, but,* or *or.*
- **Subordinating conjunctions** can appear at the beginning or in the middle of a complex sentence. If the sentence begins with a subordinating conjunction, a comma should follow the last word of the **dependent,** or **subordinate, clause**.

  When spring is near, I hang a new bird feeder in the tree.

  I hang a new bird feeder in the tree when spring is near.

Use the subordinating conjunction in parentheses to combine the two simple sentences into one complex sentence.

1. I was worried about the dog. She wouldn't eat. (because)

   ____

2. I told my mother. We called the vet. (after)

   ____

3. The dog walked away. We were still on the phone. (while)

   ____

4. She was acting suspicious. I followed her. (since)

   ____

5. I was concerned. She led me to a bag of food she had eaten. (until)

   ____

Read this sentence from "A Fresh Idea." Circle the subordinating conjunction. Then write a new sentence about a peaceful place. Include a different subordinating conjunction.

After they got home, Mali headed out to her backyard swing to think.

____

____

Name ______________________________

- Use a **comma** before a conjunction to separate two independent clauses in compound sentences.

  It's supposed to rain today, but I don't see any clouds in the sky.

- In complex sentences that begin with dependent clauses, add a **comma** after the last word of the dependent clause.

  After the soccer game ended, we heard thunder.

Use the conjunction in parentheses to create one compound or complex sentence from the two simple sentences. Use commas correctly.

1. My grandmother called. No one was home. (but)

   ____

2. I had a spare moment. I called her back. (when)

   ____

3. She had exciting news. I begged her to tell me. (and)

   ____

4. She wanted it to be a surprise. I promised to keep it secret. (because)

   ____

5. She had won a contest. She was taking us all on a trip! (since)

   ____

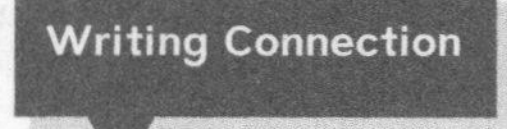

Write two complex sentences about a time you were surprised. Check to make sure that you use commas correctly.

____

____

____

____

Name ______________________________

- Use a **comma** before a conjunction to separate two independent clauses in compound sentences.
- In complex sentences that begin with dependent clauses, add a **comma** after the last word of the dependent clause.

Proofread the paragraph. On the lines below, correct mistakes in the use of conjunctions and commas.

When he heard a branch snap behind him. The explorer stopped in his tracks. Since he had just discovered the ruins he didn't know where to turn. Something made a growling noise and his heart raced with fear. Before he could turn around someone spoke. "I told you to stay at the camp but here you are," said his father. "Now we'll have to wait here, until the others return."

Name ____

Read the student draft and look for any corrections that need to be made. Then choose the best answer to each question.

(1) Since I am so tall, I signed up for basketball. (2) I played well until I hurt my ankle. (3) The doctor checked the ankle, but the injury wasn't serious. (4) If it feels better by Monday, I can practice. (5) I will sit on the bench during games, since it heals.

(6) At our next game, I watched the game from the sidelines. (7) The buzzer sounded. (8) The players jumped for the ball. (9) We passed the ball so that our fastest player could run with it. (10) The second half began. (11) We were leading the game. (12) We were about to score again. (13) The time ran out.

1. What is the **BEST** way to revise sentence 5?
   - **A** I will sit on the bench during games while it heals.
   - **B** I will sit on the bench during games, but it heals.
   - **C** I will sit on the bench during games because it heals.
   - **D** I will sit on the bench during games if it heals.

2. What is the **BEST** way to combine sentences 7 and 8?
   - **F** The buzzer sounded, the players jumped for the ball.
   - **G** As the buzzer sounded, the players jumped for the ball.
   - **H** The buzzer sounded, since the players jumped for the ball.
   - **J** Until the buzzer sounded, the players jumped for the ball.

3. What is the **BEST** way to combine sentences 10 and 11?
   - **A** If the second half began, we were leading the game.
   - **B** Because the second half began, we were leading the game.
   - **C** The second half began we were leading the game.
   - **D** When the second half began, we were leading the game.

4. What is the **BEST** way to combine sentences 12 and 13?
   - **F** We were about to score again, so that the time ran out.
   - **G** We were about to score again when the time ran out.
   - **H** We were about to score again since the time ran out.
   - **J** We were about to score again, because the time ran out.

Name ______________________________

Fold back the paper along the dotted line. Use the blanks to write each word as it is read aloud. When you finish the test, unfold the paper. Use the list at the right to correct any spelling mistakes.

	1. ________	**1. heart**
	2. ________	**2. swear**
	3. ________	**3. aboard**
	4. ________	**4. squares**
	5. ________	**5. swore**
	6. ________	**6. chart**
	7. ________	**7. scorn**
	8. ________	**8. starch**
	9. ________	**9. source**
	10. ________	**10. fare**
	11. ________	**11. barge**
	12. ________	**12. thorn**
	13. ________	**13. marsh**
	14. ________	**14. force**
	15. ________	**15. harsh**
	16. ________	**16. scarce**
	17. ________	**17. coarse**
	18. ________	**18. flare**
	19. ________	**19. course**
	20. ________	**20. sword**
Review Words	**21.** ________	**21. soothe**
	22. ________	**22. prove**
	23. ________	**23. hoof**
Challenge Words	**24.** ________	**24. uproar**
	25. ________	**25. gorge**

Name ____________________

A vowel followed by the letter *r* is called an ***r*-controlled vowel**. Three *r*-controlled vowel sounds are /är/, /âr/, and /ôr/. These sounds can have different spellings.

- ***/är/*: *darken, hearth***
- ***/âr/*: *unfair, stare, pear, scary***
- ***/ôr/*: *torn, roar, store, pour***

DECODING WORDS

The first syllable in *unfair* is a closed syllable pronounced /un/. The second syllable /fâr/ has the *r*-controlled vowel spelling *ar* pronounced /âr/. These vowel spellings must stay in the same syllable. Blend the sounds and read the word: *un/fair.*

Write the spelling words that contain the matching sound and spelling pattern.

heart	swore	source	marsh	coarse
swear	chart	fare	force	flare
aboard	scorn	barge	harsh	course
squares	starch	thorn	scarce	sword

/är/ spelled *ar*

1. ____________
2. ____________
3. ____________
4. ____________
5. ____________

/är/ spelled *ear*

6. ____________

/âr/ spelled *are*

7. ____________
8. ____________
9. ____________

/âr/ spelled *ar*

10. ____________

/âr/ spelled *ear*

11. ____________

/ôr/ spelled *our*

12. ____________
13. ____________

/ôr/ spelled *or*

14. ____________
15. ____________
16. ____________
17. ____________

/ôr/ spelled *ore*

18. ____________

/ôr/ spelled *oar*

19. ____________
20. ____________

Look through your writer's notebook for more words to sort. Create a word sort in your writer's notebook. Include at least two multisyllabic words. Then read each word aloud.

Name ______________________________

A vowel followed by the letter *r* is called an ***r*-controlled vowel**. Three *r*-controlled vowel sounds are /är/, /âr/, and /ôr/. These sounds can have different spellings.

- **/är/: darken, hearth**
- **/âr/: *unfair, stare, pear, scary***
- **/ôr/: *torn, roar, store, pour***

DECODING WORDS

The first syllable in *unfair* is a closed syllable pronounced /un/. The second syllable /fâr/ has the *r*-controlled vowel spelling *ar* pronounced /âr/. These vowel spellings must stay in the same syllable. Blend the sounds and read the word: *un/fair*.

Write the spelling words that contain the matching sound and spelling pattern.

heart	swore	your	marsh	board
bear	chart	stare	force	hairy
roar	scorn	carve	harsh	course
squares	starch	thorn	scare	rare

/är/ spelled *ar*

1. ____________
2. ____________
3. ____________
4. ____________
5. ____________

/är/ spelled *ear*

6. ____________

/âr/ spelled *are*

7. ____________
8. ____________
9. ____________
10. ____________

/âr/ spelled *air*

11. ____________

/âr/ spelled *ear*

12. ____________

/ôr/ spelled *our*

13. ____________
14. ____________

/ôr/ spelled *or*

15. ____________
16. ____________
17. ____________

/ôr/ spelled *ore*

18. ____________

/ôr/ spelled *oar*

19. ____________
20. ____________

Look through your writer's notebook for more words to sort. Create a word sort in your writer's notebook. Include at least two multisyllabic words. Then read each word aloud.

Name ______________________________

A. Write the spelling words that contain the matching sound and spelling pattern.

heartfelt	explore	source	parched	coarse
swear	uproar	fare	forcefully	flared
aboard	scorned	barge	sparsely	portfolios
awareness	starch	escorts	scarce	sword

/är/ spelled *ar*

1. ______________
2. ______________
3. ______________
4. ______________

/är/ spelled *ear*

5. ______________

/âr/ spelled *are*

6. ______________
7. ______________
8. ______________

/âr/ spelled *ar*

9. ______________

/âr/ spelled *ear*

10. ______________

/ôr/ spelled *our*

11. ______________

/ôr/ spelled *or*

12. ______________
13. ______________
14. ______________
15. ______________
16. ______________

/ôr/ spelled *ore*

17. ______________

/ôr/ spelled *oar*

18. ______________
19. ______________
20. ______________

B. Compare the words *swear* and *sweat*. How are the words similar? How are they different?

____

____

____

____

Look through your writer's notebook for more words to sort. Create a word sort in your writer's notebook. Include at least two multisyllabic words. Then read each word aloud.

Name ______________________________

heart	swore	source	marsh	coarse
swear	chart	fare	force	flare
aboard	scorn	barge	harsh	course
squares	starch	thorn	scarce	sword

A. Write the spelling word that belongs with each set of words below.

1. circles, triangles, ______________

2. blade, club, ______________

3. rose, leaf, ______________

4. diagram, graph, ______________

5. dislike, belittle, ______________

6. rare, limited, ______________

7. flash, flame, ______________

8. brain, lung, ______________

9. cruel, bleak, ______________

10. power, strength, ______________

B. Write the spelling word that best completes each sentence.

11. Only sailors are allowed ______________ the ship.

12. Many wetland animals live in the ______________.

13. She ______________ she would tell the truth at the trial.

14. You can use ______________ to make clothes stiff.

15. He likes to ______________ in and disturb my studying.

16. Do you ______________ you will keep my secret?

17. I used ______________ sandpaper to smooth the wood.

18. The ______________ of the river is a small lake.

19. Taxi ______________ from here to the airport is expensive.

20. The ______________ of our trip takes us through Kansas.

Name ______________________________

Underline the six misspelled words in the paragraphs below. Write the words correctly on the lines. Then read each spelling word out loud.

I was abored a plane headed for America. The corse of my flight would take me from my homeland to a strange new country. My hart was heavy because I was leaving my parents and sister behind.

So much surprised me when I reached America. One sores of delight was the food. Food wasn't scares in my home country. We had plenty. But there was such as variety in America! I sware there were vegetables and fruits that I had never seen or tasted before.

1. ______________ 4. ______________

2. ______________ 5. ______________

3. ______________ 6. ______________

Writing Connection

Write about an important or memorable event in your own life. Use at least four spelling words in your writing. As you check your work, remember the different spelling patterns for *r*-controlled vowels.

Name ______________________________

Remember

Words with the same *r*-controlled vowel sound can be spelled in different ways.

- ***/är/*** as in ***market, hearth***
- ***/âr/*** as in ***stairs, spare, wearing***
- ***/ôr/*** as in ***worn, boar, chore, four***

Read each example out loud. Listen carefully to the vowel sounds.

heart	swore	source	marsh	coarse
swear	chart	fare	force	flare
aboard	scorn	barge	harsh	course
squares	starch	thorn	scarce	sword

A. Fill in the missing letters to form a spelling word. Then write it on the line.

1. m __ __ sh ____________

2. h __ __ __ t ____________

3. f __ __ __ ____________

4. st __ __ ch ____________

5. th __ __ n ____________

6. ab __ __ __ d ____________

7. squ __ __ __ s ____________

8. f __ __ ce ____________

9. sw __ __ d ____________

10. b __ __ ge ____________

11. h __ __ sh ____________

12. sc __ __ n ____________

13. sc __ __ ce ____________

14. fl __ __ __ ____________

15. s __ __ __ ce ____________

B. Write these words on the lines in alphabetical order. Alphabetize them to the third letter. ***swore, coarse, chart, swear, course***

16. ____________

17. ____________

18. ____________

19. ____________

20. ____________

Name ______________________________

A **suffix** is a word part that is added to the end of a word. It changes the word's meaning or part of speech. Knowing the suffix of an unfamiliar word can help you figure out its meaning.

Example: The suffix *-ive* means **having the nature of**.

- The verb ***act*** means **do or perform something**. Adding the suffix ***-ive*** changes the word to ***active***, an adjective. ***Active*** means **full of energy, action, or movement**.

Example: The suffix *-logy* means **science, study of**, or **body of knowledge**.

- The root ***geo-*** means ***earth***. The word ***geology*** means **the study of earth and rocks**.

Use your knowledge of the suffixes *-ive* and *-logy* to determine the definition of each word.

Suffix	Word	Definition
-ive	expensive	
	inventive	
-logy	zoology	
	biology	

How many more words can you and a partner make with the suffixes *-ive* and *-logy*? Write your words and a brief definition on the lines below. Use a dictionary to help you.

____

____

____

____

____

____

Name ____

Read each passage from "Building Our Community." Underline the context clues that help you figure out the meaning of each word in bold. Then use your background knowledge, or what you know already, along with the clues to write the word's meaning on the line.

1. "Clara and I were hoping you could take us to the mall next weekend." "Sorry, Gabriela, I'm working at the hospital this weekend and next weekend," she said. "Well, then maybe Carlos could take us?" I **persisted**, not ready to give up.

   ____

2. "Second, Carlos is **volunteering** next weekend. He's giving time to help build a home for a family that needs one."

   ____

3. "Now, if Juan can get shirts for us, we need something to put on them. Any ideas?" After a lively **debate**, we settled on the slogan "Building Our Community." Clara, our class artist, agreed to draw the design.

   ____

4. "Now, if Juan can get shirts for us, we need something to put on them. Any ideas?" After a lively debate, we settled on the **slogan** "Building Our Community." Clara, our class artist, agreed to draw the design.

   ____

5. I **beamed** with pride as I handed over the gift card. Mom and Mr. Pham had both been right. Everyone can do something, and together we can accomplish something great.

   ____

Name ______________________________

- A **sentence fragment** is a group of words that does not express a complete thought.

  Went to the park. (missing a subject)

  Kayla is getting better, but she. (missing a predicate)

- A **run-on sentence** joins together two or more sentences incorrectly.

  Diego wanted to see the movie it was playing down the street.

After each sentence, write whether it is a *sentence fragment* or a *run-on sentence*.

1. She was born in 1945 she grew up in Maine. ______________
2. Took long walks along the shore. ______________
3. After moving from place to place. ______________
4. She studied biology it interested her. ______________
5. One of her most trusted friends. ______________
6. She went to Africa she made a huge discovery. ______________
7. The scientist wrote a book it was very popular. ______________
8. Made a movie about her adventures. ______________
9. Winning all sorts of prizes and awards. ______________
10. Now she lives in Iowa, and her family. ______________

Imagine the scientist described above. In your writer's notebook, write a short fictional passage about her life in Iowa. Include simple and compound sentences. Then check your work. Did you avoid sentence fragments and run-on sentences?

Name ______________________________

- Correct a **sentence fragment** by adding a **subject**, a **predicate**, or both.

  Went to the park. (fragment) *We went to the park.*

  Kayla is getting better, but she. (fragment)

  Kayla is getting better, but she needs more practice.

- You can correct a **run-on sentence** by rewriting it as two separate sentences or as one **compound** or **complex sentence**.

  Diego will see the movie it is playing down the street. (run-on)

  Diego will see the movie. It is playing down the street.

  Diego will see the movie, and it is playing down the street.

  Diego will see the movie because it is playing down the street.

After each group of words, write the strategy that would best correct each sentence error. Write *add a subject, add a predicate, add both subject and predicate, add a comma,* or *make a compound sentence.*

1. My new model airplane kit. ______________________
2. Inside the box on the kitchen table. ______________________
3. Found all kinds of small parts and pieces. ______________________
4. There were no instructions I didn't know what to do. ______________________
5. When Mom offered to help me I happily accepted. ______________________

Read this excerpt from "Building Our Community." Underline two lines of dialogue that are fragments. Then rewrite the fragments as complete sentences.

"Great idea!" Mr. Pham said enthusiastically. "Now, if Juan can get shirts for us, we need something to put on them. Any ideas?"

____

____

Name ______________________________

- You can correct a **run-on sentence** or **comma splice** by rewriting it as two separate sentences using **periods** or as either a compound or complex sentence. You can also use a **semicolon** to connect the sentences.

  The blossoms looked beautiful, they were in full bloom. (comma splice)

  The blossoms looked beautiful; they were in full bloom.
- Use a **comma** before a conjunction to separate two independent clauses in compound sentences.
- In complex sentences that begin with dependent clauses, add a **comma** after the last word of the dependent clause.

Rewrite each run-on sentence or comma splice as instructed in the parentheses. Add any conjunctions or punctuation that is needed.

1. The ship left at dawn it sailed to the east. (separate sentences)

   ____

2. The voyage would be long there was plenty of food. (compound sentence)

   ____

3. We spotted a storm ahead we tried to sail around it. (complex sentence)

   ____

4. I stayed in my cabin the crew raced about. (complex sentence)

   ____

5. We found calm seas, it was clear sailing all the way home. (separate sentences)

   ____

Write a short passage about a voyage to outer space. Include simple, compound, and complex sentences. Then edit and proofread your work. Did you avoid run-on sentences, comma splices, and fragments?

Name ______________________________

- You can correct a **run-on sentence** by rewriting it as a **compound sentence,** a **complex sentence,** or two separate sentences.
- Use a **comma** before a conjunction to separate two independent clauses in compound sentences.
- In complex sentences that begin with dependent clauses, add a **comma** after the last word of the dependent clause.

  After the rain stopped, I saw a rainbow in the sky.

Proofread the paragraph. On the lines below, correct any fragments and run-on sentences. Use commas and conjunctions properly where needed.

Our class would like to make a movie we need a few supplies. A video camera and a computer. My classmates are writing a script I will help out with costumes. Wants to be an actor some day. All of us work on the scenery. We want the room to look like a cave we will make rocks and boulders out of plaster. Sheets with streaks of black and gray. We will work all week long I can't wait for opening night of our blockbuster movie!

____

____

____

____

____

____

____

____

____

____

Name ____________________

Read the student draft and look for any corrections that need to be made. Then choose the best answer to each question.

(1) All different kinds of jobs. (2) Firefighters often face danger they have to be alert. (3) Medicine is complicated doctors must study hard. (4) Teaching can be exhausting it is often rewarding. (5) My father is a teacher, and he.

1. What is the **BEST** way to revise sentence 1?
   - **A** I read a book about all different kinds of jobs.
   - **B** I read a book; about all different kinds of jobs.
   - **C** All kinds of jobs.
   - **D** I read a book, it was about all different kinds of jobs.

2. What is the **BEST** way to revise sentence 2?
   - **F** Firefighters often face danger, they have to be alert.
   - **G** They have to be alert. Firefighters often face danger.
   - **H** Firefighters often face danger; they have to be alert.
   - **J** Firefighters often face danger have to be alert.

3. What is the **BEST** way to revise sentence 3?
   - **A** Medicine is complicated, doctors must study hard.
   - **B** Because medicine is complicated, doctors must study hard.
   - **C** Medicine is complicated, but doctors must study hard.
   - **D** Although medicine is complicated, doctors must study hard.

4. What is the **BEST** way to revise sentence 4?
   - **F** Teaching can be exhausting; it is rewarding.
   - **G** Teaching can be exhausting, often rewarding.
   - **H** Until teaching can be exhausting, it is often rewarding.
   - **J** Teaching can be exhausting, but it is often rewarding.

5. What is the BEST way to revise sentence 5?
   - **A** My father is a teacher, he loves his job.
   - **B** My father is a teacher, loves his job.
   - **C** My father is a teacher, and he loves.
   - **D** My father is a teacher, and he loves his job.

Name ______________________________

Fold back the paper along the dotted line. Use the blanks to write each word as it is read aloud. When you finish the test, unfold the paper. Use the list at the right to correct any spelling mistakes.

	1. ________	**1.** word
	2. ________	**2.** nerve
	3. ________	**3.** squirt
	4. ________	**4.** verse
	5. ________	**5.** surf
	6. ________	**6.** lurk
	7. ________	**7.** work
	8. ________	**8.** stern
	9. ________	**9.** spurts
	10. ________	**10.** lurch
	11. ________	**11.** blurt
	12. ________	**12.** thirst
	13. ________	**13.** spur
	14. ________	**14.** learning
	15. ________	**15.** shirt
	16. ________	**16.** midterm
	17. ________	**17.** return
	18. ________	**18.** squirm
	19. ________	**19.** swerve
	20. ________	**20.** yearns
Review Words	**21.** ________	**21.** aboard
	22. ________	**22.** barge
	23. ________	**23.** scarce
Challenge Words	**24.** ________	**24.** merging
	25. ________	**25.** rehearse

Name ____________________

When the vowels *e, i,* and *u* are followed by *r,* the sound is usually **/ûr/**. You will find this ***r*-controlled vowel** in words like ***her, dirt,*** and ***fur***.

Read the following words out loud: ***verb, winter, sir, firm, blur, turnip***. Notice how the same sound can be spelled with different vowels.

You will sometimes hear **/ûr/** when an *r* follows the vowel *o* or the vowels *ea*: ***worth, heard***.

DECODING WORDS

When a vowel is followed by *r,* the sounds change and the vowel and *r* stay in the same syllable. In *turnip,* the *u* is followed by an *r.* Blend the sounds, keeping /ûr/ together: /tûr/ /nip/.

Write the spelling words that contain the matching spelling pattern.

word	surf	spurts	spur	return
nerve	lurk	lurch	learning	squirm
squirt	work	blurt	shirt	swerve
verse	stern	thirst	midterm	yearns

/ûr/ spelled *er*

1. ____________________
2. ____________________
3. ____________________
4. ____________________
5. ____________________

/ûr/ spelled *ir*

6. ____________________
7. ____________________
8. ____________________
9. ____________________

/ûr/ spelled *ear*

10. ____________________
11. ____________________

/ûr/ spelled *ur*

12. ____________________
13. ____________________
14. ____________________
15. ____________________
16. ____________________
17. ____________________
18. ____________________

/ûr/ spelled *or*

19. ____________________
20. ____________________

Look through this week's readings for more words to sort. Create a word sort in your writer's notebook. Include at least two multisyllabic words. Then read each word out loud.

Name ______________________________

When the vowels *e, i,* and *u* are followed by *r,* the sound is usually **/ûr/**. You will find this ***r*-controlled vowel** in words like ***her, dirt,*** and ***fur***.

Read the following words out loud: ***winter, serve, fir, sir, blur, turnip***. Notice how the same sound can be spelled with different vowels.

You will sometimes hear **/ûr/** when an *r* follows the vowel *o* or the vowels *ea*: ***worth, heard***.

DECODING WORDS

When a vowel is followed by *r,* the sounds change and the vowel and *r* stay in the same syllable. In *turnip,* the *u* is followed by an *r.* Blend the sounds, keeping /ûr/ together: /tûr/ /nip/.

Write the spelling words that contain the matching spelling pattern.

word	surf	curve	spur	nurse
nerve	curl	burn	learn	bird
squirt	work	blurt	shirt	swerve
verb	stern	thirst	stir	fern

/ûr/ spelled *er*

1. ______________
2. ______________
3. ______________
4. ______________
5. ______________

/ûr/ spelled *ir*

6. ______________
7. ______________
8. ______________
9. ______________
10. ______________

/ûr/ spelled *ear*

11. ______________

/ûr/ spelled *ur*

12. ______________
13. ______________
14. ______________
15. ______________
16. ______________
17. ______________
18. ______________

/ûr/ spelled *or*

19. ______________
20. ______________

Look through this week's readings for more words to sort. Create a word sort in your writer's notebook. Include at least two multisyllabic words. Then read each word out loud.

Name ______________________________

A. Write the spelling words that contain the matching spelling pattern.

wordsmith	surface	plural	courage	return
spurts	lurk	lurch	learning	squirm
squirrel	working	urban	shirt	swerve
verse	western	thirsty	earthworm	yearns

/ûr/ spelled *er*

1. ____________

2. ____________

3. ____________

/ûr/ spelled *ir*

4. ____________

5. ____________

6. ____________

7. ____________

/ûr/ spelled *ear*

8. ____________

9. ____________

/ûr/ spelled *ur*

10. ____________

11. ____________

12. ____________

13. ____________

14. ____________

15. ____________

16. ____________

/ûr/ spelled *or*

17. ____________

18. ____________

/ûr/ spelled *our*

19. ____________

/ûr/ spelled *ear* and *or*

20. ____________

B. Compare the words *western* and *yearns*. How are they alike? How are they different?

____

____

____

____

____

____

Look through this week's readings for more words to sort. Create a word sort in your writer's notebook. Include at least two multisyllabic words. Then read each word out loud.

Name ______________________________

word	surf	spurts	spur	return
nerve	lurk	lurch	learning	squirm
squirt	work	blurt	shirt	swerve
verse	stern	thirst	midterm	yearns

A. Write the spelling word that matches each definition below.

1. a unit of speech ______________
2. a test ______________
3. clothing for the upper body ______________
4. to come back ______________
5. confidence ______________
6. serious ______________

B. Write the spelling word that best completes each sentence.

7. Water shot out from the old faucet in ______________.
8. What is your favorite ______________ in this poem?
9. Juice quenches my ______________ in the morning.
10. I had to ______________ to miss a bump in the road.
11. What type of ______________ does a vet's assistant do?
12. The kitten will ______________ if I hold it too long.
13. I changed clothes on the ______________ of the moment.
14. The dentist may ______________ water in your mouth.
15. The shy boy will often ______________ in the background.
16. I will ______________ today if the waves are high enough.
17. While ______________ any new skill, you must be patient.
18. Don't ______________ out your opinion when I am speaking!
19. She ______________ for ice cream in the summer.
20. The old train car will ______________ from side to side.

Name ______________________________

Underline the three misspelled words in each paragraph below. Write the words correctly on the lines.

When it comes to skiing, count me out! The slopes are crowded. You have to swearve around other skiers. I'd rather stay inside near the fire and quench my thurst with some tasty apple cider. Then when the weather warms up, I'll go to the beach and serf.

1. ____________ **2.** ____________ **3.** ____________

Skiing is my favorite sport. I can't wait to retern to the mountain again! Who wants to lirk inside when you can ski down snowy slopes? My brother yerns to go to the beach, but I'd much rather be skiing!

4. ____________ **5.** ____________ **6.** ____________

Writing Connection

Write an opinion about a sport. Tell what you like or dislike about it. Use at least four spelling words in your writing. Edit and proofread your work using the spelling patterns for /ûr/.

Name ______________________________

Remember

A vowel followed by an *r* creates a unique vowel sound. One of those sounds is /ûr/, as in *girl*. The *r*-controlled vowel sound /ûr/ can be spelled in different ways. Read each example out loud.

- *er*: ***under, winner***
- *ir*: ***swirl, skirt***
- *or*: ***worse, labor***
- *ur*: ***curl, fur***
- *ear*: ***pearl, earth***

word	surf	spurts	spur	return
nerve	lurk	lurch	learning	squirm
squirt	work	blurt	shirt	swerve
verse	stern	thirst	midterm	yearns

A. Fill in the missing letters in each word to form a spelling word. Then write the spelling word on the line.

1. st __ __ n ____________
2. squ __ __ m ____________
3. l __ __ __ ning ____________
4. v __ __ se ____________
5. l __ __ k ____________
6. y __ __ __ ns ____________
7. l __ __ ch ____________
8. th __ __ st ____________
9. n __ __ ve ____________
10. ret __ __ n ____________
11. sp __ __ ts ____________
12. sw __ __ ve ____________
13. bl __ __ t ____________
14. s __ __ f ____________
15. squ __ __ t ____________

B. Write these words on the lines in reverse alphabetical order: ***midterm, word, work, shirt, spur.***

16. ____________
17. ____________
18. ____________
19. ____________
20. ____________

Name ____

Content words are words that are specific to a field of study. For example, words like *energy, scanners,* and *pollution* are science content words.

Authors use content words to explain a concept or idea. Sometimes you can figure out what a content word means by using context clues. You can also use a dictionary to help you find the meaning of unfamiliar content words.

Go on a word hunt with a partner. Find as many content words related to public transportation as you can. Write them in the chart.

CONNECT TO CONTENT

"The Future of Transportation" presents two different points of view about public transportation. Each author gives facts to support his or her argument. The authors use content words that help you understand this science topic.

Circle two words that you were able to figure out the meaning of by using context clues. Write the words and what they mean on the lines.

____

____

____

____

____

Name ____

A **prefix** is added to the beginning of a word to change its meaning. Many words in English have prefixes that come from ancient Greek and Latin. You can use the prefix as a clue to the meaning of the word.

Read each passage from "Driverless Cars" and underline each correct word choice. Then write a definition of the word you chose.

1. Technology has often provided new and unique products that help humans in all sorts of ways. One of the latest things that science and the (automobile, immobile, transmobile) industry are experimenting with is driverless cars.

____

____

2. Today's cars already are becoming much safer. Driverless cars are not a good form of (exportation, importation, transportation). We should stick to cars with drivers.

____

____

3. The biggest benefit is that driverless cars cannot be (detracted, distracted, subtracted). They do not text or make phone calls.

____

____

Name ______________________________

- A **noun** names a person, place, thing, event, or idea. A **common noun** names any person, place, thing, or event: *professor, farm, scissors, concert.*
- A **proper noun** names a specific person, place, or thing and begins with a capital letter. Some proper nouns may contain more than one word. Days of the week, months of the year, and holidays are proper nouns.

  George Washington, Wyoming, The Library of Congress, Thursday, February, Fourth of July

Read each sentence. Underline each common noun and circle each proper noun.

1. Hillside Library has many books.
2. The entrance is on Spring Street.
3. Our class visited on Tuesday.
4. Mrs. Young gave a tour of the sections.
5. My friend asked for novels by Louisa May Alcott.
6. The materials must be returned by the end of October.

Connect to Community

Talk to a parent or another trusted adult about why libraries are good for your community. Then write a paragraph about why you think libraries are important. Edit your paragraph to make sure you capitalize proper nouns.

____

____

____

____

____

____

____

Name ______________________________

- A **concrete noun** names a person, place, or thing. It is something you can see, hear, smell, taste, or feel: *fog, thunder, scent, apple, feathers.*
- An **abstract noun** is an idea or concept. You cannot see, hear, smell, taste, or feel it: *personality, bravery, childhood, birthday, future, energy.*

Read each sentence. Write whether the underlined noun is *concrete* or *abstract*.

1. The new factory will open in June. ______________
2. My brother will look for a job there. ______________
3. He has a good understanding of machinery. ______________
4. The company makes engines for airplanes. ______________
5. Our neighbor has worked for them before. ______________
6. She was a manager during the construction process. ______________
7. We liked to watch the tractors and cranes at the site. ______________
8. The main building was finished in three months. ______________

Reading/Writing Connection

Read this excerpt from "Creating a Nation." Circle the abstract nouns. Can you find them all? Then, write a sentence that contains an abstract noun. After you finish, read the sentence aloud to a partner and explain why it is an abstract noun.

Jefferson knew he had to convince many colonists of the need for independence. As a result, he combined a variety of ideas to make his case. Individuals, he explained, had certain rights. These included life, liberty, and the pursuit of happiness.

____

____

Name ______________________________

- A **proper noun** always begins with a capital letter. When proper nouns contain more than one word, capitalize each important word.
- Capitalize the names of days, months, holidays, historical events, geographical names, nationalities, and organizations.

  Naomi, Sunday, August, Presidents' Day, Shays's Rebellion, Denver, Spanish, American Heart Association
- Some proper nouns are abbreviated, or shortened. An initial is the first letter of a name. Initials and titles are capitalized and end with a period. Abbreviations of days and months are also capitalized.

  E.B. White, Mrs. Jackson, Thurs., Aug.

Rewrite each sentence correctly by capitalizing any proper nouns.

1. My family will travel to mexico next july.

   ____

2. Our flight takes off from midway airport in chicago.

   ____

3. We will leave on a monday and return the next thursday.

   ____

4. The hansons will take care of our cat teddy while we are gone.

   ____

5. We plan to go hiking in copper canyon on independence day.

   ____

6. We won't forget to write mr. hanson and j.r. hanson, his son, a thank-you note.

   ____

In your writer's notebook, write a short passage about an organization that helps people. Include three proper nouns. Then check your work to make sure that any organizations, initials, and abbreviations you include use proper capitalization and punctuation.

Name ______________________________

- A **proper noun** always begins with a capital letter. When proper nouns contain more than one word, capitalize each important word.
- Capitalize the names of days, months, holidays, historical events, geographical names, nationalities, and organizations.
- Capitalize titles, initials, and abbreviations of days and months.

Proofread the paragraph. On the lines below, correct mistakes in the use of proper nouns and capitalization.

The band township tunes will perform a benefit concert at cascade arena next tuesday, august 23, at 7:30. Mayor alice lee will introduce the group. All proceeds from the Event will be donated to the falls village foundation. This group will help rebuild areas of falls village that were destroyed by flooding along the wells river last Spring. For more information, read dr. j.c. perez's article in this week's *falls village times*.

COMMON ERRORS

Seasons are not proper nouns. They should not be capitalized: *autumn, winter.*

____

____

____

____

____

____

____

____

____

____

____

Name ____

A. Read the paragraph. Then answer the questions.

(1) The author of *Camper Comedy* visited our class. (2) Mr. Binkle read the first chapter aloud. (3) One of the main characters' names is Sid. (4) The writer used his own family for inspiration. (5) The author grew up in Texas, but the story is set in Maine.

1. Which word in sentence 3 is a proper noun?

A One

B main

C characters'

D Sid

2. Which word in sentence 4 is an abstract noun?

F writer

G his

H family

J inspiration

B. Read the student draft and look for any corrections that need to be made. Then choose the best answer to each question.

(1) Our team plays the conway cougars on Saturday. (2) The game is at Dover Stadium and is being organized by the youth sports Association. (3) To get there, take Elm Street across Flint River. (4) The Dover Brass Attack will perform songs at Halftime. (5) The winner takes home the t.j. ellis Trophy.

3. What change, if any, should be made to sentence 1?

A Change ***team*** to **Team**

B Change ***Saturday*** to **saturday**

C Change ***conway cougars*** to **Conway Cougars**

D Make no change

4. What change, if any, should be made to sentence 2?

F Change ***Dover Stadium*** to **dover stadium**

G Change ***youth sports*** to **Youth Sports**

H Change ***Association*** to **association**

J Make no change

5. What change, if any, should be made to sentence 4?

A Change ***Dover*** to **dover**

B Change ***Brass Attack*** to **brass attack**

C Change ***Halftime*** to **halftime**

D Make no change

6. What change, if any, should be made to sentence 5?

F Change ***winner*** to **Winner**

G Change ***t.j. ellis*** to **T.J. Ellis**

H Change ***Trophy*** to **trophy**

J Make no change

Name ______________________________

Fold back the paper along the dotted line. Use the blanks to write each word as it is read aloud. When you finish the test, unfold the paper. Use the list at the right to correct any spelling mistakes.

	1.	________	**1. joint**
	2.	________	**2. foul**
	3.	________	**3. coil**
	4.	________	**4. hoist**
	5.	________	**5. stout**
	6.	________	**6. dawdle**
	7.	________	**7. mouthful**
	8.	________	**8. counter**
	9.	________	**9. brought**
	10.	________	**10. bawl**
	11.	________	**11. fountain**
	12.	________	**12. sprawls**
	13.	________	**13. douse**
	14.	________	**14. clause**
	15.	________	**15. sprouts**
	16.	________	**16. cautious**
	17.	________	**17. turmoil**
	18.	________	**18. scrawny**
	19.	________	**19. foundation**
	20.	________	**20. turquoise**
Review Words	**21.**	________	**21. work**
	22.	________	**22. thirst**
	23.	________	**23. squirm**
Challenge Words	**24.**	________	**24. buoyant**
	25.	________	**25. renown**

Name ______________________________

The **variant vowel** /ô/ is the sound you hear in the word *dawn*. It can be spelled in different ways.

- **/ô/**: ***lawn, pause, bought, chalk***

Diphthongs are gliding vowel sounds. They combine two vowel sounds into one syllable. When you say the word *boil*, you start with one vowel sound and then glide to another. /oi/ and /ou/ are two common diphthongs. They can be spelled in different ways. Read the following words out loud.

- **/oi/**: ***soil, enjoy***
- **/ou/**: ***account, town***

DECODING WORDS

The word *enjoy* has two syllables: /en/ and /joi/. In the second syllable, the letters *o* and *y* stand for the diphthong /oi/. Blend the sounds to read the word: *en/joy*.

Write the spelling words that contain the matching sound and spelling patterns. Then read each word out loud.

joint	stout	brought	douse	turmoil
foul	dawdle	bawl	clause	scrawny
coil	mouthful	fountain	sprouts	foundation
hoist	counter	sprawls	cautious	turquoise

/ô/ spelled *aw*

1. ______________
2. ______________
3. ______________
4. ______________

/ô/ spelled *ough*

5. ______________

diphthong spelled *oi*

6. ______________
7. ______________
8. ______________
9. ______________
10. ______________

/ô/ spelled *au*

11. ______________
12. ______________

diphthong spelled *ou*

13. ______________
14. ______________
15. ______________
16. ______________
17. ______________
18. ______________
19. ______________
20. ______________

Look through this week's readings for more words to sort. Include at least two multisyllabic words. Read each word out loud. Then create a word sort in your writer's notebook.

Name ______________________________

The **variant vowel** /ô/ is the sound you hear in the word *dawn*. It can be spelled in different ways.

- ***/ô/**: lawn, pause, bought, chalk*

Diphthongs are gliding vowel sounds. They combine two vowel sounds into one syllable. When you say the word *boil*, you start with one vowel sound and then glide to another. /oi/ and /ou/ are two common diphthongs. They can be spelled in different ways. Read the following words out loud.

- ***/oi/**: soil, joy*
- ***/ou/**: account, town*

DECODING WORDS

The word *enjoy* has two syllables: /en/ and /joi/. In the second syllable, the letters *o* and *y* stand for the diphthong /oi/. Blend the sounds to read the word: *en/joy*.

Write the spelling words that contain the matching sound and spelling patterns. Then read each word out loud.

joint	round	brought	south	turmoil
foul	dawn	hawks	sauce	scrawny
coil	mouthful	fountain	sprouts	bounce
join	counter	straws	cause	point

/ô/ spelled *aw*

1. ______________
2. ______________
3. ______________
4. ______________

/ô/ spelled *ough*

5. ______________

diphthong spelled *oi*

6. ______________
7. ______________
8. ______________
9. ______________
10. ______________

/ô/ spelled *au*

11. ______________
12. ______________

diphthong spelled *ou*

13. ______________
14. ______________
15. ______________
16. ______________
17. ______________
18. ______________
19. ______________
20. ______________

Look through this week's readings for more words to sort. Include at least two multisyllabic words. Read each word out loud. Then create a word sort in your writer's notebook.

Name ______________________________

A. Write the spelling words that contain the matching sound and spelling patterns. Then read each word out loud.

loiter	stout	wrought	douse	turmoil
outnumber	dawdle	bawl	clause	scrawny
poise	mouthful	fountain	scour	foundations
hoist	council	sprawls	cautious	renowned

/ô/ spelled *aw*

1. ______________
2. ______________
3. ______________
4. ______________

/ô/ spelled *ough*

5. ______________

diphthong /oi/ spelled *oi*

6. ______________
7. ______________
8. ______________
9. ______________

/ô/ spelled *au*

10. ______________
11. ______________

diphthong /ou/ spelled *ou*

12. ______________
13. ______________
14. ______________
15. ______________
16. ______________
17. ______________
18. ______________
19. ______________

diphthong /ou/ spelled *ow*

20. ______________

B. Compare the words *cautious* and *wrought*. How are they alike? How are they different?

____

____

____

Look through this week's readings for more words to sort. Include at least two multisyllabic words. Read each word out loud. Then create a word sort in your writer's notebook.

Name ______________________________

joint	stout	brought	douse	turmoil
foul	dawdle	bawl	clause	scrawny
coil	mouthful	fountain	sprouts	foundation
hoist	counter	sprawls	cautious	turquoise

A. Write the spelling word that matches each definition below.

1. blue gemstone ____________
2. to move slowly ____________
3. thin and bony ____________
4. spreads out ____________
5. water feature ____________
6. place where two parts are joined ____________
7. past tense of *bring* ____________
8. base; support ____________
9. quantity of food ____________
10. part of a written agreement ____________

B. Write the spelling word that best completes each analogy.

11. *Calm* is to *peace* as *disorder* is to ____________.
12. *Untie* is to *knot* as *straighten* is to ____________.
13. *Table* is to *dining room* as ____________ is to *kitchen*.
14. *Float* is to *sink* as ____________ is to *drop*.
15. *Cold* is to *hot* as ____________ is to *pleasant*.
16. *Chuckle* is to *laugh* as ____________ is to *cry*.
17. *Grows* is to ____________ as *droops* is to *wilts*.
18. *Reckless* is to ____________ as *dangerous* is to *safe*.
19. ____________ is to *thin* as *tall* is to *short*.
20. ____________ is to *soak* as *watch* is to *look*.

Name ______________________________

Underline the six misspelled words in the paragraphs below. Write the words correctly on the lines.

Zinnia flowers brawt a lot of butterflies to my backyard last year. You might want to try planting some of these colorful flowers near the fowndation of your own home this spring. Just be sure to plant them where there is plenty of sun, or the stems will be weak and scrauny.

A zinnia seed sprowts in seven to ten days. Keep the young plants watered, but don't dowse them. Be catious! Too much water is just as bad as too little. The plants will grow quickly, and they bloom until fall.

1. ______________________ 4. ______________________

2. ______________________ 5. ______________________

3. ______________________ 6. ______________________

Writing Connection

Write information about a plant or an insect that interests you. Use at least four spelling words in your writing. Proofread your work using the spelling patterns for /ô/, /oi/, and /ou/.

____

____

____

____

____

____

____

____

____

____

____

____

Name ____________________

Remember

The variant vowel /ô/ can be spelled in different ways.

- ***/ô/*: *fawn, applause, bought, talk***

The diphthongs /oi/ and /ou/ glide from one vowel sound to another. These sounds can be spelled in different ways, too. Read the following examples out loud. Listen for the glide.

- ***/oi/*: *avoid, annoy***
- ***/ou/*: *astound, brown***

joint	stout	brought	douse	turmoil
foul	dawdle	bawl	clause	scrawny
coil	mouthful	fountain	sprouts	foundation
hoist	counter	sprawls	cautious	turquoise

A. Fill in the missing letters to form a spelling word. Write the spelling word on the line. Then read the words out loud. Listen to the different vowel sounds.

1. scr ___ ___ ny ____________________

2. d ___ ___ dle ____________________

3. j ___ ___ nt ____________________

4. f ___ ___ ntain ____________________

5. turm ___ ___ l ____________________

6. c ___ ___ tious ____________________

7. f ___ ___ l ____________________

8. c ___ ___ nter ____________________

9. spr ___ ___ ts ____________________

10. b ___ ___ l ____________________

11. h ___ ___ st ____________________

12. st ___ ___ t ____________________

13. c ___ ___ l ____________________

14. cl ___ ___ se ____________________

15. d ___ ___ se ____________________

B. Write these spelling words on the lines in reverse alphabetical order: *turquoise, foundation, brought, mouthful, sprawls.*

16. ____________________

17. ____________________

18. ____________________

19. ____________________

20. ____________________

Name ____

Content words are words that are specific to a field of study. For example, words like *government, colonists,* and *patriots* are social studies content words.

Authors use content words to explain a concept or idea. Sometimes you can figure out what a content word means by using context clues. You can also use a dictionary to help you find the meaning of unfamiliar content words.

Go on a word hunt with a partner. Find as many content words related to the conflict between American colonies and Great Britain. Write them in the chart.

Social Studies Words

CONNECT TO CONTENT

"Creating a Nation" gives facts about the events that led up to the American Revolution. It tells examples of the colonists' problems with Great Britain. The author uses content words that help you understand this social studies topic.

Circle two words that you were able to figure out the meaning of using context clues. Write the words and what they mean on the lines.

____

____

____

____

____

____

Name ____

Use the words in the box and the clues below to help you solve the crossword puzzle. If you get stuck, you can use a dictionary to help you.

drawbacks	reasoning	retrace	decipher
advance	data	analysis	cite
counterpoint	captivated	indicated	access

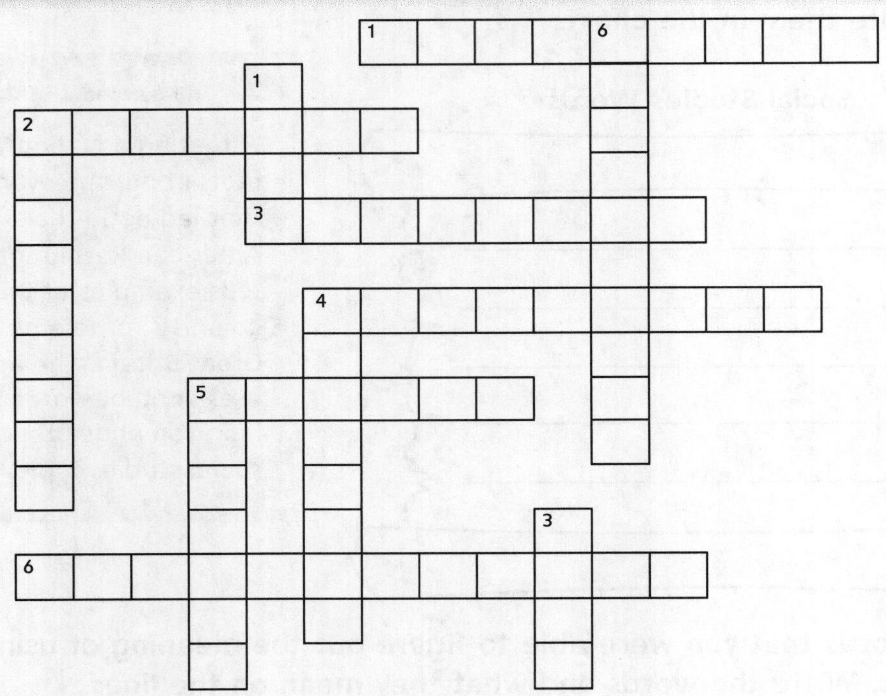

Across

1. showed a sign
2. to go back over
3. careful examination or study of something
4. problems or disadvantages
5. to get or make contact with
6. opposing, or disagreeing, point of view

Down

1. facts, figures, and other kinds of information
2. the ability to think in a logical way
3. mention as proof or evidence
4. to figure out something that is difficult to understand
5. to move forward or make progress
6. influenced by charm, art, or skill

Name ____

- A **singular noun** names one person, place, idea, or thing.
- A **plural noun** names more than one person, place, idea, or thing. Most plural nouns are formed by adding *-s* or *-es*: *song, songs; inch, inches.*
- A noun can function in a sentence as a subject, a direct object of an action verb, or an object of a preposition.

  My parents walked the dog around the neighborhood.

Read each sentence. Draw one line under each singular noun. Draw two lines under each plural noun.

1. The campers told stories around the campfire.
2. Bright sparks drifted up into the sky.
3. The wind blew through the branches of the trees.
4. A full moon peeked above the top of the mountain.
5. The first story was about two boys on a raft.
6. My friend told a tale about knights and dragons.
7. Two girls spoke about training horses on a ranch.
8. The counselors added more logs to the flames.
9. Another hour passed before the fire went out.
10. The campers headed back to the cabins beside the lake.

Use the sentences as a model. In your writer's notebook, write about a place you visited. Draw one line under each singular noun and two lines under each plural noun. Can you figure out the function of each noun? Is it a subject, a direct object of an action verb, or an object of a preposition? Discuss with a partner.

Name ______________________________

- Add -es to form the plural of singular nouns that end in *s, sh, ch,* or *x.*

  bus, buses; wish, wishes; lunch, lunches; box, boxes

- To form the plural of nouns ending in a consonant and the letter *y,* change the *y* to *i* and add *-es*: *reply, replies.*
- To form the plural of nouns ending in a vowel and *y,* add *-s*: *key, keys.*

Complete each sentence by writing the plural form of each noun in parentheses.

1. My father worked at two different (ranch) last year. ______________
2. One had many cattle, horses, and (donkey). ______________
3. I spent several (day) working with him. ______________
4. We saw two baby (fox) playing in a field. ______________
5. They disappeared into the (bush) after a while. ______________
6. Both of my dad's (boss) watched the weather. ______________
7. There were some snow (flurry) early one morning. ______________
8. The tree (branch) were laced with white. ______________

Read this excerpt from "Wordsmiths." Some of the nouns are underlined. Write the plural form of each underlined noun on the lines below.

> Wheatley is remembered as the first African American to publish a <u>collection</u> of poetry. She also wrote and sent a <u>poem</u> to General George Washington in 1775 that praised him for his <u>success</u>. His <u>response</u> to her shows how highly regarded Wheatley was.

____

____

Name ____

- Add *-es* to form the plural of singular nouns that end in *s, sh, ch,* or *x.*
- To form the plural of nouns ending in a consonant and the letter *y,* change the *y* to *i* and add *-es.*
- To form the plural of nouns ending in a vowel and *y,* add *-s.*

Complete each sentence by writing the plural form of each noun in parentheses.

1. The explorer shared (picture) of his trip to the rain forest. ____________
2. The first slide showed two (monkey) in a tree. ____________
3. He wanted to photograph (gorilla) as well. ____________
4. He showed us some close-ups of (butterfly). ____________
5. Many had colorful (patch) on their wings. ____________
6. Did he see any scary (snake) on his visit? ____________
7. Some slithered along the leaves and (moss). ____________
8. The explorer put five (box) on the table. ____________
9. Each was filled with samples from his (study). ____________
10. If I had three (wish), one would be to visit the rain forest. ____________

Imagine that you take a trip to a rain forest. Write three sentences about what you see there. Include at least three plural nouns. Underline them. Then read through your work and correct any misspellings.

____

____

____

____

____

Name ______________________________

- Add *-es* to form the plural of singular nouns that end in *s, sh, ch,* or *x*.
- To form the plural of nouns ending in a consonant and the letter *y,* change the *y* to *i* and add *-es*.
- To form the plural of nouns ending in a vowel and *y,* add *-s*.

Proofread the paragraph. On the lines below, correct mistakes in plural nouns and their endings.

Most homes should have one or two toolboxs on hand in case of emergencyes. Hammeres and screwdrivers are the most useful tools. A good set of wrenchs is helpful for fixing sinks and faucets. Power tool, such as drills and sawes, can solve many problems, such as broken furniture. Some appliancees run on batterys and can be used outdoors. Many hobby require an assortment of tools. A toolbox is one of the best wayes to store them.

COMMON ERRORS

Certain nouns, such as *information, milk, bread,* and *furniture,* always take the singular form. Example: *There is too much furniture in this room.*

Name ______________________________

Read the student draft and look for any corrections that need to be made. Then choose the best answer to each question.

(1) All the fan cheer for the players on the field. (2) Their team is behind by two points. (3) The winner of the game goes on to the finals. (4) The bases are loaded, and Big Bill steps up to the plate. (5) Bill swings and misses the first two pitches.

(6) The pitcher has heard storys about Bill's home runs. (7) Bill sends the next ball soaring up into the cloudes. (8) The coachs jump up and down with joy. (9) There will be many party in town tonight!

1. What change, if any, should be made in sentence 1?

A Change ***fan*** to **fans**

B Change ***cheer*** to **cheers**

C Change ***players*** to **playeres**

D Make no change

2. What change, if any, should be made in sentence 2?

F Change ***team*** to **teams**

G Change ***is*** to **are**

H Change ***points*** to **point**

J Make no change

3. What change, if any, should be made in sentence 6?

A Change ***pitcher*** to **pitchers**

B Change ***storys*** to **stories**

C Change ***home*** to **homes**

D Make no change

4. What is the correct way to write sentence 7?

F Bill sends the next ball soaring up into the cloud.

G Bill sends the next balls soaring up into the cloud.

H Bill sends the next ball soaring up into the clouds.

J Bill send the next ball soaring up into the clouds.

5. What change, if any, should be made in sentence 8?

A Change ***coachs*** to **coaches**

B Change ***jump*** to **jumps**

C Change ***joy*** to **joys**

D Make no change

6. What is the correct way to write sentence 9?

F There will be many party in towns tonight!

G There will be many partys in town tonight!

H There will be many parties in town tonight!

J There will be many parties in towns tonight!

Name ____

Fold back the paper along the dotted line. Use the blanks to write each word as it is read aloud. When you finish the test, unfold the paper. Use the list at the right to correct any spelling mistakes.

1. ________________ 1. rattlers
2. ________________ 2. fangs
3. ________________ 3. countries
4. ________________ 4. liberties
5. ________________ 5. potatoes
6. ________________ 6. rodeos
7. ________________ 7. taxes
8. ________________ 8. reptiles
9. ________________ 9. surroundings
10. ________________ 10. beliefs
11. ________________ 11. difficulties
12. ________________ 12. batches
13. ________________ 13. abilities
14. ________________ 14. lashes
15. ________________ 15. identities
16. ________________ 16. losses
17. ________________ 17. possibilities
18. ________________ 18. notches
19. ________________ 19. zeroes
20. ________________ 20. eddies

Review Words

21. ________________ 21. brought
22. ________________ 22. counter
23. ________________ 23. coil

Challenge Words

24. ________________ 24. mangoes
25. ________________ 25. sinews

Name ______________________________

- Most nouns are made plural by adding *-s* to the end of the word, as in ***rocks***.
- Words that end in *-sh, -ch, -s, -ss,* or *-x* are made plural by adding *-es* to the end of the word, as in ***dishes***, ***inches***, ***losses***, and ***foxes***. Adding *-es* also adds an extra syllable. Read the words out loud.
- Words that end with a consonant + *y* are usually made plural by changing *y* to *i* and adding *-es*, as in ***libraries*** and ***duties***.
- Words that end with a vowel + *y* are made plural by adding *-s*, as in ***essays*** and ***bays***.

RULE REVIEW

- If a noun ends in a vowel and *o*, add *-s*: *radios, zoos*. If a noun ends in a consonant and *o*, add *-s* or *-es*: *pianos, tomatoes*.
- Some nouns, such as *scissors* and *clothes*, are always plural.

Write the spelling words that contain the matching spelling patterns.

rattlers	potatoes	surroundings	abilities	possibilities
fangs	rodeos	beliefs	lashes	notches
countries	taxes	difficulties	identities	zeroes
liberties	reptiles	batches	losses	eddies

form the plural by adding *-s*

1. ______________
2. ______________
3. ______________
4. ______________
5. ______________

form the plural by adding *-es*

6. ______________
7. ______________
8. ______________
9. ______________
10. ______________
11. ______________
12. ______________

form the plural by changing *y* to *i* and adding *-es*

13. ______________
14. ______________
15. ______________
16. ______________
17. ______________
18. ______________
19. ______________

when used as a noun, this word is always plural

20. ______________

Look through this week's readings for more plurals to sort. Create a word sort for a partner in your writer's notebook.

Name ____

- Most nouns are made plural by adding *-s* to the end of the word, as in ***rocks***.
- Words that end in *-sh, -ch, -s, -ss,* or *-x* are made plural by adding *-es* to the end of the word, as in ***dishes, inches, losses,*** and ***foxes***. Adding *-es* also adds an extra syllable. Read the words out loud.
- Words that end with a consonant + *y* are usually made plural by changing *y* to *i* and adding *-es,* as in ***libraries*** and ***duties***.
- Words that end with a vowel + *y* are made plural by adding *-s,* as in ***essays*** and ***bays***.

RULE REVIEW

- If a noun ends in a vowel and *o,* add *-s*: *radios, zoos*. If a noun ends in a consonant and *o,* add *-s* or *-es*: *pianos, tomatoes*.
- Some nouns, such as *scissors* and *clothes,* are always plural.

Write the spelling words that contain the matching spelling patterns.

rattlers	couches	snakes	cities	berries
fangs	rodeos	beliefs	lashes	bunches
babies	taxes	enemies	families	zeroes
liberties	reptiles	batches	losses	trophies

form the plural by adding *-s*

1. ______________
2. ______________
3. ______________
4. ______________
5. ______________
6. ______________

form the plural by adding *-es*

7. ______________
8. ______________
9. ______________
10. ______________
11. ______________
12. ______________
13. ______________

form the plural by changing *y* to *i* and adding *-es*

14. ______________
15. ______________
16. ______________
17. ______________
18. ______________
19. ______________
20. ______________

Look through this week's readings for more plurals to sort. Create a word sort for a partner in your writer's notebook.

Name ______________________________

rattlers	potatoes	surroundings	mangoes	possibilities
molecules	canopies	beliefs	mosquitoes	notches
countries	geniuses	difficulties	identities	zeroes
calamities	reptiles	crutches	losses	eddies

A. Write the spelling words that contain the matching spelling patterns.

form the plural by adding *-s*

1. ____________

2. ____________

3. ____________

4. ____________

form the plural by adding *-es*

5. ____________

6. ____________

7. ____________

8. ____________

9. ____________

10. ____________

11. ____________

12. ____________

form the plural by changing *y* to *i* and adding *-es*

13. ____________

14. ____________

15. ____________

16. ____________

17. ____________

18. ____________

19. ____________

when used as a noun, this word is always plural

20. ____________

B. Compare the words *calamities* and *losses*. How are they alike? How are they different?

____

____

____

Look through this week's readings for more plurals to sort. Create a word sort for a partner in your writer's notebook.

Name ______________________________

rattlers	potatoes	surroundings	abilities	possibilities
fangs	rodeos	beliefs	lashes	notches
countries	taxes	difficulties	identities	zeroes
liberties	reptiles	batches	losses	eddies

A. Write the spelling word that matches each definition below.

1. small whirls ______________
2. snake teeth ______________
3. rattlesnakes ______________
4. defeats; failures ______________
5. freedoms ______________
6. skills; talents ______________
7. bunches or groups ______________
8. eyelid hairs ______________
9. nations ______________
10. accepted truths ______________

B. Write the spelling word that best completes each sentence.

11. The cook put ______________ and carrots in the stew.
12. Are crocodiles and alligators ______________?
13. Many ______________ have riding and roping events.
14. The travelers were happy in their new ______________.
15. Our ______________ will be used to build new schools.
16. The numeral *100* has two ______________.
17. He searched the paper for job ______________.
18. You can use an ax to put ______________ in a log.
19. The clever criminal had many different ______________.
20. Pioneers faced many ______________ in the wilderness.

Name ____________________

Underline the six misspelled words in the paragraphs below. Using the rules about forming plurals, write the words correctly on the lines.

Once upon a time, a prince was held captive in a high tower. Knights from many countrys used their powers and abilitys to try to free him, but none could. The tower was surrounded by prickly bushes and guarded by a fierce dragon. How could a prince be rescued from these surrounding?

A clever princess heard about the prince's difficultes and decided to rescue him. She didn't wear armor or carry a sword. She simply put on gloves and chopped through the bushes with hedge cutters. And the dragon? Well, she wasn't afraid of flying reptilies with fanges. She merely ordered the dragon to scram, and it did!

1. ____________________ 4. ____________________

2. ____________________ 5. ____________________

3. ____________________ 6. ____________________

Writing Connection

Write a passage for a fairy tale. It can be a new fairy tale or a retelling of an old tale you know. Use at least four spelling words in your writing. Edit and proofread your work.

Name ______________________________

Remember

- Most plural nouns are made by adding *-s* or *-es* to the end of the word. When you add *-es* to many of these words, you also add an extra syllable. Try reading these words out loud: ***books, socks, doors; benches, guesses.***
- If a noun ends with *o*, add *-s* or *-es*: ***pianos, mangoes.***
- If a noun ends with a consonant + *y*, change *y* to *i* and add *-es*: ***lobbies.***
- If a noun ends with a vowel + *y*, add *-s*: ***trays, chimneys.***

rattlers	potatoes	surroundings	abilities	possibilities
fangs	rodeos	beliefs	lashes	notches
countries	taxes	difficulties	identities	zeroes
liberties	reptiles	batches	losses	eddies

A. Change each word to make a plural spelling word. Write the spelling word on the line. Then read each word out loud.

1. country ____________
2. belief ____________
3. tax ____________
4. difficulty ____________
5. zero ____________
6. liberty ____________
7. fang ____________
8. notch ____________
9. rattler ____________
10. ability ____________
11. loss ____________
12. identity ____________
13. batch ____________
14. eddy ____________
15. lash ____________

B. Write these spelling words on the lines in alphabetical order to the third letter: *surroundings, possibilities, potatoes, reptiles, rodeos.*

16. ____________
17. ____________
18. ____________
19. ____________
20. ____________

Name ____

A **dictionary** lists words in alphabetical order. You use a dictionary to look up the meaning, or denotation, of an unfamiliar word. A **glossary** lists words and definitions related to a specific text or subject. You can find glossaries in the back of textbooks or other nonfiction books, or online.

- The **guide words** show the first and last words on the page. Words on the page appear alphabetically between guide words.
- The **entry words** show the spelling and syllables.
- The **pronunciation** of each word is shown in parentheses. **Syllabication** separates syllables by bullets and shows how many syllables a word has.
- The word's **origin**, such as the language it comes from, is often shown.

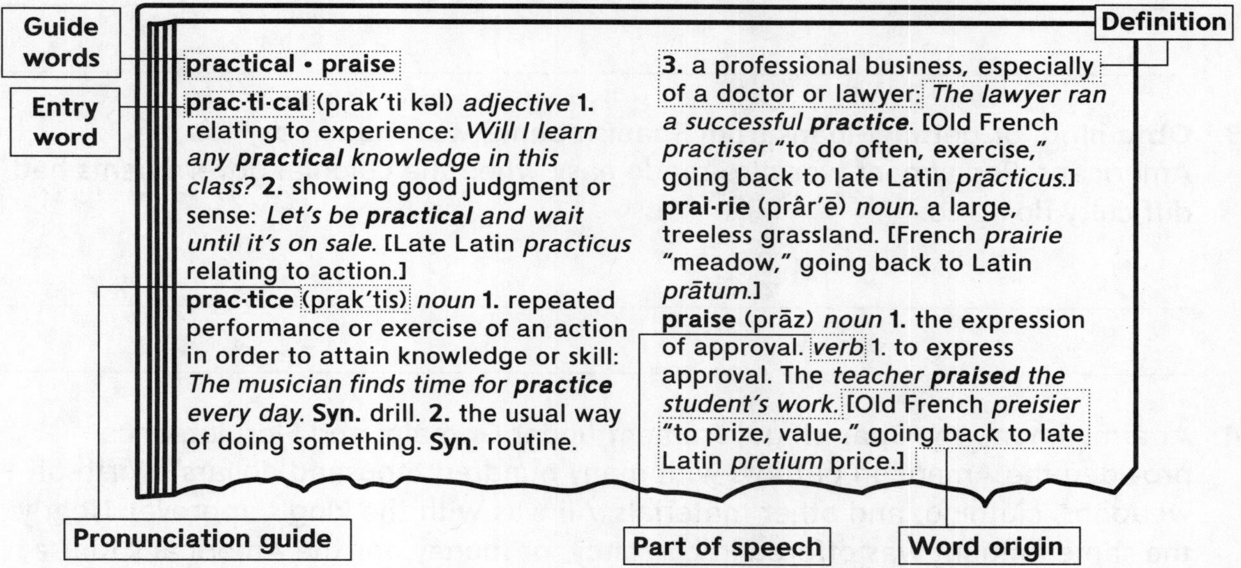

Use the dictionary entry and context clues to figure out the meaning of each word in bold. Write the meaning, part of speech, and word origin on the lines.

1. It is standard **practice** for the company to offer refunds to unhappy customers.

____

2. Rosa had a successful business, but she was **practical** about spending money.

____

Read each dictionary entry aloud with a partner. Sound out each word carefully. How many syllables are in each word? How do you know?

Name ______________________________

Read each passage from "Secret Help from Spain." Underline context clues that help you figure out the meaning of each word in bold. Then write a new sentence using the bold word.

1. They were aristocrats who served kings. **Aristocrats**, or nobles, are people born into high social positions.

____

____

2. Floridablanca continued with bayonets, shoes, and blankets. Spain also provided the colonists with **funds**, or money, from its national treasury.

____

____

3. **Obtaining**, or getting, loans from Spanish banks was made easy for the Americans. Repayment was also made easy when the colonial governments had difficulty doing so.

____

____

4. At a minimum, the Spanish government under Grimaldi and Floridablanca provided the American patriots with many hundred thousand dollars' worth of weapons, clothing, and other materials. All was with the king's approval. Nearly the same amount was offered in **currency,** or money, for the Americans to use as they wished.

____

____

Name ____

- To form the plural of some nouns ending in *f* or *fe,* change the *f* to *v* and add *-es*: *leaf, leaves.*
- To form the plural of nouns ending in a vowel followed by *o,* add *-s*: *videos.* To form the plural of nouns ending in a consonant followed by *o,* add *-s* or *-es*: *pianos, potatoes.*
- Some nouns name a group. These nouns are called **collective nouns**. A collective noun can be either singular or plural. Usually a collective noun has a singular verb because it refers to a group as a whole.

  My basketball team is the second best in the state.

A. Complete each sentence by writing the plural form of each noun in parentheses.

1. The (hoof) of the horses struck the stone roads. ____________________
2. People heard the (echo) from far away. ____________________
3. Had the (hero) returned from their journey? ____________________
4. They had risked their (life) to defend the town. ____________________

B. Read each sentence. Underline each collective noun.

5. Our family camps at Bright Lake every year.
6. We swam through a school of tiny fish.
7. A flock of ducks had built their nests nearby.
8. My sister ran away from a swarm of biting flies.

Write a short passage in your writer's notebook about a performance or presentation at school. Use the following collective nouns: *class, audience,* and *group*. Underline these collective nouns and any others that you include. Edit and proofread your work.

Name ______________________________

- Some nouns have a special plural form that does not end in *-s: women, teeth, feet.*
- Some nouns stay the same whether they are singular or plural: *trout, deer, moose, sheep.*

Complete each sentence by writing the plural form of each noun in parentheses.

1. The (child) packed their bags for the long trip. ________________

2. They washed their hands and brushed their (tooth). ________________

3. They put sneakers and shoes on their (foot). ________________

4. Two (man) gave the family directions to the park. ________________

5. They drove past fields full of cows and (sheep). ________________

6. Flocks of (goose) honked at them from above. ________________

7. They waved at (person) along the country roads. ________________

8. They stopped to let a team of (ox) cross. ________________

Writing Connection

Write a paragraph using the plural form of the following nouns: *cactus, oasis, species,* and *mouse*. You may use a dictionary when you edit and proofread your work.

____

____

____

____

____

____

Name ____

- Some nouns have special plural forms that do not end in *-s* or *-es*.
- Some nouns stay the same whether they are singular or plural.
- **Appositives** tell more about the nouns they follow. Use commas within a sentence to set off many appositives: *The photographer's camera, the newest on the market, broke after one month.*

Rewrite each sentence correctly by using the correct plural forms or adding commas where they belong.

1. Our town Grantsville will host this year's summer celebration.

   ____

2. The mayor has asked our school's childs to help.

   ____

3. Mrs. Munson the principal had many great idea.

   ____

4. We will have a parade on Founder's Day the first Saturday in June.

   ____

Reading/Writing Connection

Read this excerpt from "The Magical Lost Brocade." Rewrite one sentence to include an appositive. You can use your imagination to add new information.

> Next, Ping approached the Mountain of the Sun. He rode up the steep mountain grasping the reins for dear life! Finally, he reached the top and dismounted at the palace door.

____

____

____

Name ______________________________

- To form the plural of some nouns ending in *f* or *fe,* change the *f* to *v* and add *-es.* To form the plural of nouns ending in a vowel followed by *o,* add *-s.* To form the plural of nouns ending in a consonant followed by *o,* add *-s* or *-es.*
- Some nouns have special plural forms that do not end in *-s* or *-es.* Some nouns stay the same whether they are singular or plural.
- **Appositives** tell more about the nouns they follow. Use commas to set off many appositives.

Proofread the paragraph. On the lines below, correct mistakes in plural nouns and comma usage.

I interviewed one of our school's heros the chef in the cafeteria. She takes ingredients off the kitchen shelfs and makes delicious lunchs for all the childrens. Our chef believes that the proper handling of knifes is important. She once worked in a bakery making dozenes of loafs of bread every day. She learned from other great chef. I took photoes of her making her favorite meal lasagna. I can't wait to sink my tooths into one of her latest dishs!

COMMON ERRORS

Some plural nouns that end in *f* do not follow this rule. Instead, simply add *-s*: *roofs, chiefs, beliefs.*

____

____

____

____

____

____

____

____

____

Name ______________________________

A. Read the paragraphs. Then answer the questions.

(1) The leaves fell from the trees on the ground. (2) My family worked together to rake them. (3) My father suggested that we work harder.

(4) Then a noise like thunder filled the air around us. (5) A herd of bison ran across the plains in the distance. (6) Brown clouds of dust rose up like smoke behind them. (7) The bison stopped when they reached the river's edge.

1. Which word in sentence 2 is a collective noun?

A my

B whole

C family

D them

2. Which other sentence contains a collective noun?

F Sentence 4

G Sentence 5

H Sentence 6

J Sentence 7

B. Read the student draft and look for any corrections that need to be made. Then choose the best answer to each question.

(1) My uncle visits zoo around the country. (2) He loves to see animals and their babies. (3) He once saw an elk and her two new calf. (4) Our local zoo features two timber wolves. (5) They also have four moose in a fenced area. (6) Yesterday I took some photo of all the goose in the park. (7) My uncle and I enjoy learning about the lives of animals.

3. What change, if any, should be made to sentence 1?

A Change ***uncle*** to **uncles**

B Change ***zoo*** to **zoos**

C Change ***country*** to **countries**

D Make no change

4. What is the correct way to write sentence 3?

F He once saw an elk and her two new calfs.

G He once saw an elks and her two new calf.

H He once saw some elk and her two new calf.

J He once saw an elk and her two new calves.

5. What change, if any, should be made to sentence 5?

A Change ***moose*** to **mooses**

B Change ***fenced*** to **fences**

C Change ***area*** to **areas**

D Make no change

6. What is the correct way to write sentence 6?

F Yesterday I took some photos of all the geese in the park.

G Yesterday I took some photos of all the goose in the park.

H Yesterday I took some photos of all the gooses in the park.

J Yesterday I took some photo of all the geese in the park.

Name ____________________

Fold back the paper along the dotted line. Use the blanks to write each word as it is read aloud. When you finish the test, unfold the paper. Use the list at the right to correct any spelling mistakes.

1. ________	**1.**	jogging
2. ________	**2.**	dripping
3. ________	**3.**	skimmed
4. ________	**4.**	accepted
5. ________	**5.**	amusing
6. ________	**6.**	easing
7. ________	**7.**	regretted
8. ________	**8.**	forbidding
9. ________	**9.**	referred
10. ________	**10.**	injured
11. ________	**11.**	deserved
12. ________	**12.**	applied
13. ________	**13.**	relied
14. ________	**14.**	renewing
15. ________	**15.**	complicated
16. ________	**16.**	qualified
17. ________	**17.**	threatening
18. ________	**18.**	gnarled
19. ________	**19.**	envied
20. ________	**20.**	fascinated
Review Words 21. ________	**21.**	difficulties
22. ________	**22.**	notches
23. ________	**23.**	rodeos
Challenge Words 24. ________	**24.**	adoring
25. ________	**25.**	diaries

Name ______________________________

The inflectional endings *-ed* and *-ing* change the verb tense. ***-ed***: happened; ***-ing***: happening now

- When a base word ends with a consonant and *e*, drop the *e* and add *-ed* or *-ing*: ***raked, raking*** (*rake*).
- When a base word ends with a vowel and a consonant, double the final consonant before adding *-ed* or *-ing*: ***gripped, gripping*** (*grip*).
- When a word ends in *y*, change the *y* to *i* before adding *-ed*: ***fried*** (*fry*).

SPELLING TIP

Adding *-ed* or *-ing* to some base words does not change the base word: ***wished, wishing*** (*wish*).

Write the spelling words that contain the matching spelling patterns. Then read each word out loud.

jogging	amusing	referred	relied	threatening
dripping	easing	injured	renewing	gnarled
skimmed	regretted	deserved	complicated	envied
accepted	forbidding	applied	qualified	fascinated

add *-ed* without a spelling change

1. ______________
2. ______________

add *-ing* without a spelling change

3. ______________
4. ______________

drop final *e* and add *-ed*

5. ______________
6. ______________
7. ______________
8. ______________

double final consonant and add *-ed*

9. ______________
10. ______________
11. ______________

change *y* to *i* and add *-ed*

12. ______________
13. ______________
14. ______________
15. ______________

drop final *e* and add *-ing*

16. ______________
17. ______________

double final consonant and add *-ing*

18. ______________
19. ______________
20. ______________

Name ___________________________________

The inflectional endings *-ed* and *-ing* change the verb tense. ***-ed***: happened; ***-ing***: happening now

- When a base word ends with a consonant and *e*, drop the *e* and add *-ed* or *-ing*: ***raked, raking*** (*rake*).
- When a base word ends with a vowel and a consonant, double the final consonant before adding *-ed* or *-ing*: ***gripped, gripping*** (*grip*).
- When a word ends in *y*, change the *y* to *i* before adding *-ed*: ***fried*** (*fry*).

SPELLING TIP

Adding *-ed* or *-ing* to some base words does not change the base word: ***wished, wishing*** (*wish*).

Write the spelling words that contain the matching spelling patterns. Then read each word out loud.

jogging	amusing	referred	relied	awaiting
dripping	saving	injured	renewing	checked
skimmed	flipped	deserved	dared	pitied
raking	swimming	applied	studied	traced

add *-ed* without a spelling change

1. ____________

add *-ing* without a spelling change

2. ____________

3. ____________

drop final *e* and add *-ed*

4. ____________

5. ____________

6. ____________

7. ____________

double final consonant and add *-ed*

8. ____________

9. ____________

10. ____________

change *y* to *i* and add *-ed*

11. ____________

12. ____________

13. ____________

14. ____________

drop final *e* and add *-ing*

15. ____________

16. ____________

17. ____________

double final consonant and add *-ing*

18. ____________

19. ____________

20. ____________

Name ______________________________

Write the spelling words that contain the matching spelling patterns. Then read each word out loud.

accepted	amusing	referred	unified	threatening
shredding	easing	portrayed	soothing	gnarled
skimmed	regretted	dedicated	complicated	envied
recognizing	forbidding	applied	qualified	fascinated

add *-ed* without a spelling change

1. ______________________

2. ______________________

3. ______________________

add *-ing* without a spelling change

4. ______________________

drop final *e* and add *-ed*

5. ______________________

6. ______________________

7. ______________________

double final consonant and add *-ed*

8. ______________________

9. ______________________

10. ______________________

change *y* to *i* and add *-ed*

11. ______________________

12. ______________________

13. ______________________

14. ______________________

drop final *e* and add *-ing*

15. ______________________

16. ______________________

17. ______________________

18. ______________________

double final consonant and add *-ing*

19. ______________________

20. ______________________

Look through this week's readings for more words to sort. Create a word sort for a partner in your writer's notebook. Can you find any words that do not follow these spelling rules?

Name ____________________

jogging	amusing	referred	relied	threatening
dripping	easing	injured	renewing	gnarled
skimmed	regretted	deserved	complicated	envied
accepted	forbidding	applied	qualified	fascinated

A. Write the spelling word that has the same, or almost the same, meaning.

1. entertaining ____________
2. twisted ____________
3. scanned ____________
4. disallowing ____________
5. amazed ____________
6. dribbling ____________
7. sliding ____________
8. depended ____________
9. suitable ____________
10. hostile ____________

B. Write the spelling word that best completes each sentence.

11. The boy was ____________ when he fell off his bike.
12. Rick stays in shape by ____________ every day.
13. The confusing game has ____________ rules.
14. I ____________ lending my jacket to a careless friend.
15. Kendra filled out several forms when she ____________ for a job.
16. I ____________ her talent for learning new languages.
17. He thanked his supporters when he ____________ the award.
18. Amy is now ____________ all her library books online.
19. He worked hard and ____________ the raise.
20. Marta ____________ to an encyclopedia for information.

Name ______________________________

Underline the six misspelled words in the paragraphs below. Write the words correctly on the lines.

The room was filling up. Some of the best scientists in the world were easeing into their seats. Dr. Lee skimed his notes one last time to make sure he was ready. Was he qualifyed to speak in front of these men and women? Yes, he thought he was.

Dr. Lee opened his talk with an amussing story. It relaxed him, even though it didn't get a big laugh. Then he began to present his ideas to the group. He refered to studies that had been done, as well as his own experiments. Within minutes, the audience was fascinateed.

1. ____________________ 4. ____________________

2. ____________________ 5. ____________________

3. ____________________ 6. ____________________

Writing Connection

Write about a time when you or someone you know had to do something challenging. Use at least four spelling words in your writing. Edit and proofread your work using the spelling rules for adding inflectional endings.

____

____

____

____

____

____

____

____

____

____

Name ____________________

Remember

- Adding *-ed* or *-ing* to some base words does not change the spelling of the base word: ***fished, fishing*** (*fish*).
- When a base word ends with a consonant and *e*, drop the final *e* before adding *-ed* and *-ing*: ***hired, hiring*** (*hire*).
- When a base word ends with a vowel and a consonant, double the final consonant before adding *-ed* or *-ing*: ***dropped, dropping*** (*drop*).
- When a base word ends in *y*, change *y* to *i* before adding *-ed*: ***tried*** (*try*).

jogging	amusing	referred	relied	threatening
dripping	easing	injured	renewing	gnarled
skimmed	regretted	deserved	complicated	envied
accepted	forbidding	applied	qualified	fascinated

A. Add the ending to each word to form a spelling word. Write the spelling word on the line. Then read each word out loud.

1. renew + ing = ____________
2. deserve + ed = ____________
3. skim + ed = ____________
4. forbid + ing = ____________
5. amuse + ing = ____________
6. qualify + ed = ____________
7. fascinate + ed = ____________
8. refer + ed = ____________
9. drip + ing = ____________
10. apply + ed = ____________
11. regret + ed = ____________
12. complicate + ed = ____________
13. accept + ed = ____________
14. rely + ed = ____________
15. threaten + ing = ____________

B. Write the words on the lines in reverse alphabetical order. Alphabetize them to the second letter. ***injured, easing, gnarled, jogging, envied***

16. ____________
17. ____________
18. ____________
19. ____________
20. ____________

Name ___

Expand your vocabulary by adding or removing inflectional endings, prefixes, or suffixes to a base word to create different forms of a word.

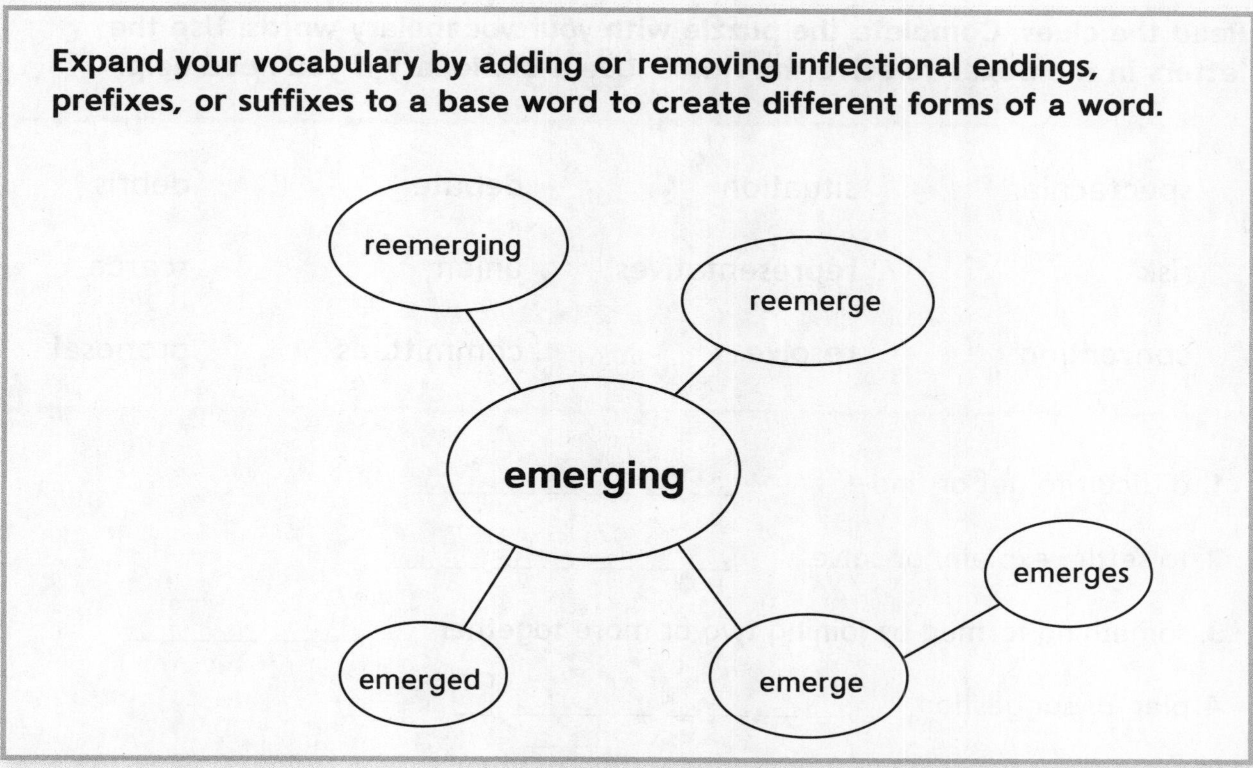

Write as many related words as you can on the notepad below. After you finish, read each word out loud. Do any of the new endings change the sound of the final *t* in *detect*? Which related word would change the /t/ to /sh/? Discuss with a partner. Use a dictionary to help you.

Name ____

Read the clues. Complete the puzzle with your vocabulary words. Use the letters in the boxes to solve the riddle. Use a dictionary if you need help.

spectacular	situation	debate	debris
risk	representatives	union	scarce
convention	resolve	committees	proposal

1. difficult to get or find ___ ___ ___ ___ ___ ___
2. to settle, explain, or solve ___ ___ ___ ___ ___ ☐ ___
3. something formed by joining two or more together ___ ___ ___ ☐ ___
4. plan or suggestion ___ ___ ___ ___ ___ ___ ___ ☐
5. formal meeting for a special purpose ☐ ___ ___ ___ ___ ___ ___ ___ ___ ___
6. chance of loss or harm ___ ___ ___ ___
7. condition or state of affairs ___ ___ ___ ☐ ___ ___ ___ ___ ___
8. people chosen to speak or act for others

   ___ ___ ___ ___ ___ ___ ☐ ___ ___ ___ ___ ___ ___ ___ ___
9. groups of people chosen to do certain work ___ ☐ ___ ___ ___ ___ ___ ___ ___ ___
10. to argue or discuss ___ ☐ ___ ___ ___ ___
11. unusual and impressive ___ ___ ___ ___ ___ ___ ___ ___ ___ ___ ___
12. scattered remains of something ___ ___ ___ ___ ___ ☐

Australia is the only continent in the world that does not have:

☐ ☐ ☐ ☐ ☐ ☐ ☐ ☐ ☐

Name ______________________________

- A **possessive noun** is a noun that shows who or what owns or has something.
- Form a singular possessive noun by adding an **apostrophe** (') and an *-s* to a singular noun: *the squirrel's tail; Maria's suitcase.*
- A person's name or a **collective noun** that ends in *-s* also has an apostrophe (') and an *-s* in the possessive form: *Lucas's bicycle; the class's final project.*

Complete each sentence by writing the possessive form of the noun in parentheses.

1. My (sister) paintings are being sold in a gallery. ______________
2. We will attend the (show) opening tonight. ______________
3. An invitation arrived from the (gallery) owner. ______________
4. The paintings show scenes from our (family) history. ______________
5. My (mother) favorite is the portrait of my father. ______________
6. (Dad) favorite shows Aunt Bess on a bicycle. ______________
7. (Aunt Bess) bicycle is painted many different colors. ______________
8. You can see the (paintbrush) strokes in the sky. ______________
9. Each (painting) price appears on a tiny card. ______________
10. The (crowd) reaction has been quite positive so far. ______________

In your writer's notebook, write a short passage about a special event that you attended. Include five singular possessive nouns. Try to include at least one collective noun. Check to make sure that you use apostrophes correctly.

Name ______________________________

- A **plural possessive noun** is a plural noun that shows ownership.
- To form the possessive of a plural noun that ends in *-s,* add an **apostrophe**: *the athletes' uniforms.*
- To form the possessive of a plural noun that does not end in *-s,* add an apostrophe and *-s*: *the people's hometown.*

Stop the presses! These newspaper headlines need editing. Read each one and correct the plural possessive noun. Write your answers on the lines.

Local Athlete Wins Womens' Olympic Medal ____________

Three Authors Books Offer Clues for Lost Crown ____________

Ten Year's Worth of Research Leads to New Medicine ____________

Two Fishs Mission to Swim Upstream Fails ____________

Read the sentence from "The Fox and the Snail." Circle the possessive noun. Then write a sentence using the plural possessive form of the word you circled.

The snail crawled as quickly as he could onto the fox's bushy tail just as the fox yelled "Ten!" and set off in a run.

____

____

Name ______________________

- When a singular noun ends in *-s,* show the **possessive form** by adding an apostrophe and *-s*: *the atlas's index.*
- The possessive form of a plural noun that ends in *-s* adds only an **apostrophe**: *the socks' design.* To form the possessive of a plural noun that does not end in *-s,* add an apostrophe and *-s*: *the oxen's horns.*
- Do not confuse plural nouns with possessive nouns.

Complete each sentence by writing the correct form of the noun in parentheses.

1. They lined up near the (circus) main entrance. ______________
2. The teachers purchased the two (class) tickets. ______________
3. An usher pointed toward the (child) seats. ______________
4. The (child) laughed when two clowns appeared. ______________
5. The pair of (clown) wore oversized clothes. ______________
6. The two (clown) costumes filled up with air. ______________
7. One (clown) suit exploded with a burst of confetti. ______________
8. Each (class) students laughed with delight. ______________

Imagine that you go to the circus with family and friends. Write three sentences about what you see there. Include two plural nouns and two possessive plural nouns.

____

____

____

____

____

Name ______________________________

- To form the possessive of a plural noun that ends in *-s,* add an apostrophe. To form the possessive of a plural noun that does not end in *-s,* add an apostrophe and *-s.*
- When a singular noun ends in *-s,* show the possessive form by adding an apostrophe and *-s.* To form the possessive of a plural noun that does not end in *-s,* add an apostrophe and *-s.*

Proofread the paragraph. On the lines below, correct mistakes in the formation of possessive nouns or the use of apostrophes.

My classes debate team has had three straight loss's. We started the season with two wins' and a tie. Three teachers' at school offered to coach the team. We listened to the teachers presentations at our meeting yesterday. They will help us prepare for next weeks match. The final three week's scores will determine the champions. I hope our class performs better than the other five school's teams.

COMMON ERRORS

Sometimes an apostrophe is included by mistake. If a plural noun does not have or own something, then it is not possessive and should not have an apostrophe.

____

____

____

____

____

____

____

____

____

____

Name ____

A. Read the paragraphs. Then answer the questions.

(1) We have one week's passes to the state fair. (2) One pass's corner was torn by accident. (3) I can't make out the passes' expiration dates. (4) I doubt the passes are good for more than two weeks.

(5) Our school library owns three large atlases. (6) One atlas contains mostly photographs. (7) That atlas's cover shows Earth from outer space. (8) The other atlases' covers are maps of the world.

1. Which sentence in paragraph 1 has a plural possessive noun?

A Sentence 1

B Sentence 2

C Sentence 3

D Sentence 4

2. Which sentence in paragraph 2 has a singular possessive noun?

F Sentence 5

G Sentence 6

H Sentence 7

J Sentence 8

B. Read the student draft and look for any corrections that need to be made. Then choose the best answer to each question.

(1) I am researching my familys history for my homework. (2) First, I borrowed my grandparents' photo albums. (3) Next, I sent e-mails to my three cousins' addresses. (4) Dad let me read parts of his father's journal. (5) He also told me some of Uncle Gus travel stories. (6) Mom had postcards from Grandma's home country. (7) With both my parents help, I created an amazing report. (8) I can't wait to hear all the other families stories!

3. What change, if any, should be made to sentence 1?

A Change ***familys*** to **family's**

B Change ***familys*** to **families'**

C Change ***familys*** to **familys'**

D Make no change.

4. What change, if any, should be made to sentence 3?

F Change ***cousins'*** to **cousin's**

G Change ***cousins'*** to **cousins's**

H Change ***cousins'*** to **cousins**

J Make no change.

5. What change, if any, should be made to sentence 5?

A Change ***Uncle Gus*** to **Uncle Guses**

B Change ***Uncle Gus*** to **Uncle Gus'**

C Change ***Uncle Gus*** to **Uncle Gus's**

D Make no change.

6. What change, if any, should be made to sentence 7?

F Change ***parents*** to **parent's**

G Change ***parents*** to **parents'**

H Change ***parents*** to **parents's**

J Make no change.

Name ____________________

Fold back the paper along the dotted line. Use the blanks to write each word as it is read aloud. When you finish the test, unfold the paper. Use the list at the right to correct any spelling mistakes.

1.	________	**1. you've**
2.	________	**2. she'd**
3.	________	**3. that's**
4.	________	**4. what's**
5.	________	**5. doesn't**
6.	________	**6. there's**
7.	________	**7. you're**
8.	________	**8. wasn't**
9.	________	**9. we'll**
10.	________	**10. we've**
11.	________	**11. we're**
12.	________	**12. couldn't**
13.	________	**13. I've**
14.	________	**14. didn't**
15.	________	**15. they're**
16.	________	**16. shouldn't**
17.	________	**17. wouldn't**
18.	________	**18. he'd**
19.	________	**19. don't**
20.	________	**20. isn't**
Review Words 21.	________	**21. dripping**
22.	________	**22. applied**
23.	________	**23. diaries**
Challenge Words 24.	________	**24. won't**
25.	________	**25. aren't**

Name ______________________________

Two words can be shortened to make one word. These shortened words are called **contractions**. An **apostrophe** (') takes the place of the missing letter or letters.

- Some contractions connect a verb (such as *have, had, is, are, will*) and the word *not*.

  Example: *could not* becomes *couldn't*

- Other contractions connect a pronoun (such as *she, he, they*) and a verb.

  Example: *you will* becomes *you'll*

SPELLING TIP

To know where to put the apostrophe in a contraction, ask yourself where the missing letters would go. In the contraction *wouldn't*, the apostrophe replaces the *o* in *not*. **Note:** The contraction of *will not*, ***won't***, is irregular.

Write the spelling words that are formed using the words listed below.

you've	doesn't	we'll	I've	wouldn't
she'd	there's	we've	didn't	he'd
that's	you're	we're	they're	don't
what's	wasn't	couldn't	shouldn't	isn't

is

1. ______________

2. ______________

3. ______________

would

4. ______________

5. ______________

have

6. ______________

7. ______________

8. ______________

will

9. ______________

are

10. ______________

11. ______________

12. ______________

not

13. ______________

14. ______________

15. ______________

16. ______________

17. ______________

18. ______________

19. ______________

20. ______________

Look through this week's readings for two different contractions. Write the sentences in your writer's notebook.

Name ______________________________

Two words can be shortened to make one word, which is called a **contraction**. An **apostrophe** (') takes the place of the missing letter or letters.

- Some contractions connect a verb (such as *have, had, is, are, will*) and the word *not.*

  Example: *could not* becomes *couldn't*
- Other contractions connect a pronoun (such as *she, he, they*) and a verb.

  Example: *you will* becomes *you'll*

SPELLING TIP

To know where to put the apostrophe in a contraction, ask yourself where the missing letters would go. In the contraction *wouldn't,* the apostrophe replaces the *o* in *not.* **Note:** The contraction of *will not, **won't,*** is irregular.

Write the spelling words that are formed using the words listed below.

he'd	doesn't	we'll	I've	wouldn't
she'd	there's	we've	didn't	you've
that's	you're	we're	they're	don't
what's	wasn't	couldn't	shouldn't	isn't

is

1. ______________
2. ______________
3. ______________

would

4. ______________
5. ______________

have

6. ______________
7. ______________
8. ______________

will

9. ______________

are

10. ______________
11. ______________
12. ______________

not

13. ______________
14. ______________
15. ______________
16. ______________
17. ______________
18. ______________
19. ______________
20. ______________

Look through this week's readings for two different contractions. Write the sentences in your writer's notebook.

Name ______________________

A. Write the spelling words that are formed using the words listed below.

you've	doesn't	we'll	I've	wouldn't
she'd	there's	we've	didn't	he'd
that's	you're	we're	they're	don't
what's	wasn't	couldn't	shouldn't	isn't

is

1. ______________
2. ______________
3. ______________

would

4. ______________
5. ______________

have

6. ______________
7. ______________
8. ______________

will

9. ______________

are

10. ______________
11. ______________
12. ______________

not

13. ______________
14. ______________
15. ______________
16. ______________
17. ______________
18. ______________
19. ______________
20. ______________

B. Compare the words *we'll* and *we're*. How are they alike? How are they different?

____

____

____

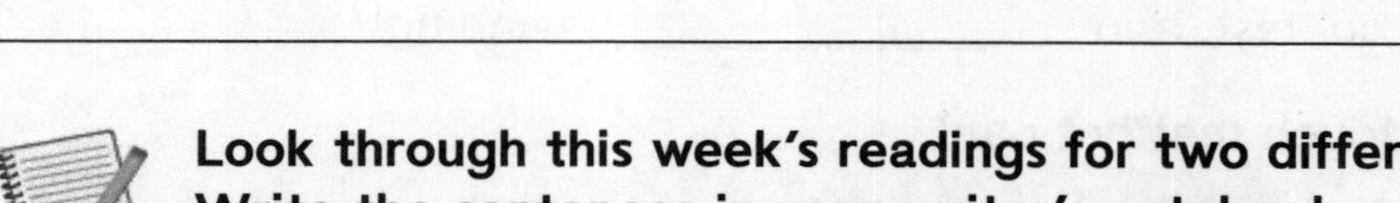

Look through this week's readings for two different contractions. Write the sentences in your writer's notebook.

Name ______________________________

you've	doesn't	we'll	I've	wouldn't
she'd	there's	we've	didn't	he'd
that's	you're	we're	they're	don't
what's	wasn't	couldn't	shouldn't	isn't

A. Write the spelling word that is the opposite of each word or phrase below.

1. would ________________
2. is ________________
3. did ________________
4. could ________________
5. should ________________
6. he would not ________________
7. you are not ________________
8. they are not ________________

B. Write the spelling word that best completes each sentence.

9. Molly said that ________________ help me with my homework.
10. The old car ________________ have good brakes.
11. ________________ tried my best to teach my dog to sit.
12. ________________ be on vacation next week.
13. ________________ the biggest pumpkin I've ever seen!
14. I had to study, so I ________________ at the game.
15. ________________ the answer to the last question?
16. Brett and I are in the contest, and ________________ winning!
17. ________________ touch that hot pan!
18. Did you say ________________ never seen the Grand Canyon?
19. The reporter said ________________ a chance of rain today.
20. We can rest now that ________________ finished our work.

Name ______________________________

Underline the six misspelled words in the paragraphs below. Some of them are high-frequency words. Write the words correctly on the lines.

One day an old man decided hed make soup for dinner. He went out to his garden to pull up some carrots. He pulled up two small carrots without difficulty, but he had trouble with the third. It was huge and wouldn't come out of the ground. "Iv'e tried and tried," the old man said. "This carrot is'nt coming up!"

A chipmunk saw the old man struggling and offered to help. The old man just laughed. A little chipmunk could'nt do much! But the chipmunk didnt hesitate. It dug around the carrot to loosen it so the man could pluck it from the ground. "You're pretty smart!" said the old man. "Youv'e shown that two can work better than one."

1. ______________________ 4. ______________________

2. ______________________ 5. ______________________

3. ______________________ 6. ______________________

Writing Connection

Write a passage for a folktale. It can be a new folktale or a retelling of an old tale you know. Use at least four spelling words in your writing.

____

____

____

____

____

____

____

____

____

____

Name ____________________

Remember

A **contraction** is a shortened form of two words. An apostrophe (') takes the place of the missing letter or letters.

- Some contractions connect a verb (such as *have, had, is, are, will*) and the word *not*. For example: *have not* becomes *haven't; will not* becomes *won't*.
- Other contractions connect a pronoun (such as *she, he, they*) and a verb. For example: *they will* becomes *they'll*.

you've	doesn't	we'll	I've	wouldn't
she'd	there's	we've	didn't	he'd
that's	you're	we're	they're	don't
what's	wasn't	couldn't	shouldn't	isn't

A. Combine the two words to make a contraction. Write the spelling word on the line.

1. I + have = ____________
2. could + not = ____________
3. you + are = ____________
4. was + not = ____________
5. we + will = ____________
6. they + are = ____________
7. what + is = ____________
8. you + have = ____________
9. should + not = ____________
10. he + would = ____________
11. is + not = ____________
12. we + are = ____________
13. would + not = ____________
14. we + have = ____________
15. she + would = ____________

B. Write these spelling words on the lines in alphabetical order. Alphabetize them to the third letter. *doesn't, there's, don't, didn't, that's*

16. ____________
17. ____________
18. ____________
19. ____________
20. ____________

Name ______________________________

You can figure out the meaning of an unfamiliar word if you know what the root means.

- The root ***geo*** means **earth, soil,** and **ground**.
- The word ***geography*** means **the study of earth, soil,** and **ground.**
- The root ***photo*** means **light**.
- The word ***photography*** means **the process of making images using a camera that directs the image onto a light-sensitive surface.**

How many words can you make with the roots *geo* and *photo*? Use a dictionary to help you. Write your words in the houses. Compare words with a partner.

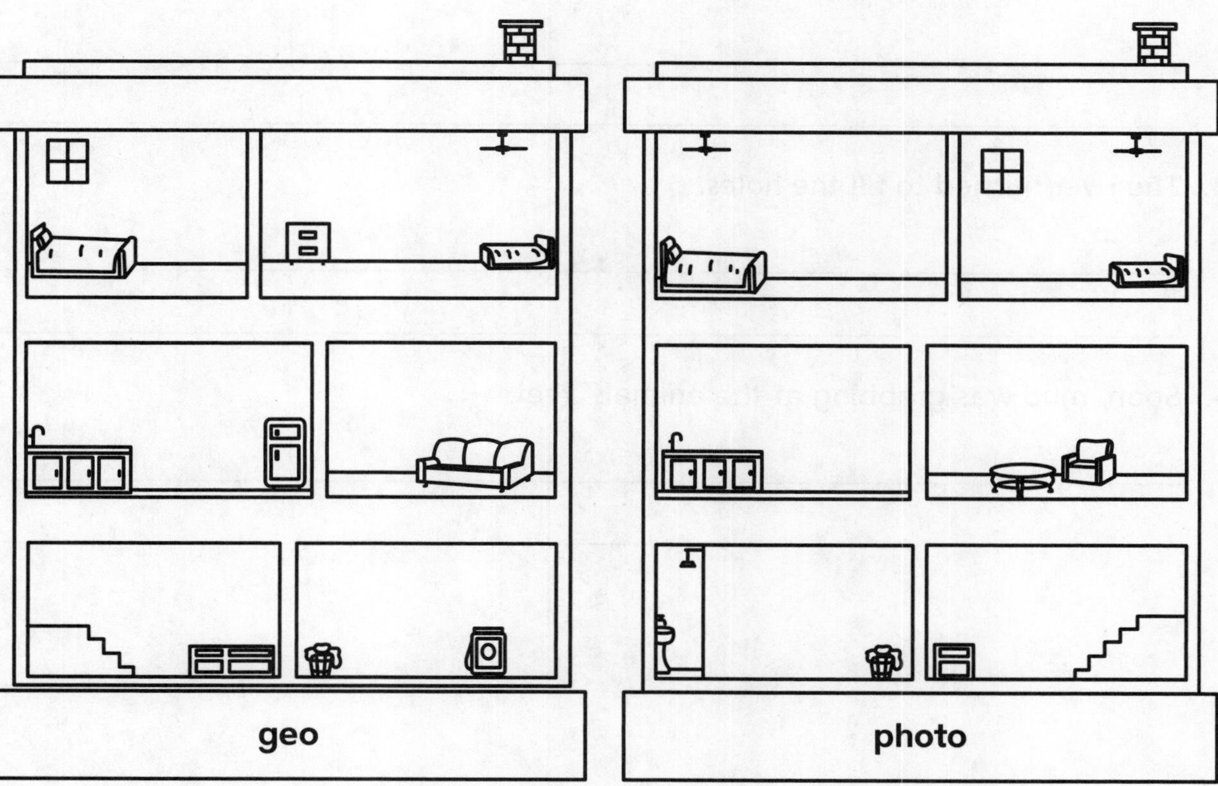

Name ____________________

Read each passage. Underline the word or words that show personification. Remember that personification is a kind of figurative language that gives human abilities or feelings to nonhuman objects, animals, or ideas. Then write a sentence about the mental picture you have of the thing described.

1. Long ago, a river wandered through a large forest.

____

____

2. It offered its water freely to all who needed it.

____

____

3. The more the animals drank, the more the water retreated.

____

____

4. The river hurried to fill the holes.

____

____

5. Soon, mud was grabbing at the animals' feet.

____

____

Name ______________________________

- A **prepositional phrase** is a group of words that tells more about an important part of a sentence.
- A prepositional phrase begins with a **preposition**, such as *about, during, in, near, under,* or *with*. It ends with a noun or pronoun: *near the door.*
- A prepositional phrase can function as an **adjective** or an **adverb**.

  The dog with brown fur barked loudly. (adjective)

  The dog barks at the park. (adverb)

Read each sentence. Underline each prepositional phrase and circle each preposition.

1. The sun shone in the sky.
2. I hiked up the mountain.
3. The view from the top was incredible.
4. Hawks flew over the treetops.
5. I could see the lake in the distance.
6. Sailboats moved across the water.
7. A man with red hair joined me.
8. He told a story about a bear he had seen.

Writing Connection

Write three sentences about something you see outside. Each sentence should include a prepositional phrase. Underline each prepositional phrase and circle each preposition. Edit your work.

____

____

____

____

____

Name ____

- The **object of a prepositional phrase** is the noun or pronoun that follows the preposition: *over the ledge; by her.*
- The most important word in a prepositional phrase is often the noun or pronoun at the end: *The key is under the **doormat**.*
- When a prepositional phrase comes between the subject and a verb, the verb should agree with the subject, not the object of a preposition.

Read each sentence. Underline each prepositional phrase and circle the object of each preposition.

1. The new bakery opens in a week.
2. My father knows the owner of the store.
3. They met during a talent contest.
4. They both sang with musical groups.
5. One of his friends won the top prize.

Reading/Writing Connection

Read the lines from "Blue Ribbon Dreams," a poem about a young horse. Underline two prepositional phrases and circle the object of each preposition. Then write two more lines of poetry. Include two prepositional phrases. Edit your work.

But I intend to demonstrate
That small things can be truly great.
So every morning, and again at night
I train Little Red with all my might.
Again, again, and yet again
I lead him all 'round the pen.

____

____

Name ______________________________

- Use **quotation marks** around the title of a song, part of a book, or a short story: *The name of the first chapter is "The Quiet Skies."*
- Use **italics** or **underlining** with the title of a long work, such as a book or newspaper. You can also use italics or underlining to show emphasis.

  Have you ever read <u>The Secret Garden</u>?

  My brother was the *only* person in class to get an A on the paper.

  This is <u>great</u> news!
- Use **commas** after the **greeting** and **closing** in a friendly letter and in the date and address. In a business letter, use a **colon** after the greeting.

Insert commas, quotation marks, or underlining where needed.

1. June 5 2018
2. Dear Aunt Kay
3. Thank you for sending me A Treasury of New Tales.
4. The Haunted Window is one of my favorite stories.
5. We also read the story Race to the North in school.
6. Have you ever read the novel A Light on the River?
7. It was a lot like the song Catching the Sun on page 45.
8. My mother gave me the book Suncatcher to read.
9. Believe it or not, Chapter 2 is called Write to Your Relatives.
10. Sincerely yours

Write a short thank-you letter about a gift a relative gives you. Include the title of a song or book, and make sure that one word shows emphasis. Then edit your letter to make sure you used quotation marks, underlining, and commas correctly.

Name ____

- Use **quotation marks** around the title of a song, short story, or part of a book. Use **italics** or **underlining** with the title of a long work. Italics and underlining may also be used for emphasis.
- Use **commas** after the **greeting** and **closing** in a friendly letter and in dates and addresses. In a business letter, use a **colon** after the greeting.
- **Appositives** tell more about the nouns they follow. Use commas to set off many appositives.
- Form a singular possessive noun by adding an **apostrophe (')** and an *-s* to a singular noun. A person's name or a collective noun that ends in *-s* also has an apostrophe (') and an *-s* in the possessive form.

Proofread the paragraph. On the lines below, correct mistakes in the use of quotation marks, commas, colons, and underlining.

Dear Members of Bookends Middle City's Book Club

Our groups next meeting will be on Friday November 15 2019. We had planned to read Fields of Flowers Shawna Ross' new book. Let's focus on Chapter One <u>Planting the Seeds</u>. We can then choose between "The Lonely Star" and "Ten New Tales" for our December selection. The first story The Neighbors Dog takes place in our town Middle City! This is a <u>surprise</u>!

With all best wishes

____

____

____

____

____

____

____

____

Name ______________________________

A. Read the paragraph. Then answer the questions.

(1) I wrote an article about the new club. (2) The editor of the newspaper wanted to publish it. (3) We reviewed the article in her office. (4) Her comments on the first paragraph were helpful. (5) I revised the article on Saturday. (6) My friends from other states can read it online.

1. What is the prepositional phrase in sentence 2?
   A editor of the
   B of the newspaper
   C the newspaper wanted
   D to publish it

2. Which word in sentence 6 is an object of a preposition?
   F friends
   G from
   H states
   J it

B. Read the student draft and look for any corrections that need to be made. Then choose the best answer to each question.

(1) The article about the club will appear in The Five Lakes Herald. (2) Look for the article "New Club Forms in City." (3) Another article, History Lovers will feature an interview of the group. (4) After weeks of hard work, I will finally have my first article published!

3. What is the correct way to write sentence 1?
   A The article about the club will appear in, The Five Lakes Herald.
   B The article about the club will appear in: The Five Lakes Herald.
   C The article about the club will appear in "The Five Lakes Herald."
   D The article about the club will appear in <u>The Five Lakes Herald</u>.

4. What is the correct way to write sentence 3?
   F Another article, "History Lovers" will feature an interview over the group.
   G Another article, "History Lovers," will feature an interview with the group.
   H Another article "History Lovers" will feature an interview on the group.
   J Another article: History Lovers, will feature an interview of the group.

5. What is the BEST way to show emphasis in sentence 4?
   A After weeks *of* hard work, I will finally have my first article published!
   B After weeks of hard work, I will finally *have* my first article published!
   C After weeks of hard work, I will *finally* have my first article published!
   D After weeks of hard work, I will finally have my first *article* published!

Name ____________________

Fold back the paper along the dotted line. Use the blanks to write each word as it is read aloud. When you finish the test, unfold the paper. Use the list at the right to correct any spelling mistakes.

	1. ________	**1.** dentist
	2. ________	**2.** jogger
	3. ________	**3.** fifteen
	4. ________	**4.** flatter
	5. ________	**5.** submit
	6. ________	**6.** mustang
	7. ________	**7.** absent
	8. ________	**8.** hollow
	9. ________	**9.** empire
	10. ________	**10.** blizzard
	11. ________	**11.** culture
	12. ________	**12.** goggles
	13. ________	**13.** summon
	14. ________	**14.** excite
	15. ________	**15.** kennel
	16. ________	**16.** valley
	17. ________	**17.** fragment
	18. ________	**18.** gallop
	19. ________	**19.** vulture
	20. ________	**20.** pigment
Review Words	21. ________	**21.** won't
	22. ________	**22.** shouldn't
	23. ________	**23.** we're
Challenge Words	24. ________	**24.** clammy
	25. ________	**25.** hammock

Name ______________________________

A **closed syllable** is a syllable that ends in one or more consonants and usually has a short vowel sound. When dividing a word that starts with a closed syllable, look for the consonants after the first short vowel sound.

- Words divided between a double consonant: *run/ner, cot/ton, hap/pen*
- Words divided between different consonants: *thun/der, lap/top, tim/ber*

Read these examples out loud.

DECODING WORDS

The word *update* has one closed syllable and one VC*e* syllable. The syllables divide between the two consonants *p* and *d* in the middle. Blend the sounds in the syllables together: /up/ /dāt/. **Note:** If the two consonants represent one sound (*sh, ch, th*), divide after the consonants: *wish/ful, lock/er.*

Write the spelling words that contain the matching syllable pattern.

dentist	submit	empire	summon	fragment
jogger	mustang	blizzard	excite	gallop
fifteen	absent	culture	kennel	vulture
flatter	hollow	goggles	valley	pigment

words divided between a double consonant

1. ______________
2. ______________
3. ______________
4. ______________
5. ______________
6. ______________
7. ______________
8. ______________
9. ______________

words divided between different consonants

10. ______________
11. ______________
12. ______________
13. ______________
14. ______________
15. ______________
16. ______________
17. ______________
18. ______________
19. ______________
20. ______________

Look through this week's readings for words with closed syllables. Record them in your writer's notebook. Draw a slash between the syllables, and circle any VC*e* syllables. Then read the words aloud.

Name ______________________________

A **closed syllable** is a syllable that ends in one or more consonants and usually has a short vowel sound. When dividing a word that starts with a closed syllable, look for the consonants after the first short vowel sound.

- Words divided between a double consonant: *run/ner, cot/ton, hap/pen*
- Words divided between different consonants: *thun/der, lap/top, en/tire*

Read these examples out loud.

DECODING WORDS

The word *update* has one closed syllable and one VC*e* syllable. The syllables divide between the two consonants *p* and *d* in the middle. Blend the sounds in the syllables together: /up/ /dāt/. **Note:** If the two consonants represent one sound (*sh, ch, th*), divide after the consonants: *wish/ful, lock/er.*

Write the spelling words that contain the matching syllable pattern.

garden	basket	empire	dinner	fragment
jogger	mustang	blizzard	checkers	gallop
fifteen	absent	corner	injure	vulture
bottom	arrow	goggles	valley	clatter

words divided between a double consonant

1. ______________
2. ______________
3. ______________
4. ______________
5. ______________
6. ______________
7. ______________
8. ______________
9. ______________

words divided after different consonants

10. ______________

words divided between different consonants

11. ______________
12. ______________
13. ______________
14. ______________
15. ______________
16. ______________
17. ______________
18. ______________
19. ______________
20. ______________

Look through this week's readings for words with closed syllables. Record them in your writer's notebook. Draw a slash between the syllables, and circle any VC*e* syllables. Then read the words aloud.

Name ______________________________

A. Write the spelling words that contain the matching syllable pattern.

swerving	muttered	clammy	summon	fragment
jogger	stubble	suspend	whinnied	gallop
cinder	whimper	culture	kennel	vulture
flattery	hollow	stallion	canyon	pigment

words divided between a double consonant

1. ______________________

2. ______________________

3. ______________________

4. ______________________

5. ______________________

6. ______________________

7. ______________________

8. ______________________

9. ______________________

10. ______________________

11. ______________________

words divided between different consonants

12. ______________________

13. ______________________

14. ______________________

15. ______________________

16. ______________________

17. ______________________

18. ______________________

19. ______________________

20. ______________________

B. Compare the words *cinder* and *summon*. How are they alike? How are they different?

____

____

____

____

Look through this week's readings for words with closed syllables. Record them in your writer's notebook. Draw a slash between the syllables, and circle any VC*e* syllables. Then read the words aloud.

Name ________________________________

dentist	submit	empire	summon	fragment
jogger	mustang	blizzard	excite	gallop
fifteen	absent	culture	kennel	vulture
flatter	hollow	goggles	valley	pigment

A. Write the spelling word that matches each definition below.

1. to call for ______________
2. eye protection ______________
3. color in paint ______________
4. bird of prey ______________
5. not present ______________
6. tooth doctor ______________
7. to praise or compliment __________
8. small wild horse ______________
9. hand in ______________
10. place to board dogs ______________
11. person who runs ______________
12. one more than fourteen ____________

B. Write the spelling word that best completes each analogy.

13. *All* is to *everything* as *piece* is to ________________.
14. *Wind* is to *gust* as *snowstorm* is to ________________.
15. *First* is to *last* as ________________ is to *bore.*
16. *Empty* is to *full* as ________________ is to *solid.*
17. *Kingdom* is to ________________ as *nation* is to *country.*
18. *Walk* is to *stroll* as *run* is to ________________.
19. *Low* is to *high* as ________________ is to *hill.*
20. *Custom* is to *tradition* as ________________ is to *society.*

Name ______________________________

Underline the six misspelled words in the paragraphs below. Write the words correctly on the lines.

When Edgar was young, he was a sports champion. He is now in his 60s, but he prides himself on staying in shape. Edgar is a daily joger. Each morning you will see him stretch and galop out the front door to the valey.

1. ____________ **2.** ____________ **3.** ____________

Last week, Edgar awoke to a howling blizard. It was fiveteen degrees outside, and blowing snow made it impossible to see more than a few feet. "I can't let a little snow stop me!" Edgar said to himself. He got out his cross-country skis, put on his gogles, and went for a trek around the neighborhood.

4. ____________ **5.** ____________ **6.** ____________

Writing Connection

Write a passage for a story about another determined person. Use at least four spelling words in your writing.

Name ____

Remember

A **closed syllable** is a syllable that ends in one or more consonants and has a short vowel sound. The word *subject* has two closed syllables: *sub* and *ject*. The following words contain at least one closed syllable.

- Words divided by a double consonant: *mam/mal, rot/ten, rab/bit.*
- Words divided by different consonants: *prob/lem, pic/nic, Mon/day.*

Blend the sounds in the two closed syllables in *picnic*: /pik/ /nik/.

dentist	submit	empire	summon	fragment
jogger	mustang	blizzard	excite	gallop
fifteen	absent	culture	kennel	vulture
flatter	hollow	goggles	valley	pigment

A. Fill in the missing letters of each word to form a spelling word. Then write the word on the line. Draw a slash after the first closed syllable.

1. mu ___ ___ ang ____________________
2. e ___ ___ ire ____________________
3. vu ___ ___ ure ____________________
4. de ___ ___ ist ____________________
5. e ___ ___ ite ____________________
6. a ___ ___ ent ____________________
7. go ___ ___ les ____________________
8. cu ___ ___ ure ____________________
9. fra ___ ___ ent ____________________
10. bli ___ ___ ard ____________________
11. va ___ ___ ey ____________________
12. pi ___ ___ ent ____________________
13. fla ___ ___ er ____________________
14. su ___ ___ on ____________________
15. su ___ ___ it ____________________

B. Write these spelling words on the lines in reverse alphabetical order: *jogger, fifteen, hollow, gallop, kennel.*

16. ____________________
17. ____________________
18. ____________________
19. ____________________
20. ____________________

Name ______________________________

Expand your vocabulary by adding or removing inflectional endings, prefixes, or suffixes to a base word to create different forms of a word.

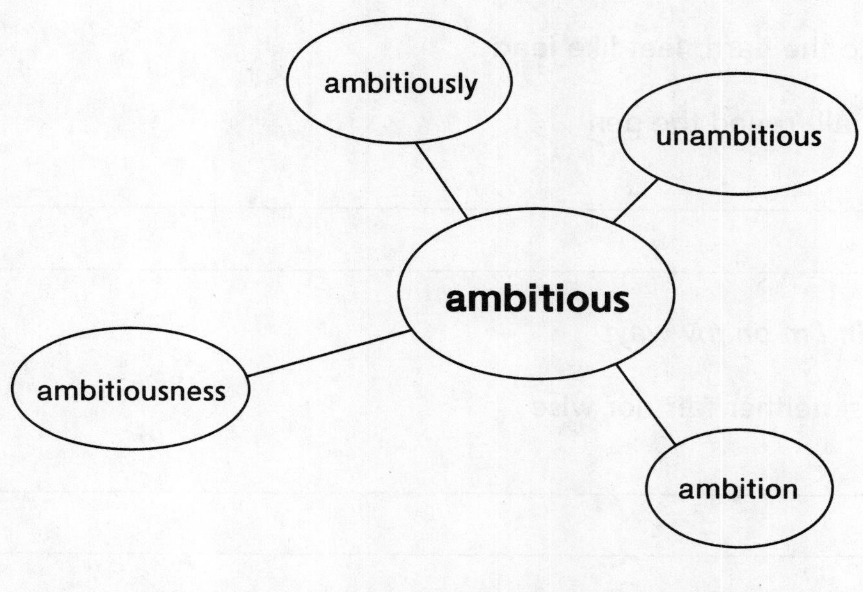

Write as many related words as you can on the lines below. Use a dictionary to help you.

______________ ______________ ______________

______________ ______________

satisfaction

Name ______________________________

Read each pair of passages from "Blue Ribbon Dreams." Then, on the line below each pair, give the two definitions of the homographs in bold. Homographs are words that are spelled the same but have different meanings and may be pronounced differently.

1. Trudging to the barn, feet like **lead**

I **lead** him all ′round the pen

____

____

2. *County* ***fair****, I'm on my way!*

Some folks, neither **fair** nor wise

____

____

3. By the **entrance** hangs a bit

As always, he **entrances** me

____

____

4. **Might** judge us simply by our size

I train Little Red with all my **might**

____

____

Name ______________________________

- A **verb** shows what the subject does or is. An **action verb** expresses action: *The girl builds a sand castle. The waves knock it down.*
- Commonly misused verbs include *lie/lay, sit/set,* and *rise/raise.*

  Lie, sit, and *rise* do not use a direct object. You lie down. You sit on the chair. You rise in the morning.

  Lay, set, and *raise* require a direct object. You lay a **book** on the table. You set a **glass** down. You raise your **hand**.

Read each sentence. Write each verb on the line provided.

1. The farmer scatters seeds on the ground. ________________
2. The lazy dog raises his head. ________________
3. He rises from the ground and barks. ________________
4. One child lays a stick in front of the dog. ________________
5. The dog just sits and stares at it. ________________

Reading/Writing Connection

Read the excerpt from "A Reluctant Traveler." Circle three action verbs. Then write two sentences about an unusual place you see. Include at least two action verbs.

> "You know, that *is* pretty cool," Paul admitted.
>
> Around noon, they piled back into the car and drove to the most unusual neighborhood Paul had seen yet.

____

____

____

Name ______________________________

- A verb must **agree** with its subject: a singular subject takes a singular verb. A plural subject takes a plural verb.
- Add *-s* or *-es* to most verbs in the **present tense** if the subject is singular.

  The scientist looks through the microscope.

  Raul's father watches from the stands.
- A **prepositional phrase** that comes between a subject and a verb does not affect subject-verb agreement: *The box of toys collects dust.* (singular verb)
- **Collective nouns**, such as *class* and *government*, describe a group of people or things. They take a singular verb when they refer to the group as a whole.

  The team trains every day.

  A flock of birds flies over the river. (The prepositional phrase "of birds" does not change the verb. The subject, *flock*, takes a singular verb.)
- If the subject is *I*, *you*, or plural, do not add *-s* to the verb.

  I listen to music. You travel a lot. The club members meet after class.

Read each sentence. Write the correct present-tense form of the verb in parentheses on the line.

1. The principal (wait) for the students on the stage. ______________
2. She (announce) that the show will begin now. ______________
3. The students (begin) to sing a song. ______________
4. One student from the front rows (rush) onto the stage. ______________
5. He (raise) his hands above his head. ______________
6. The audience (clap) along to the beat. ______________

Write a short passage describing a performance. Include at least one collective noun and one prepositional phrase. Edit and proofread your work. Make sure that all subjects and verbs agree.

Name ______________________________

- A verb must **agree** with its subject.
- Add *-s* or *-es* to most verbs in the present tense if the subject is singular. If the subject is *I* or *you*, do not add *-s* or *-es* to the verb.
- If the subject is plural, the verb is plural. Do not add *-s* or *-es* to the verb.
- A **compound subject** with the conjunction ***and*** takes a plural verb.

  Audrey and her sister play catch in the field.
- In **compound sentences**, each subject must agree with the verb that follows it.

  My sisters practice basketball, and my little brother watches.
- If a clause or phrase intervenes, or comes between, the subject and verb, the subject and verb must still agree. *The girls, including Miriam, leave tomorrow.*

Read each sentence. Write the correct present-tense form of the verb in parentheses on the line.

1. The firefighters put on their helmets, and the helicopter (lift) off the ground. ______________
2. The helicopter (bring) gallons of water to the fire. ______________
3. Flames (leap) up from the treetops. ______________
4. The water, rushing like two waterfalls, (gush) out of two huge containers. ______________

Talk to a parent or another trusted adult about how firefighters help your community. Write a paragraph about what you learn. Include one compound sentence. Vary your sentence structure. Then edit your work for subject-verb agreement.

____

____

____

____

____

Name ______________________________

- A verb must **agree** with its subject. In **compound sentences,** each subject must agree with the verb that follows it.
- Add *-s* or *-es* to most verbs in the present tense if the subject is singular. If the subject is *I* or *you,* do not add *-s* or *-es* to the verb.
- A **compound subject** with the conjunction ***and*** takes a plural verb.

Proofread the paragraph. On the lines below, correct mistakes in subject-verb agreement.

My brother take his bike to school. I needs to fix my bike. The seat wobble on bumpy roads. The pedals slips a lot, and the chain is loose. I tell my father about the problems. He offer to help and get out his toolbox. Dad and I tightens many of the screws and bolts. I fills the tires with air, and Dad adjusts the chain. Now my brother and I enjoys riding to school together.

COMMON ERRORS

A **compound subject** with the conjunction ***or*** takes a singular verb when each noun is singular: *Either Mom or Dad rings the doorbell.*

____

____

____

____

____

____

____

____

____

____

____

Name ____

Read the student draft and look for any corrections that need to be made. Then choose the best answer to each question.

(1) The three surfers paddles out toward the waves. (2) A lifeguard watch from his tall chair. (3) Along the shoreline, dozens of seagulls searches for their next meal. (4) A young boy and his dog walks past the lifeguard. (5) The dog chase the seagulls along the beach. (6) The flock of birds fly away over the ocean.

1. What change needs to be made in sentence 1?
   - **A** Change ***surfers*** to **surfer**
   - **B** Change ***paddles*** to **paddle**
   - **C** Change ***out*** to **over**
   - **D** Change ***waves*** to **wave**

2. What is the correct way to write sentence 2?
   - **F** A lifeguards watches from his tall chair.
   - **G** A lifeguard watch from his tall chair.
   - **H** A lifeguard watch from his tall chairs.
   - **J** A lifeguard watches from his tall chair.

3. What change needs to be made in sentence 3?
   - **A** Change ***shoreline*** to **shorelines**
   - **B** Change ***seagulls*** to **seagull**
   - **C** Change ***searches*** to **search**
   - **D** Change ***meal*** to **meals**

4. What change, if any, should be made in sentence 4?
   - **F** Change ***boy*** to **boys**
   - **G** Change ***dog*** to **dogs**
   - **H** Change ***walks*** to **walk**
   - **J** Make no change

5. What is the correct way to write sentence 5?
   - **A** The dog chase the seagulls along the beaches.
   - **B** The dog chases the seagulls along the beach.
   - **C** The dogs chases the seagull along the beach.
   - **D** The dog chase them seagulls along the beach.

6. What change, if any, should be made in sentence 6?
   - **F** Change ***flock*** to **flocks**
   - **G** Change ***fly*** to **flies**
   - **H** Change ***over*** to **overs**
   - **J** Change ***ocean*** to **oceans**

Name ____________________

Fold back the paper along the dotted line. Use the blanks to write each word as it is read aloud. When you finish the test, unfold the paper. Use the list at the right to correct any spelling mistakes.

	1. ______	1. minus
	2. ______	2. loser
	3. ______	3. humor
	4. ______	4. closet
	5. ______	5. recent
	6. ______	6. student
	7. ______	7. equal
	8. ______	8. profile
	9. ______	9. local
	10. ______	10. comet
	11. ______	11. vacant
	12. ______	12. punish
	13. ______	13. cavern
	14. ______	14. shiver
	15. ______	15. decent
	16. ______	16. linen
	17. ______	17. legal
	18. ______	18. panic
	19. ______	19. smoky
	20. ______	20. tyrant
Review Words	21. ______	21. valley
	22. ______	22. fifteen
	23. ______	23. culture
Challenge Words	24. ______	24. fatigue
	25. ______	25. fugitive

Name ______________________________

Syllables can divide after the first vowel (V/CV). These syllables, which end in vowels, are called **open syllables**. In open syllables, the vowel sound is usually long. ***to**/ken, **ti**/ny, **si**/lent*

Syllables can divide after the consonant that follows the first vowel (VC/V). These syllables, which end in consonants, are called **closed syllables**. In closed syllables, the vowel sound is usually short. ***riv**/er, **sol**/id, **nov**/el*

DECODING WORDS

The word *motel* has two syllables. The first syllable, *mo*, ends with the long *o* sound. It is an open syllable. The second syllable, *tel*, ends with a consonant and has a short *e* sound. It is a closed syllable. Blend the two syllables together: /mō/ /tel/.

Write the spelling words that match each syllable pattern.

minus	recent	local	cavern	legal
loser	student	comet	shiver	panic
humor	equal	vacant	decent	smoky
closet	profile	punish	linen	tyrant

long vowel sound in first syllable

1. ______________
2. ______________
3. ______________
4. ______________
5. ______________
6. ______________
7. ______________
8. ______________
9. ______________
10. ______________
11. ______________
12. ______________

short vowel sound in first syllable

13. ______________
14. ______________
15. ______________
16. ______________
17. ______________
18. ______________
19. ______________
20. ______________

Look through this week's readings for more words to sort. Create a word sort in your writer's notebook. Draw a slash (/) after each open syllable. Then read the words aloud.

Name ______________________________

Syllables can divide after the first vowel (V/CV). These syllables, which end in vowels, are called **open syllables**. In open syllables, the vowel sound is usually long. ***to/ken, ti/ny, si/lent***

Syllables can divide after the consonant that follows the first vowel (VC/V). These syllables, which end in consonants, are called **closed syllables**. In closed syllables, the vowel sound is usually short. ***riv/er, sol/id, nov/el***

DECODING WORDS

The word *motel* has two syllables. The first syllable, *mo,* ends with the long *o* sound. It is an open syllable. The second syllable, *tel,* ends with a consonant and has a short *e* sound. It is a closed syllable. Blend the two syllables together: /mō/ /tel/.

Write the spelling words that match each syllable pattern.

minus	camel	local	human	decent
loser	student	comet	shiver	amaze
humor	equal	parade	legal	fancy
closet	hero	punish	linen	tyrant

long vowel sound in first syllable

1. ______________
2. ______________
3. ______________
4. ______________
5. ______________
6. ______________
7. ______________
8. ______________
9. ______________
10. ______________

short vowel sound in first syllable

11. ______________
12. ______________
13. ______________
14. ______________
15. ______________
16. ______________
17. ______________
18. ______________
19. ______________
20. ______________

Look through this week's readings for more words to sort. Create a word sort in your writer's notebook. Draw a slash (/) after each open syllable. Then read the words aloud.

Name ______________________________

A. Write the spelling words that match each syllable pattern.

relevant	recent	bayonets	caverns	biceps
separate	utensil	comet	stamen	panic
license	vinyl	vacant	decent	smoky
rehearse	profile	punished	tirade	tyrant

long vowel sound in first syllable

1. ______________
2. ______________
3. ______________
4. ______________
5. ______________
6. ______________
7. ______________
8. ______________
9. ______________
10. ______________
11. ______________
12. ______________
13. ______________
14. ______________

short vowel sound in first syllable

15. ______________
16. ______________
17. ______________
18. ______________
19. ______________
20. ______________

B. Compare the words *profile* and *panic*. How are they alike? How are they different?

____

____

____

Look through this week's readings for more words to sort. Create a word sort in your writer's notebook. Draw a slash (/) after each open syllable. Then read the words aloud.

Name ______________________________

minus	recent	local	cavern	legal
loser	student	comet	shiver	panic
humor	equal	vacant	decent	smoky
closet	profile	punish	linen	tyrant

A. Write the spelling word that is the opposite of each word below.

1. reward ____________________
2. national ____________________
3. full ____________________
4. outdated ____________________
5. clear ____________________
6. teacher ____________________
7. disgraceful ____________________
8. calm ____________________

B. Write the spelling word that best completes each sentence.

9. We keep our umbrellas in the hall ____________________.
10. Is it ____________________ to park on the street overnight?
11. My younger brother has a childish sense of ____________________.
12. Kim turned to the side so we could see her ____________________.
13. She came in third, but she didn't feel like a ____________________.
14. It was cold and damp in the underground ____________________.
15. He acts like a ____________________ when he wants to get his way.
16. The icy winter wind made Jason ____________________.
17. How much is ninety ____________________ forty-five?
18. You can see the bright ____________________ in the sky at night.
19. Her blouse is made of the finest ____________________.
20. How many ounces are ____________________ to one pound?

Name ____

Underline the six misspelled words in the paragraphs below. Write the words correctly on the lines.

Miles loved working with animals. When a part-time job opened up at a locale vet clinic, he applied for it. He had read a rescent story about the clinic owner, Dr. Susan Hoffman. Dr. Hoffman sounded like a desant person who offered animal care at prices that everyone could afford.

1. ____________ 2. ____________ 3. ____________

Dr. Hoffman knew that Miles was a stoodent who needed time for homework and soccer practice. She didn't act like a tirant by demanding that he work long hours. And she had a good sense of huemor. It was the perfect job for Miles!

4. ____________ 5. ____________ 6. ____________

Writing Connection

Write a passage for a story about a student who works at another part-time job. Use at least four spelling words in your writing.

____

____

____

____

____

____

____

____

____

____

____

____

Name ______________________________

Remember

- **Open syllables** divide after the first vowel (V/CV). These syllables end in a vowel and usually have a long vowel sound: ***pho**/to, **sa**/fer, **ru**/ler.*
- **Closed syllables** divide after the consonant that follows the first vowel (VC/V). These syllables end in a consonant and usually have a short vowel sound: ***pal**/ace, **cab**/in, **sal**/ad.* Read these words aloud.

minus	recent	local	cavern	legal
loser	student	comet	shiver	panic
humor	equal	vacant	decent	smoky
closet	profile	punish	linen	tyrant

A. Write the missing letters to form a spelling word. Write the word on the line. Then draw a slash to divide the syllables in each word. Read the words aloud.

1. c __ __ et ______________
2. h __ __ or ______________
3. c __ __ ern ______________
4. pr __ __ ile ______________
5. p __ __ ic ______________
6. m __ __ us ______________
7. d __ __ ent ______________
8. cl __ __ et ______________
9. l __ __ al ______________
10. r __ __ ent ______________
11. __ __ ual ______________
12. p __ __ ish ______________
13. t __ __ ant ______________
14. v __ __ ant ______________
15. st __ __ ent ______________
16. l __ __ en ______________

B. Write these spelling words on the lines in alphabetical order. Alphabetize them to the third letter. ***local, smoky, shiver, loser***

17. ______________
18. ______________
19. ______________
20. ______________

Name ______________________________

Expand your vocabulary by adding or removing inflectional endings, prefixes, or suffixes to a base word to create different forms of a word.

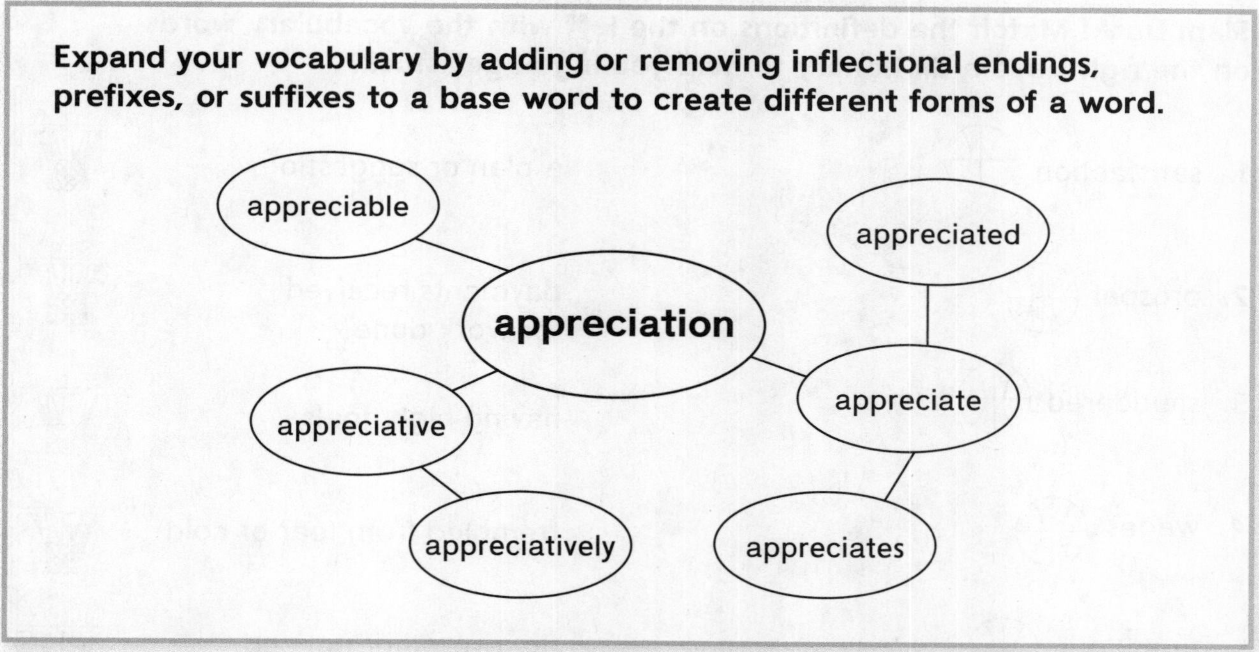

Add balloons to the banner to write as many related words as you can. Use a print or digital dictionary to help you. In your writer's notebook, use each word in a sentence.

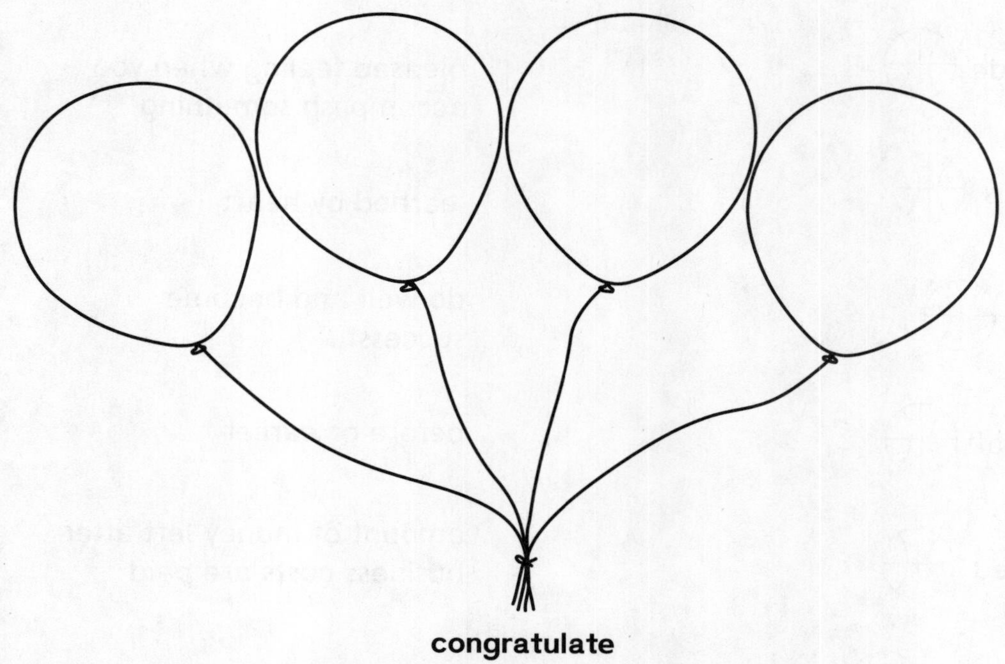

Name ____

Slam Dunk! Match the definitions on the left with the vocabulary words on the right. Use a dictionary to help you if you get stuck.

1. satisfaction
2. prosper
3. shuddered
4. wages
5. ambitious
6. profit
7. gratitude
8. previous
9. afford
10. proposal
11. detected
12. memorized

a plan or suggestion

payments received for work done

having high goals

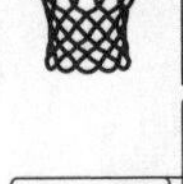

trembled from fear or cold

discovered or noticed

have enough money to pay for something

pleased feeling when you accomplish something

learned by heart

do well and become successful

before or earlier

amount of money left after business costs are paid

feeling of thankfulness

Name ____

- The **tense** of a verb tells when an action takes place.
- A **present-tense verb** tells what is happening now. To form the present tense of most verbs in the third person singular, add *-s*: *draws.* Add *-es* to verbs that end in *s, ss, ch, sh, x,* or *zz*: *wishes, misses.* If a verb ends with a consonant and the letter *y,* change *y* to *i* before adding *-es: tries.*
- The **present progressive tense** shows action that is continuing over time. To form the present progressive, use the verb *be* plus a **present participle**. Adding *-ing* to a verb creates a present participle.

  Malik is trying. We are playing hockey.

Read each sentence. Choose the correct form of the verb to complete the sentence. Write it on the line.

1. My mother (carrys, carries) boxes to the attic. ____________________
2. She (asking, asks) me to help her. ____________________
3. She is (trying, tries) to lift a heavy carton. ____________________
4. Each one of us (grabs, grab) one end. ____________________
5. We are (climb, climbing) the stairs when the box breaks. ____________________
6. Books (tumble, tumbling) down the stairs. ____________________
7. Mom (watchs, watches) them fall around us. ____________________
8. She and I are (picks, picking) them up carefully. ____________________

In your writer's notebook, write a short passage about helping someone. Include at least two present-tense verbs and two present participles. Remember the rules for forming verbs in the present tense.

Name ______________________________

- **Past-tense verbs** tell about actions in the past. Add *-ed* to most verbs to show past tense: *looked.* If a verb ends in *e,* drop the *e* and add *-ed*: *liked.* If a verb ends in a vowel and consonant, double the consonant and add *-ed*: *slipped.* If it ends in a consonant + *y,* change *y* to *i* and add *-ed*: *fried.*
- **Future-tense verbs** are formed with the helping verb *will*: *He will stop.*
- The **past progressive** and **future progressive tenses** use present participles to show action that was or will be continuing.

  She was helping. My friend will be attending.

Read each sentence. Underline each complete verb. Then write whether the tense is *present, past,* or *future* on the line.

1. Our class will visit the museum next week. ______________
2. I am making a list of interesting exhibits. ______________
3. One display shows historical inventions. ______________
4. Several devices provided light and heat. ______________
5. My classmates and I will be asking many questions. ______________

Read the excerpt from "A Reluctant Traveler." Look for the past progressive tense. Underline the helping verb and present participle in that sentence. Then write a sentence about a sunset using the past progressive tense.

Paul never realized how surrounded by water New York was. Many hours later, as the plane was landing in Buenos Aires, Paul noticed similar outlines of a city on the water, and bright lights, just like home.

____

____

Name ____________________

- When talking or writing about the **past**, **present**, or **future**, always use the correct verb tense.
- Take care not to mix verb tenses when describing the same incident.

Monique will look in the bushes, and Andre will check the grass.

Rewrite each sentence so that the second verb matches the tense of the first verb in the sentence.

1. The milk spills and poured off the edge of the table.

____

2. The cat raced over and licks it up.

____

3. The dog will come in and chases the cat.

____

4. I find a mop and cleaned up the puddle.

____

5. Dad will return soon, and the floor shines.

____

Writing Connection

Write a paragraph about an accident that you or someone you know had. Describe the event using action verbs. Make sure to avoid shifting verb tenses across the paragraph.

____

____

____

____

____

____

Name ______________________________

- Take care not to mix verb tenses when describing the same incident.
- To form the **present tense** of most verbs in the third-person singular, add *-s.* Add *-es* to verbs that end in *s, ss, ch, sh, x,* or *zz.* If a verb ends with a consonant and the letter *y,* change *y* to *i* before adding *-es.*
- Add *-ed* to most verbs to show **past tense**. If a verb ends in *e,* drop the *e,* then add *-ed.* If a verb ends in a vowel and consonant, double the consonant and add *-ed.* If it ends in a consonant and *y,* change *y* to *i* and add *-ed.*
- **Future-tense verbs** are formed with the helping verb *will.*

Proofread the paragraph. On the lines below, correct mistakes in spelling and verb tenses.

Sundale School will celebrates its tenth anniversary next year. At yesterday's assembly, the principal asks students for ideas. I will raise my hand and suggest a play. Beginning next week, students writing scenes from the school's history. At first, the founders of the school expect little interest in their plans. They were worry about the costs. I hoping to play the part of a founder. The school mean a great deal to me.

____

____

____

____

____

____

____

____

____

____

Name ______________________________

Read the student draft and look for any corrections that need to be made. Then choose the best answer to each question.

(1) The two sisters boarding a train in Italy. (2) They were traveled to the coast of Spain. (3) Their parents will join them next week. (4) Yesterday, the girls send an e-mail to their parents telling them about a museum they visited. (5) After reading the e-mail, their parents shares the photos with their friends.

(6) The train shuddered and pull out of the station. (7) I talked and shared stories with my cousin. (8) I last saw her two years ago! (9) We took silly pictures of ourselves and laugh for hours and hours.

1. In order to write sentence 1 in the past tense, what change needs to be made?

A Change ***boarding*** to **will board**

B Change ***boarding*** to **board**

C Change ***boarding*** to **boarded**

D Change ***boarding*** to **are boarding**

2. What is the correct way to write sentence 2 in the past progressive tense?

F They were travels to the coast of Spain.

G They were travelers to the coast of Spain.

H They were traveling to the coast of Spain.

J They traveling to the coast of Spain.

3. What change, if any, should be made to sentence 3 or 4?

A Change ***will join*** to **joined** in sentence 3

B Change ***send*** to **sent** in sentence 4

C Change ***telling*** to **told** in sentence 4

D Make no change

4. What change needs to be made in sentence 5?

F Change ***shares*** to **shared**

G Change ***shares*** to **sharing**

H Change ***reading*** to **reads**

J Change ***their*** to **they're**

5. What change, if any, should be made to sentence 6 or 7?

A Change ***pull*** to **pulled** in sentence 6

B Change ***talked*** to **talk** in sentence 7

C Change ***shared*** to **share** in sentence 7

D Make no change

6. What change, if any, should be made to sentence 8 or 9?

F Change ***saw*** to **seen** in sentence 8

G Change ***took*** to **take** in sentence 9

H Change ***laugh*** to **laughed** in sentence 9

J Make no change

Name ______________________________

Fold back the paper along the dotted line. Use the blanks to write each word as it is read aloud. When you finish the test, unfold the paper. Use the list at the right to correct any spelling mistakes.

	1. ______	1. video
	2. ______	2. poet
	3. ______	3. riot
	4. ______	4. piano
	5. ______	5. diary
	6. ______	6. radio
	7. ______	7. ideas
	8. ______	8. ruin
	9. ______	9. diet
	10. ______	10. patriot
	11. ______	11. fluid
	12. ______	12. rodeo
	13. ______	13. cruel
	14. ______	14. genuine
	15. ______	15. casual
	16. ______	16. trial
	17. ______	17. fuel
	18. ______	18. meteor
	19. ______	19. diameter
	20. ______	20. meander
Review Words	21. ______	21. recent
	22. ______	22. closet
	23. ______	23. minus
Challenge Words	24. ______	24. situation
	25. ______	25. variety

Name ________________________________

When two vowels together make two different sounds, they divide into separate syllables. Words such as ***duet*** and ***patio*** have this V/V syllable pattern. These words have an **open syllable** followed by a syllable that starts with a vowel.

In ***duet***, the V/V pattern divides the two vowels as follows: *du/et*. In ***patio***, the V/V pattern divides the vowels *io*: *pa/ti/o*.

DECODING WORDS

In the word *duet*, the first syllable, *du*, is open. It has a long *u* sound. The second syllable, *et*, is closed. It has a short *e* vowel sound. Blend the two syllables together: /dü/ /et/.

Write the spelling words that contain the matching V/V pattern.

video	diary	diet	cruel	fuel
poet	radio	patriot	genuine	meteor
riot	ideas	fluid	casual	diameter
piano	ruin	rodeo	trial	meander

ea

1. ____________
2. ____________

eo

3. ____________
4. ____________
5. ____________

ia

6. ____________
7. ____________
8. ____________
9. ____________

ie

10. ____________

io

11. ____________
12. ____________
13. ____________

oe

14. ____________

ua

15. ____________

ue

16. ____________
17. ____________

ui

18. ____________
19. ____________
20. ____________

Look through this week's readings for words with a V/V syllable division pattern. Record them in your writer's notebook. Draw a slash (/) to indicate the V/V pattern. Then read the words aloud.

Name ______________________________

When two vowels together make two different sounds, they divide into separate syllables. Words such as ***duet*** and ***patio*** have this V/V syllable pattern. These words have an **open syllable** followed by a syllable that starts with a vowel.

In ***duet,*** the V/V pattern divides the two vowels as follows: *du/et*. In ***patio,*** the V/V pattern divides the vowels *io*: *pa/ti/o*.

DECODING WORDS

In the word *duet,* the first syllable, *du,* is open. It has a long *u* sound. The second syllable, *et,* is closed. It has a short *e* vowel sound. Blend the two syllables together: /dü/ /et/.

Write the spelling words that contain the matching V/V pattern.

video	diary	diet	cruel	fuel
poet	radio	giant	lion	science
riot	ideas	dial	casual	quiet
piano	ruin	rodeo	trial	prior

ea

1. ____________________

eo

2. ____________________
3. ____________________

ia

4. ____________________
5. ____________________
6. ____________________
7. ____________________
8. ____________________

ie

9. ____________________
10. ____________________
11. ____________________

io

12. ____________________
13. ____________________
14. ____________________
15. ____________________

oe

16. ____________________

ua

17. ____________________

ue

18. ____________________
19. ____________________

ui

20. ____________________

Look through this week's readings for words with a V/V syllable division pattern. Record them in your writer's notebook. Draw a slash (/) to indicate the V/V pattern. Then read the words aloud.

Name ______________________________

A. Write the spelling words that contain the matching V/V pattern.

dialect	calcium	glorious	cruelly	variety
grueling	pioneers	patriot	genuine	meteor
riot	ideas	fluidity	casual	diameter
radiance	ruined	evaluate	trials	meander

ea

1. ______________
2. ______________

eo

3. ______________

ia

4. ______________
5. ______________
6. ______________
7. ______________

ie

8. ______________

iu

9. ______________

io

10. ______________
11. ______________
12. ______________
13. ______________

ua

14. ______________
15. ______________

ue

16. ______________
17. ______________

ui

18. ______________
19. ______________
20. ______________

B. Read each word. Draw a slash (/) between the two vowels that form the V/V pattern. Then write the sound of the first vowel in the pattern.

1. **meander** ______________________________
2. **genuine** ______________________________

Look through this week's readings for words with a V/V syllable division pattern. Record them in your writer's notebook. Draw a slash (/) to indicate the V/V pattern. Then read the words aloud.

Name ______________________________

video	diary	diet	cruel	fuel
poet	radio	patriot	genuine	meteor
riot	ideas	fluid	casual	diameter
piano	ruin	rodeo	trial	meander

A. Write the spelling word that matches each definition below.

1. rock in space ______________
2. poetry writer ______________
3. usual food ______________
4. court case ______________
5. distance across center of a circle ______________
6. device on which music is heard ______________
7. supporter of one's country ______________
8. musical instrument with keys ______________
9. Western competition ______________
10. material burned for heat or power ______________

B. Write the spelling word that best completes each analogy.

11. *Schedule* is to *timetable* as *journal* is to ______________.
12. *Party* is to *celebration* as *uprising* is to ______________.
13. *Mend* is to *repair* as *wreck* is to ______________.
14. *Loose* is to *tight* as ______________ is to *formal.*
15. *Mist* is to *fog* as ______________ is to *liquid.*
16. *Sprint* is to *run* as ______________ is to *wander.*
17. *False* is to ______________ as *phony* is to *real.*
18. *Thoughts* is to ______________ as *behavior* is to *actions.*
19. *Heartless* is to *caring* as ______________ is to *kind.*
20. *Car* is to *automobile* as ______________ is to *movie.*

Name ____________________

Underline the six misspelled words in the paragraphs below. Using the V/V patterns you learned, write the words correctly on the lines.

We walked along a river that flowed with a sparkling green flued. Soft music filled the air, even though there wasn't a radeo around for miles. A red moon rose above the horizon, and a bright metear flashed by in the sky.

1. ____________ 2. ____________ 3. ____________

We needed a fire for warmth, but we had no fuil to burn. The trees around us were huge—at least 50 feet in diometer. It would be impossible to cut them. I looked at my friends. "Any idias?" I asked.

4. ____________ 5. ____________ 6. ____________

Writing Connection

Write a passage that includes an unusual setting. Select a genre, such as a fantasy story or a narrative poem. Brainstorm ideas in your writer's notebook to plan your particular topic. Use at least four spelling words in your writing.

____

____

____

____

____

____

____

____

____

____

____

Name ______________________________

Remember

Words such as ***chaos*** and ***cereal*** have a V/V syllable pattern. These words have an **open syllable** (a syllable that ends in a vowel) followed by a syllable that starts with a vowel.

- In ***chaos,*** the V/V patterns divides the two vowels as follows: *cha/os.*
- In ***cereal,*** the V/V pattern comes in the second and third syllables: *ce/re/al.*

Read the words out loud. Listen to the syllable division between the vowels.

video	diary	diet	cruel	fuel
poet	radio	patriot	genuine	meteor
riot	ideas	fluid	casual	diameter
piano	ruin	rodeo	trial	meander

A. Fill in the missing letters to form a spelling word. Then write the spelling word.

1. cas ___ ___ l ______________

2. p ___ ___ t ______________

3. rad ___ ___ ______________

4. d ___ ___ meter ______________

5. vid ___ ___ ______________

6. p ___ ___ no ______________

7. cr ___ ___ l ______________

8. gen ___ ___ ne ______________

9. fl ___ ___ d ______________

10. d ___ ___ ry ______________

11. id ___ ___ s ______________

12. patr ___ ___ t ______________

13. f ___ ___ l ______________

14. d ___ ___ t ______________

15. tr ___ ___ l ______________

B. Write these spelling words on the lines in reverse alphabetical order: *riot, meteor, rodeo, meander, ruin.*

16. ______________

17. ______________

18. ______________

19. ______________

20. ______________

Name ____

An **adage** is a short, often old, saying that expresses a common observation or piece of wisdom. Two popular adages are "Don't judge a book by its cover" (don't judge something based on its appearance), and "Slow and steady wins the race" (careful and consistent effort leads to success).

You can figure out the meaning of an adage by looking at the surrounding words and sentences and thinking about what you already know.

Read each passage below. Underline the context clues that help you determine the meaning of each adage in bold. Then write the meaning in your own words on the lines provided.

As Brody crossed the finish line, he knew his mom had been right—**every cloud has a silver lining**. Losing last year's race had upset him, but it also made him train harder for this year's race. As a result of his hard work, he won first place.

____

____

____

____

As I was running out the door, my dad told me to grab my umbrella in case it rained. I looked outside. It was cloudy, so I grabbed it and put it in my backpack just in case. After all, my dad always says that **it's better to be safe than sorry**!

____

____

____

____

Write a short passage in your writer's notebook using one of the adages from the activity above.

Name ______________________________

Read each passage from "Potluck or Potlatch?" Underline the context clues that help you figure out the meaning of each word in bold. Look for clues within or beyond the sentence that have a cause-and-effect relationship with the word. Then tell what the word means.

1. Mrs. Wright placed a warm hand on Alex's shoulder, which made him feel a little less **nervous**.

____

____

2. "What a lovely thought," she said. "I think there may have been a **miscommunication**, though. We're having a potlatch today, not a potluck."

____

____

3. Alex still looked **confused**, so Wakiash explained that the Kwakiutl people believe that wealth should be shared.

____

____

4. The feast was delicious, and Alex was having so much fun that he lost track of time. As he helped himself to a second brownie, he was **startled** to see his mother at the front door because he felt as if she had just dropped him off.

____

____

Name ______________________________

- The **main verb** shows what the subject does or is.
- A **helping verb** helps the main verb show an action or make a statement. Some helping verbs include *has, had, have, am, is, are, was,* and *were.*
  A storm is coming.
- Sentences can be in the active or passive voice. In the **active voice**, the subject is doing something. In the **passive voice**, the subject is the object of an action.

  Janelle ate the pasta. (active)

  The pasta was eaten by Janelle. (passive)

Read each sentence. Underline each main verb and circle each helping verb. Then write on the line whether the sentence is in the *active voice* or *passive voice.*

1. I am helping my sister with her science project. ______________
2. She had decided on a model of the solar system. ______________
3. I was comparing the sizes of the planets on a diagram. ______________
4. The diagram was printed in an encyclopedia. ______________
5. Our parents have suggested some other sources. ______________
6. Some Web sites were mentioned by her teacher. ______________
7. A great deal of work was required on the model. ______________
8. My sister was awarded an "A" for the project. ______________

In your writer's notebook, write instructions for a plan you have to complete a school assignment or project. Include at least four helping verbs. After each sentence, write whether it is active or passive voice. Read the instructions to a partner, and then ask your classmate to restate them.

Name ______________________________

- The **progressive tenses** take a form of the verb *be* and a **present participle**: *I am cooking.* (present progressive) *My daughter was waiting.* (past progressive) *They will be arriving.* (future progressive)
- **Past participles** for regular verbs take the same form as the past tense: *worked, stayed.* Irregular verbs have irregular past participles: *eaten, brought, sung.*
- The three **perfect tenses** (present, past, future) use a form of the verb *have* and the past participle to show a completed action.

  She has practiced. She had practiced. She will have practiced.

Read each sentence. Underline the complete verb and circle each participle. Write the tense of the complete verb on the line.

1. We have selected a terrier for our next pet. ______________
2. Our parents are assigning jobs for each of us. ______________
3. I had requested meal preparations. ______________
4. My sister was hoping for evening walks. ______________
5. The puppy will be arriving tomorrow morning. ______________
6. As of tomorrow, we will have planned for this for a full month. ______________

Reading/Writing Connection

Read the sentence from "Gulf Spill Superheroes." It uses the present perfect tense. Underline the complete verb and circle the participle. Then write two sentences about a plan you have. Include two perfect tenses. Edit and proofread your work.

As we have seen, the Deepwater Horizon accident required heroic efforts of all kinds.

____

____

____

Name ______________________________

- Special **helping verbs**, called **modals**, express possibility or obligation. The principal modals are *can, could, may, might, must, ought, shall, should, will,* and *would: I may join you later.*
- A **contraction** is a shortened form of two words. It can be formed from a helping verb and the word *not* or from a pronoun and a verb: *aren't, can't, she's, they're.* An **apostrophe** (') indicates the missing letter or letters.
- Avoid confusing *its* with *it's* and *your* with *you're. Its* and *your* are used to show possession.

A. Rewrite each sentence, forming a contraction from the two separate words in each one.

1. He had been wandering the forest for months now.

____

2. The members of his expedition had not been able to find him.

____

3. They cannot be certain, but a new clue may lead them to him.

____

B. Circle the principal modal in each sentence. Underline the main verb.

4. There ought to be clear rules for a fire drill.

5. We may go to the aquarium next week.

6. The children would like to help with the recycling project.

Write a paragraph in your writer's notebook about a problem that needs to be solved. Include two contractions. Be sure to use apostrophes correctly.

Name ______________________________

- The three **progressive tenses** take a form of the verb *be* and a **present participle** to show a continuing action.
- The three **perfect tenses** (present, past, future) use a form of the verb *have* and the **past participle** to show a completed action.
- A **contraction** is a shortened form of two words. It can be formed from a helping verb and the word *not* or from a pronoun and a verb. An apostrophe (') indicates the missing letter or letters.

Proofread the paragraph. On the lines below, correct mistakes in spelling, verb tenses, and contractions. Look out for misspelled high-frequency words.

A crowd was form outside the courtroom an our ago. Some people hadnt picked up the morning paper yet. Others wer'nt paying attention when the results were displayd on the television screen. The jury did'nt take long to reach they're verdict. Even though the trial had lasting too months, they had decideed quickly. In a moment, we hear what they have to say. We ar'not expect any surprises.

COMMON ERRORS

The high-frequency words *they're, their,* and *there* are often confused because they sound the same. Remember: *they're* is a contraction for *they are,* whereas *their* shows possession. *There* describes a location or idea.

____

____

____

____

____

____

____

____

Name ____

Read the selection and look for any corrections that need to be made. Then choose the best answer to each question.

(1) My brother would liked a room of his own. (2) Our parents had contacting a builder last month. (3) They is setting aside money for the new construction. (4) The contractors will beginning the renovation in April. (5) The work should not take very long. (6) My brother is'nt been this excited about anything in years!

1. What is the correct way to write sentence 1?

A My brother would like a room of his own.

B My brother has would like a room of his own.

C My brother would have like a room of his own.

D My brother would liking a room of his own.

2. How does sentence 2 need to be changed?

F Change ***had*** to **have**

G Change ***had*** to **haven't**

H Change ***contacting*** to **contacted**

J Change ***contacting*** to **contact**

3. What is the correct way to write sentence 3?

A They was setting aside money for the new construction.

B They are setting aside money for the new construction.

C They is setted aside money for the new construction.

D They has set aside money for the new construction.

4. How does sentence 4 need to be changed?

F Change ***will*** to **is**

G Change ***will*** to **has**

H Change ***beginning*** to **begin**

J Change ***beginning*** to **began**

5. What is the correct way to write sentence 5?

A The work should not taking very long.

B The work should not taken very long

C The work should not takes very long.

D Sentence 5 is written correctly.

6. How does sentence 6 need to be changed?

F Change ***is'nt*** to **isn't**

G Change ***is'nt*** to **hasn't**

H Change ***excited*** to **exciting**

J Change ***excited*** to **excite**

Name ____

Fold back the paper along the dotted line. Use the blanks to write each word as it is read aloud. When you finish the test, unfold the paper. Use the list at the right to correct any spelling mistakes.

	1. ________	1. footprint
	2. ________	2. fairground
	3. ________	3. although
	4. ________	4. laughter
	5. ________	5. appoint
	6. ________	6. coastal
	7. ________	7. bleachers
	8. ________	8. grownup
	9. ________	9. encounter
	10. ________	10. grouchy
	11. ________	11. flawless
	12. ________	12. lawyer
	13. ________	13. entertain
	14. ________	14. applause
	15. ________	15. faucet
	16. ________	16. caution
	17. ________	17. boundary
	18. ________	18. doubting
	19. ________	19. southern
	20. ________	20. roughness
Review Words	21. ________	21. poet
	22. ________	22. radio
	23. ________	23. fuel
Challenge Words	24. ________	24. nowadays
	25. ________	25. distraught

Name ______________________________

When a vowel sound is spelled with more than one letter, the syllable is called a **vowel team syllable**. Two, three, or four letters can work together to form a single vowel sound: ***sound, spoon, frighten, sleigh, rainbow***.

In *frighten*, three letters form one sound, /ī/. Two letters that form one sound, such as *ou* in *found*, are called **digraphs**.

DECODING WORDS

Eighteen has two vowel team spellings—*eigh* and *ee*. Vowel team spellings, like the digraph *ee*, must stay in the same syllable. Blend the syllables together: *eigh-teen*, /ā/ /tēn/.

Write the spelling words that contain the matching vowel team pattern.

footprint	appoint	encounter	entertain	boundary
fairground	coastal	grouchy	applause	doubting
although	bleachers	flawless	faucet	southern
laughter	grownup	lawyer	caution	roughness

ai
1. ______________

au
2. ______________
3. ______________
4. ______________
5. ______________

aw
6. ______________
7. ______________

ea
8. ______________

oa
9. ______________

oi
10. ______________

oo
11. ______________

ou
12. ______________
13. ______________
14. ______________
15. ______________
16. ______________
17. ______________
18. ______________
19. ______________

ow
20. ______________

Look through this week's readings for more words to sort. Record the words in your writer's notebook. Circle the vowel team syllables that are digraphs. Then read your list to a partner.

Name ______________________________

When a vowel sound is spelled with more than one letter, the syllable is called a **vowel team syllable**. Two, three, or four letters can work together to form a single vowel sound: ***sound, spoon, frighten, sleigh, rainbow***.

In *frighten,* three letters form one sound, /ī/. Two letters that form one sound, such as *ou* in *found,* are called **digraphs**.

DECODING WORDS

Eighteen has two vowel team spellings—*eigh* and *ee*. Vowel team spellings, like the digraph *ee,* must stay in the same syllable. Blend the syllables together: *eigh-teen,* /ā/ /tēn/.

Write the spelling words that contain the matching vowel team pattern.

footprint	appoint	counter	entertain	caution
fairground	coastal	grouchy	applause	boundary
although	bleachers	flawless	faucet	doubting
August	grownup	lawyer	laundry	southern

ai

1. ______________

au

2. ______________
3. ______________
4. ______________
5. ______________
6. ______________

aw

7. ______________
8. ______________

ea

9. ______________

oa

10. ______________

oi

11. ______________

oo

12. ______________

ou

13. ______________
14. ______________
15. ______________
16. ______________
17. ______________
18. ______________
19. ______________

ow

20. ______________

Look through this week's readings for more words to sort. Record the words in your writer's notebook. Circle the vowel team syllables that are digraphs. Then read your list to a partner.

Name ____________________

A. Write the spelling words that contain the matching vowel team pattern.

footprint	appoint	encounter	lawyer	boundary
fairground	laughter	bountiful	entertainment	applause
although	bleachers	doubting	causeway	southern
allowance	faucet	flawlessly	caution	roughness

ai

1. ____________

au

2. ____________

3. ____________

4. ____________

5. ____________

6. ____________

aw

7. ____________

8. ____________

ea

9. ____________

oi

10. ____________

oo

11. ____________

ou

12. ____________

13. ____________

14. ____________

15. ____________

16. ____________

17. ____________

18. ____________

19. ____________

ow

20. ____________

B. Compare the words *although* and *southern*. How are they alike? How are they different?

____

____

____

____

Look through this week's readings for more words to sort. Record the words in your writer's notebook. Circle the vowel team syllables that are digraphs. Then read your list to a partner.

Name ______________________________

footprint	appoint	encounter	entertain	boundary
fairground	coastal	grouchy	applause	doubting
although	bleachers	flawless	faucet	southern
laughter	grownup	lawyer	caution	roughness

A. Write the spelling word that matches each definition below.

1. perfect ______________
2. to amuse ______________
3. a nozzle ______________
4. a type of seating ______________
5. an unexpected meeting ______________
6. grumpy ______________
7. clapping ______________
8. adult ______________
9. carefulness ______________
10. to select ______________
11. an attorney ______________
12. a border ______________

B. Write the spelling word that best completes each sentence.

13. Who left that muddy ______________ on the rug?
14. Many beach lovers come to our ______________ town.
15. I am ______________ the truth of his exaggerated story.
16. I do not like the ______________ of corduroy fabric.
17. The sound of the child's ______________ made me smile.
18. Do palm trees grow in the ______________ part of your state?
19. There are many exciting rides at the ______________.
20. ______________ I was tired, I still helped Dad clean the garage.

Name ______________________________

Underline the misspelled words in the paragraphs. Using your knowledge of vowel teams and digraphs, write the words correctly on the lines.

Each October, storytellers gather in the suthern state of Tennessee for the National Storytelling Festival. The storytellers entertane audiences in giant tents set up in downtown Jonesborough. If you attend, you will encownter some of the best storytellers in the country.

1. ____________ **2.** ____________ **3.** ____________

Storytellers at the festival are experts in the craft. Tales are told with flauless precision. You can expect plenty of laghter and applawse as delighted audiences enjoy the best storytellers in the land.

4. ____________ **5.** ____________ **6.** ____________

Writing Connection

Write information about an interesting event you have attended. Use at least four spelling words in your writing. Decide which details will interest your audience. Then choose a genre, such as a personal narrative or an opinion about the event. Use at least four spelling words in your writing.

____

____

____

____

____

____

____

____

____

____

____

Name ______________________________

Remember

In a **vowel team syllable**, two or more letters work together to make one vowel sound. For example, in the word *sight*, the letters *igh* work together to make a long *i* sound. In the word *heater*, the letters *ea* make a long *e* sound. When two letters stand for a single sound, it is also called a **digraph**. Read the word *heater* aloud, keeping the digraph *ea* in the same syllable: /hē/ /tər/.

footprint	appoint	encounter	entertain	boundary
fairground	coastal	grouchy	applause	doubting
although	bleachers	flawless	faucet	southern
laughter	grownup	lawyer	caution	roughness

A. Fill in the missing letters to form a spelling word. Write the spelling word on the line. Then read each word aloud.

1. l ___ ___ yer ______________
2. gr ___ ___ chy ______________
3. r ___ ___ ghness ______________
4. appl ___ ___ se ______________
5. c ___ ___ stal ______________
6. b ___ ___ ndary ______________
7. gr ___ ___ nup ______________
8. l ___ ___ ghter ______________
9. c ___ ___ tion ______________
10. alth ___ ___ gh ______________
11. app ___ ___ nt ______________
12. bl ___ ___ chers ______________
13. fairgr ___ ___ nd ______________
14. d ___ ___ bting ______________
15. s ___ ___ thern ______________

B. Write these spelling words on the lines in alphabetical order. Alphabetize them to the third letter. *footprint, entertain, faucet, encounter, flawless*

16. ______________
17. ______________
18. ______________
19. ______________
20. ______________

Name ______________________________

Expand your vocabulary by adding or removing inflectional endings, prefixes, or suffixes to a base word to create different forms of the word.

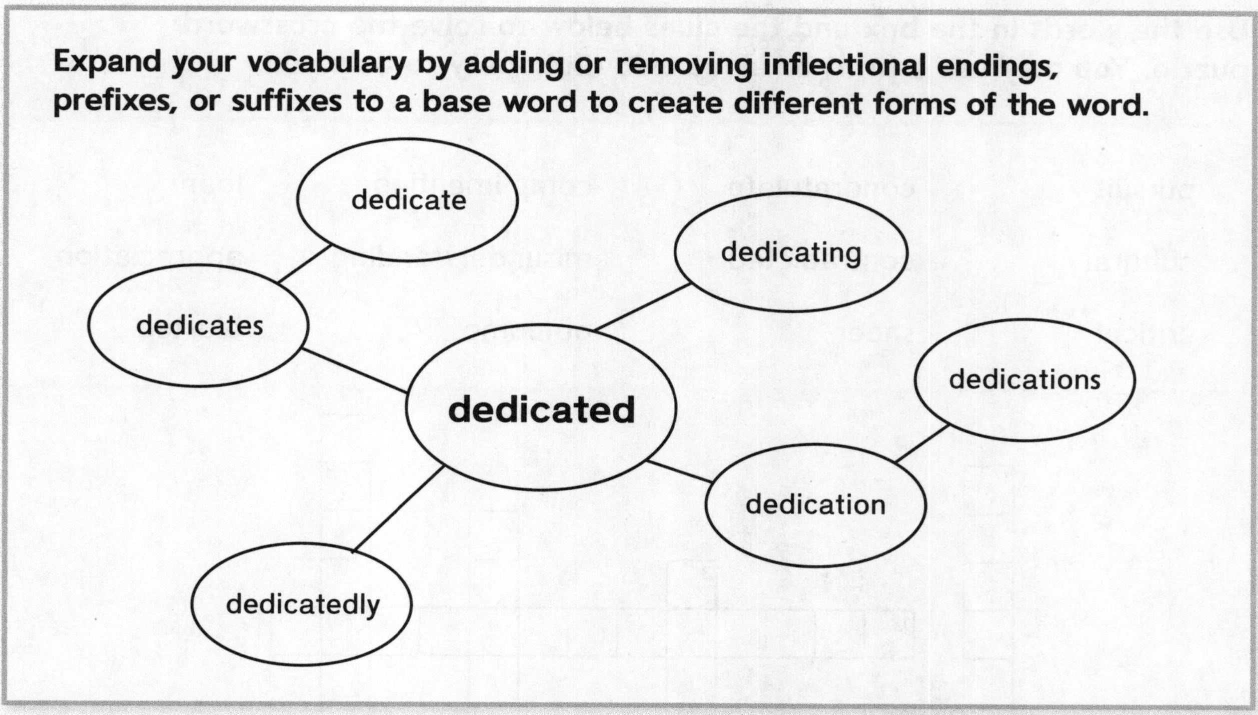

Write as many related words on the puzzle pieces as you can. Use a print or electronic dictionary to help you. Remember to drop the *e* before adding suffixes such as *-ive*.

Name ______________________________

Use the words in the box and the clues below to solve the crossword puzzle. You may use a print or electronic dictionary to help you.

pursuit	congratulate	complimenting	loan
cultural	contradicted	misunderstanding	appreciation
critical	sheer	outcome	blurted

Across

1. saying something nice about a person
2. a result or consequence
3. steep
4. understanding the value of something
5. money borrowed
6. relating to customs and beliefs

Down

1. chase
2. give good praise or good wishes
3. said suddenly
4. find fault with others
5. disagreed
6. failure to understand another

Name ______________________________

- A **linking verb** links the subject of a sentence to a noun or an adjective in the predicate. It tells what the subject is, was, or will be.
- Common linking verbs include *am, is, are, was, were,* and *will be*: *My dog is sleepy.* The verbs *seem, feel, appear, look,* and *taste* can also be used as linking verbs: *That sandwich looks delicious.*
- Subjects and linking verbs must **agree**: *The playground was empty.*
- In compound sentences, both subjects and verbs must agree.

  Those dishes are dirty, but this plate is clean.

Read each sentence and choose the correct linking verb. Write it on the line.

1. Today's speaker (is, are) a movie director. ____________
2. The students (is, are) eager to meet her. ____________
3. Her most recent movie (was, were) a documentary. ____________
4. Three major actors (was, were) narrators in the film. ____________
5. The film (was, will be) very popular last year. ____________
6. The competition is tough, but I (am, are) hopeful that it will win an award. ____________
7. Her next movie (was, will be) a comedy set in Brazil. ____________
8. The director (appear, appears) happy with it so far. ____________
9. The poster (looks, look) different from her other films' posters. ____________
10. The colors (seem, seems) much brighter on the new one. ____________

In your writer's notebook, review a movie you enjoy. Include at least five helping verbs and one compound sentence. Then edit and proofread your work. Make sure all subjects and linking verbs agree.

Name ______________________________

- A **linking verb** links the subject of a sentence to a noun or an adjective in the predicate: *The restaurant looks empty.*
- The noun that follows a linking verb renames or identifies the subject: *The woman is a politician.* (noun)
- The adjective that follows a linking verb describes the subject. It is called a **predicate adjective**: *This hike will be difficult.* (adjective)

Read this paragraph from "Helping Hands." Find the sentence that includes a linking verb. Underline the simple subject. Then circle the word in the predicate that is linked to the subject by the verb. On the line below, identify whether the word in the predicate is an adjective or a noun.

The best part of their adventure, however, came when the girls finally met Danielle Fairchild in person. Danielle showed the girls how she used the BOB-1 to draw and color with her right hand. The device was a success!

____

Reading/Writing Connection

Imagine that you are attending a big picnic on a hot day. Write a paragraph describing the event. Include at least five linking verbs. You may want to include the linking verbs *seem, feel, appear, look,* or *taste*.

____

____

____

____

____

____

____

Name ______________________________

- **Titles** always begin with a **capital letter**. All major words in the title are also capitalized: *The Washington Post*. Do not use a capital letter for articles, conjunctions, and prepositions: *Mary Poppins in the Park*.
- **Underline** or **italicize** the titles of major works, such as books, newspapers, and magazines: National Geographic. Use **quotation marks** around smaller works, such as poems, songs, and short stories: "Jack and Jill."
- Capitalize all major words in **product names:** Skylar Superball. Product names do not require underlining, italicizing, or quotation marks.

Rewrite each sentence correctly by underlining or placing quotations around any titles. Capitalize letters in titles or product names as needed.

1. I just read the book a world of wonderful words.

____

2. The book is about the inventor of the wordy wonderbot.

____

3. The author also wrote the article the seven signs of success.

____

4. Chapter five of the book is called a bumble of a spelling bee.

____

Writing Connection

Write a few sentences about a book you enjoy. Check your work for capitalization, punctuation, and mechanics.

____

____

____

____

Name ______________________________

- Subjects and linking verbs must agree.
- Titles and product names always begin with a capital letter. All major words in titles and product names are also capitalized.
- Underline or italicize the titles of major works. Use quotation marks around the titles of smaller works.

Proofread the paragraph. On the lines below, correct mistakes in linking verb usage, titles, and product names.

Is your library books always overdue? Grant Lin, author of the book Get your life On Track, can help. Lin created a new application called time on time. The program look difficult, but it were easy to use. The creation of a calendar are the first step. Mr. Lin wrote about calendars in his article The best month I ever had." You can find it in the book "always chasing Father Time." His books is available in most libraries.

Name ____________________

Read the selection and look for any corrections that need to be made. Then choose the best answer to each question.

(1) My aunt are an excellent chef. (2) Her casseroles always tastes delicious. (3) My cousins are lucky that she makes their meals. (4) She wrote the book Natural vegetable Dishes. (5) She always appear happy when she cooks. (6) We are always welcome at her home for meals. (7) We was just there for dinner last week. (8) I is looking forward to our next visit!

1. What is the correct way to write sentence 1?
   - **A** My aunt aren't an excellent chef.
   - **B** My aunt weren't an excellent chef.
   - **C** My aunt is an excellent chef.
   - **D** My aunt were an excellent chef.

2. What is the correct way to write sentence 2?
   - **F** Her casseroles always taste delicious.
   - **G** Her casseroles always are tasting delicious.
   - **H** Her casseroles always tasting delicious.
   - **J** Her casseroles always will be tasting delicious.

3. What is the correct way to write sentence 4?
   - **A** She wrote the book Natural Vegetable Dishes.
   - **B** She wrote the book "Natural Vegetable Dishes."
   - **C** She wrote the book <u>natural vegetable dishes</u>.
   - **D** She wrote the book *Natural Vegetable Dishes*.

4. What is the correct way to write sentences 5 and 6?
   - **F** She always appear happy when she cooks. We is always welcome at her home for meals.
   - **G** She always appears happy when she cooks. We are always welcome at her home for meals.
   - **H** She always appears happy when she cook. We are always welcome at her home for meal.
   - **J** She always appears happy when her cooks. We is always welcome at her home for meals.

5. What is the correct way to write sentence 7?
   - **A** Us was there for dinner last week.
   - **B** We is there for dinner last week.
   - **C** We were there for dinner last week.
   - **D** We we're there for dinner last week.

6. What change, if any, should be made to sentence 8?
   - **F** Change ***is*** to **am**
   - **G** Change ***is*** to **was**
   - **H** Change ***is*** to **were**
   - **J** Make no change

Name ____

Fold back the paper along the dotted line. Use the blanks to write each word as it is read aloud. When you finish the test, unfold the paper. Use the list at the right to correct any spelling mistakes.

1. ____________		1. stable
2. ____________		2. saddle
3. ____________		3. table
4. ____________		4. noble
5. ____________		5. cattle
6. ____________		6. stumble
7. ____________		7. terrible
8. ____________		8. beetle
9. ____________		9. kettle
10. ____________		10. eagle
11. ____________		11. royal
12. ____________		12. cripple
13. ____________		13. hospital
14. ____________		14. legal
15. ____________		15. label
16. ____________		16. vocal
17. ____________		17. journal
18. ____________		18. medal
19. ____________		19. several
20. ____________		20. sample
Review Words	21. ____________	21. entertain
	22. ____________	22. encounter
	23. ____________	23. southern
Challenge Words	24. ____________	24. impossible
	25. ____________	25. people

Name ______________________________

When a word ends with the letters *le,* the final syllable usually includes the preceding consonant. This is called a **consonant + *le* syllable.** It is **final stable syllable** that always ends with the sound /əl/. Examples include *little* (*lit/tle*) and *cable* (*ca/ble*).

Words that end in a consonant + *-el* or *-al* often divide in the same way: *tinsel* (*tin/sel*), *oval* (*o/val*).

DECODING WORDS

The word *principle* has three syllables. It ends with the final stable syllable *ple,* pronounced /pəl/. Blend the sounds in each syllable together: /prin/ /sə/ /pəl/.

Write the words whose final syllable contains the matching spelling pattern.

stable	cattle	kettle	hospital	journal
saddle	stumble	eagle	legal	medal
table	terrible	royal	label	several
noble	beetle	cripple	vocal	sample

-ble

1. ____________

2. ____________

3. ____________

4. ____________

5. ____________

-dle

6. ____________

-gle

7. ____________

-ple

8. ____________

9. ____________

-tle

10. ____________

11. ____________

12. ____________

-el

13. ____________

-al

14. ____________

15. ____________

16. ____________

17. ____________

18. ____________

19. ____________

20. ____________

Look for more words that contain consonant + *le* final stable syllables. Record them in your writer's notebook. Draw a slash (/) in between syllables. Then read the words out loud.

Name ______________________________

When a word ends with the letters *le,* the final syllable usually includes the preceding consonant. This is called a **consonant + *le* syllable**. Examples include *little* (*lit/tle*) and *cable* (*ca/ble*). It is a **final stable syllable** that ends with the sound /əl/.

Words that end in a consonant + *-el* or *-al* often divide in the same way: *tinsel* (*tin/sel*), *oval* (*o/val*).

DECODING WORDS

The word *principle* has three syllables. It ends with the final stable syllable *ple,* pronounced /pəl/. Blend the sounds in each syllable together: /prin/ /sə/ /pəl/.

Write the spelling words whose final syllable contains the matching pattern.

stable	cattle	kettle	hospital	journal
saddle	tumble	eagle	legal	medal
table	terrible	royal	label	pickle
noble	beetle	cripple	vocal	sample

-ble

1. ____________
2. ____________
3. ____________
4. ____________
5. ____________

-dle

6. ____________

-gle

7. ____________

-ple

8. ____________
9. ____________

-tle

10. ____________
11. ____________
12. ____________

-le

13. ____________

-al

14. ____________
15. ____________
16. ____________
17. ____________
18. ____________
19. ____________

-el

20. ____________

Look for more words that contain consonant + *le* final stable syllables. Record them in your writer's notebook. Draw a slash (/) in between syllables. Then read the words out loud.

Name ______________________

A. Write the spelling words whose final syllable (or second-to-final syllable) contains the matching spelling pattern.

unstable	chronicle	kettle	hospital	journalists
saddle	tumble	eagle	nocturnal	monumental
illegally	maternal	royal	label	several
noble	beetle	cripple	fundamental	castle

-ble

1. ______________
2. ______________
3. ______________

-cle

4. ______________

-dle

5. ______________

-gle

6. ______________

-ple

7. ______________

-tle

8. ______________
9. ______________
10. ______________

-al

11. ______________
12. ______________
13. ______________
14. ______________

-nal

15. ______________
16. ______________
17. ______________

-tal

18. ______________
19. ______________

-el

20. ______________

B. Read each word below. Use a slash (/) to divide the word into syllables.

believable **rental** **global** **logical** **principle**

Look through this week's readings for more words that contain consonant + *le* (or consonant + *al* or *el*) syllables. Record the words you find in your writer's notebook. Then read the words out loud.

Name ________________________________

stable	cattle	kettle	hospital	journal
saddle	stumble	eagle	legal	medal
table	terrible	royal	label	several
noble	beetle	cripple	vocal	sample

A. Write the spelling word that belongs with each group of words below.

1. tag, sticker, ________________
2. sheep, chickens, ________________
3. trophy, ribbon, ________________
4. owl, hawk, ________________
5. bank, library, ________________
6. grasshopper, ant, ________________
7. pot, pan, ________________
8. reins, stirrup, ________________
9. lawful, allowed, ________________
10. some, numerous, ________________

B. Write the spelling word that best completes each sentence.

11. A storm left our farm crops in ________________ condition.
12. The prince and princess wed in a ________________ wedding.
13. An accident on the highway can ________________ traffic for hours.
14. The tourist wrote about his travels in his ________________.
15. We enjoyed the tunes sung by the school's ________________ group.
16. How many horses do you keep in your ________________?
17. Mom asked me to set the ________________ for dinner.
18. You may have a title if you come from a ________________ family.
19. Put away your shoes or you may ________________ over them.
20. The college asks students for a ________________ of their writing.

Name ____________________

Underline the three misspelled words in each paragraph below. Write the words correctly on the lines.

Have you ever thought of keeping a journel to record ideas and important events? Severle famous explorers, including Lewis and Clark, kept track of their adventures in writing. You might want to read a sampal from their writing.

1. ________ **2.** ________ **3.** ________

You don't have to explore a new land or win an Olympic medel to write about your life. I recently read an entry from my great-grandfather's diary. In it, he describes putting a sadle on his horse and going out to round up cattale. The details of his everyday life are fascinating!

4. ________ **5.** ________ **6.** ________

Writing Connection

Give information about another type of writing. Use at least four spelling words. Check to make sure that each spelling word uses the correct final syllable spelling pattern.

Name ______________________________

Remember

In most words that end in *-le*, the final syllable includes a preceding consonant. For example, *riddle* divides as *rid/dle*. A **consonant + *le* syllable** is one example of a **final stable syllable**. The syllable always ends with /əl/.

Words that end in a consonant + *-el* or *-al* often follow the same syllable division rules, such as *tunnel* (*tun/nel*) and *tropical* (*trop/i/cal*).

Read the word *feeble* aloud: /fē/ /bəl/. In the first syllable, the digraph *ee* makes the long *e* sound. The second syllable is a final stable syllable.

stable	cattle	kettle	hospital	journal
saddle	stumble	eagle	legal	medal
table	terrible	royal	label	several
noble	beetle	cripple	vocal	sample

A. Fill in the missing letters to form a spelling word. Then write the word.

1. cat ___ ___ ___ ______________
2. crip ___ ___ ___ ______________
3. no ___ ___ ___ ______________
4. roy ___ ___ ______________
5. ea ___ ___ ___ ______________
6. jour ___ ___ ___ ______________
7. bee ___ ___ ___ ______________
8. sad ___ ___ ___ ______________
9. med ___ ___ ______________
10. sta ___ ___ ___ ______________
11. le ___ ___ ___ ______________
12. terri ___ ___ ___ ______________
13. vo ___ ___ ___ ______________
14. la ___ ___ ___ ______________

B. Write these spelling words on the lines in reverse alphabetical order: *hospital, stumble, kettle, several, table, sample*.

15. ______________
16. ______________
17. ______________
18. ______________
19. ______________
20. ______________

Name ____

Writers use figurative language to create a picture in the reader's mind. You can figure out the meaning of **similes** and **metaphors** by looking at what is being compared. Remember that a simile compares two things using *like* or *as,* whereas a metaphor does not use *like* or *as.*

Read the passage and underline the similes and metaphors. Then write the meaning of each comparison on or near its corresponding image below.

We knew we were close to the shore when we saw the "No Wake" sign. The evening sun was a giant ember fading in the horizon. The darkening water was as smooth as glass as we sailed slowly through the bay. At times, the boat cradled us like a mother's arms, gently rocking us to sleep.

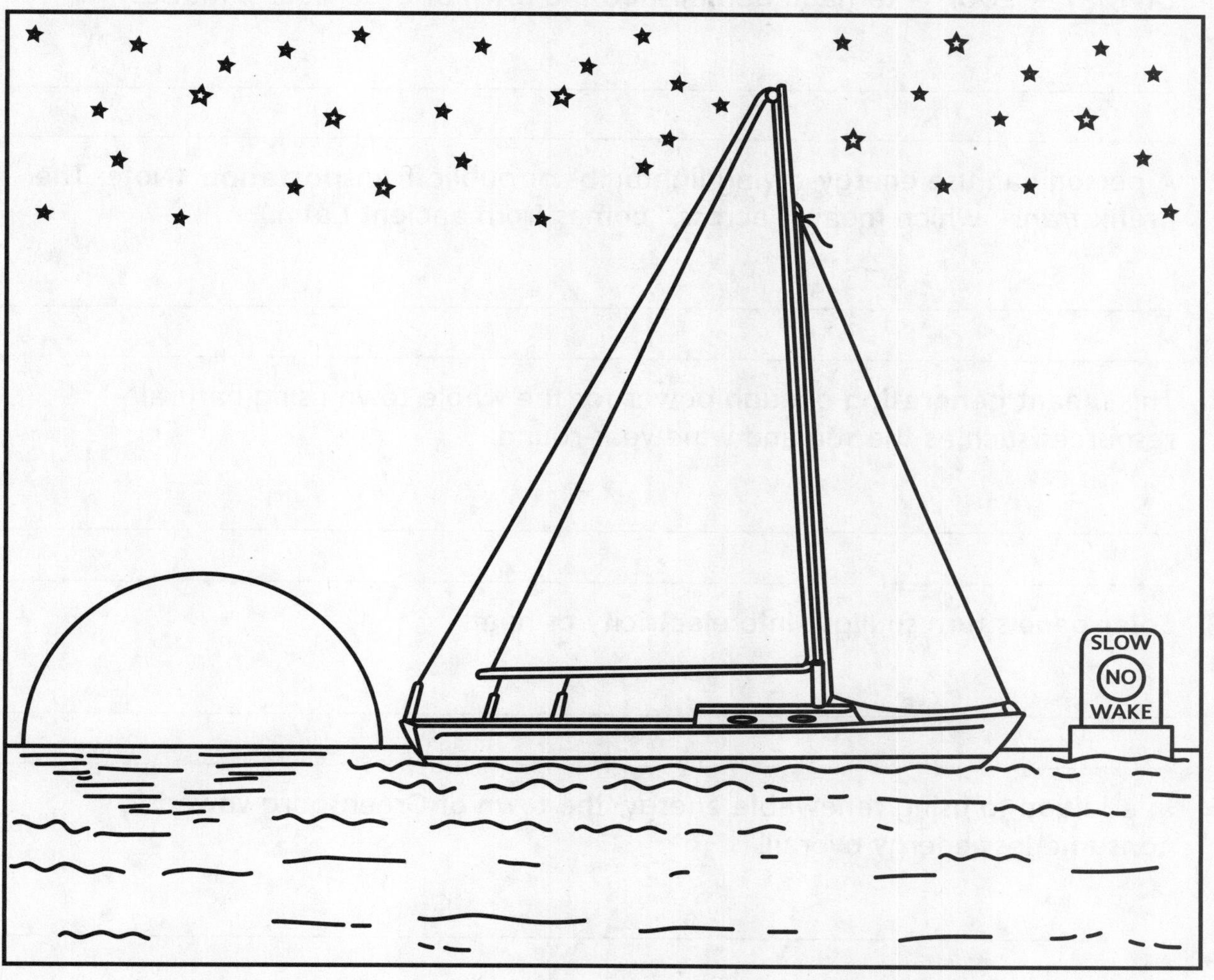

Name ______________________________

A word root can be a clue to the meaning of an unfamiliar word. Here are some roots from ancient Latin.

portare: to carry   *moliri*: to build   *sumere*: to take

generare: to produce   *sol*: sun

Read the sentences from "Building a Green Town." Use the Latin roots in the box above to identify the root in each bold word. Write the root on the line. Use context clues and your knowledge of Latin roots to determine the meaning of the word. Then write your own sentence using the word correctly.

1. On May 4, 2007, a tornado **demolished** the town of Greensburg, Kansas.

____

____

2. A person can use energy-saving lightbulbs or public **transportation**. (Note: The prefix *trans-*, which means "across," comes from ancient Latin.)

____

____

3. This meant **generating** enough power for the whole town using natural resources such as the sun and wind year-round.

____

____

4. **Solar** panels turn sunlight into electricity or heat.

____

____

5. In addition to using renewable energy, the town of Greensburg vowed to **consume** less energy overall.

____

____

Name ________________________________

- An **irregular verb** is a verb that does not add *-ed* to form the past tense.
- Some irregular verbs include *begin/began, bring/brought, catch/caught, choose/chose, do/did, drink/drank, eat/ate, fall/fell, fight/fought, get/got, go/went, keep/kept, know/knew, leave/left, make/made, read/read, run/ran, say/said, speak/spoke, think/thought, win/won,* and *write/wrote.*

Read each sentence. Write the correct past-tense form of the verb in parentheses on the line provided.

1. The game (begin) with our team at bat. ____________________
2. The player in left field (keep) his eye on the ball. ____________________
3. He (catch) the line drive near second base. ____________________
4. The next batter (think) he could hit a home run. ____________________
5. He (do) get a hit, but it fell short of the wall. ____________________
6. The player (run) to first base and stayed there. ____________________
7. After the next hit, he (go) to second base. ____________________
8. Our team scored six runs and (win) the game. ____________________
9. I met my favorite player before we (leave). ____________________
10. He (write) his name on one of the game programs. ____________________

In your writer's notebook, write about a sports game you played. Include at least four irregular verbs in the past tense. Here are some more irregular verbs you might want to use: *choose/chose, fly/flew, leap/leapt, throw/threw, slide/slid, lead/led,* and *become/became.* Check that you use the correct form of each irregular verb.

Name ____

Some **irregular verbs** have special endings when used with the helping verbs *have, has,* or *had.* Some examples are *begun, brought, chosen, drunk, eaten, fallen, given, gone, gotten, known, run, seen, spoken,* and *written.* These are called **past participles.**

Read each sentence. Write the correct form of the verb in parentheses on the line provided.

1. Mom has (speak) to her favorite author several times. ________________
2. In fact, the two of them had (go) to the same college. ________________
3. I have (wrote) an e-mail to the author as well. ________________
4. My teacher had (choose) one of her books for our class. ________________
5. My mother has (give) me a signed copy of the book. ________________
6. Have you (see) where I put it? ________________
7. I had (bring) it to class with me this morning. ________________

Read the excerpt from "How Did King Tut Die?" Circle the verb written in regular past tense. Then write a sentence about Egypt using the past participle form of the verb you circled. Remember to include a helping verb.

A tomb painting shows Tut driving a chariot. This is one way Egyptian artists showed a pharaoh. It is not realistic.

____

____

Name ______________________________

- Use the **present tenses** if the action or condition is or has been happening now. Use the **past tenses** to show an action or condition that was or had been completed in the past.
- **Irregular verbs** use forms other than adding *-ed* to show the past tense.

Read each sentence. Write the correct form of the verb in parentheses on the line provided.

1. Today, we will (write) in our journals. ______________
2. How many of you have (begin) already? ______________
3. You should have (think) about your ideas last night. ______________
4. Last week, I (leave) the final choices up to you. ______________
5. Some of you (say) you would finish this past weekend. ______________
6. I had (speak) to several of you about your topics. ______________
7. Some of you (bring) photos and pasted them in place. ______________
8. I have (keep) some journals from previous years' students. ______________

Writing Connection

Write a paragraph about something that happened in class recently. Include at least two helping verbs and two irregular verbs. Make sure you use the correct form of each verb.

____

____

____

____

____

____

Name ____

- Use the **present tenses** if the action or condition is or has been happening now. Use the **past tenses** to show an action or condition that was or had been completed in the past.
- **Irregular verbs** do not add *-ed* to show the past tense.

Proofread the paragraph. On the lines below, correct mistakes in verb tenses and spelling.

The boat had leaved England two months earlier. Some of the ship's passengers had not eated in days. They fighted with one another over the little food they have. Many had got sick. A member of the crew speak to the captain. He sayed they should stop at the next island for supplies. The captain knowed this is a good idea. He had thinked about it for a while, too.

____

____

____

____

____

____

____

____

____

____

____

Name ____________________

Read the student draft and look for any corrections that need to be made. Then choose the best answer to each question.

(1) The town fair begin earlier this morning. (2) My mother had make homemade cookies last night. (3) But my sister think we could make something to sell, too. (4) We went to the store to buy the ingredients. (5) My sister had leave her purse at home. (6) Luckily, I had bring enough money to pay for the food. (7) We get all the ingredients to make cupcakes for the fair.

1. What change needs to be made in sentence 1?

A Change ***begin*** to **begins**

B Change ***begin*** to **beginned**

C Change ***begin*** to **began**

D Change ***begin*** to **beginning**

2. How does sentence 2 need to be changed?

F Change ***make*** to **maked**

G Change ***make*** to **made**

H Change ***make*** to **makes**

J Change ***make*** to **making**

3. What change, if any, should be made in sentence 3?

A Change ***think*** to **thought**

B Change ***think*** to **thinking**

C Change ***think*** to **thoughted**

D Make no change

4. What is the correct way to write sentences 4 and 5?

F We went to the store to buy the ingredients. My sister had left her purse at home.

G We go to the store to buy the ingredients. My sister had leaved her purse at home.

H We goes to the store to buy the ingredients. My sister had left her purse at home.

J We had went to the store to buy the ingredients. My sister leaved her purse at home.

5. How does sentence 6 need to be changed?

A Change ***bring*** to **bringed**

B Change ***bring*** to **bringing**

C Change ***bring*** to **brought**

D Change ***bring*** to **brang**

6. What change, if any, should be made in sentence 7?

F Change ***get*** to **gotted**

G Change ***get*** to **gotten**

H Change ***get*** to **got**

J Make no change

Name ______________________________

Fold back the paper along the dotted line. Use the blanks to write each word as it is read aloud. When you finish the test, unfold the paper. Use the list at the right to correct any spelling mistakes.

	1. ________	**1.** perform
	2. ________	**2.** gentler
	3. ________	**3.** scissors
	4. ________	**4.** founder
	5. ________	**5.** director
	6. ________	**6.** danger
	7. ________	**7.** saucer
	8. ________	**8.** labor
	9. ________	**9.** margin
	10. ________	**10.** error
	11. ________	**11.** crater
	12. ________	**12.** pillar
	13. ________	**13.** splendor
	14. ________	**14.** peddler
	15. ________	**15.** professor
	16. ________	**16.** shatter
	17. ________	**17.** governor
	18. ________	**18.** vapor
	19. ________	**19.** equator
	20. ________	**20.** fonder
Review Words	**21.** ________	**21.** terrible
	22. ________	**22.** legal
	23. ________	**23.** journal
Challenge Words	**24.** ________	**24.** refrigerator
	25. ________	**25.** remainder

Name ______________________________

When a vowel is followed by the letter *r*, the two combine to form a special vowel sound. Both the vowel and the *r* must remain in the same syllable. Here are some examples of ***r*-controlled vowel** syllables:

ger as in ***finger*** ***flor*** as in ***floral***
gar as in ***garlic*** ***thir*** as in ***thirty***

Read each word aloud. Listen to the effect the *r* has on each vowel sound.

DECODING WORDS

The word *garlic* has two syllables. In the first syllable, the vowel *a* is followed by an *r*. That means that the letters *ar* work together to form an *r*-controlled vowel team, and the *ar* stays in the same syllable. Blend the sounds: /gär/ /lik/.

Write the spelling words that contain the matching spelling pattern for the *r*-controlled vowel syllable. Then read the words aloud.

perform	director	margin	splendor	governor
gentler	danger	error	peddler	vapor
scissors	saucer	crater	professor	equator
founder	labor	pillar	shatter	fonder

-ar

1. ______________
2. ______________

-er

3. ______________
4. ______________
5. ______________
6. ______________
7. ______________
8. ______________
9. ______________
10. ______________

-or

11. ______________
12. ______________
13. ______________
14. ______________
15. ______________
16. ______________
17. ______________
18. ______________
19. ______________

-er* and *-or

20. ______________

Look through this week's readings for more words that contain *r*-controlled vowel syllables. Record the words you find in your writer's notebook. Then read the words aloud.

Name ______________________________

When a vowel is followed by the letter *r*, the two combine to form a special vowel sound. Both the vowel and the *r* must remain in the same syllable. Here are some examples of ***r*-controlled vowel** syllables:

ger as in ***finger*** ***flor*** as in ***floral***
gar as in ***garlic*** ***thir*** as in ***thirty***

Read each word aloud. Listen to the effect the *r* has on each vowel sound.

DECODING WORDS

The word *garlic* has two syllables. In the first syllable, the vowel *a* is followed by an *r*. The letters *ar* work together to form an *r*-controlled vowel team, and the *ar* stays in the same syllable. Blend the sounds: /gär/ /lik/.

Write the spelling words that contain the matching spelling pattern for the *r*-controlled vowel syllable. Then read the words aloud.

perform	director	silver	neighbor	governor
gentler	danger	error	peddler	vapor
doctor	saucer	crater	professor	actor
margin	labor	pillar	shatter	slobber

-ar

1. ______________
2. ______________

-er

3. ______________
4. ______________
5. ______________
6. ______________
7. ______________
8. ______________
9. ______________
10. ______________

-or

11. ______________
12. ______________
13. ______________
14. ______________
15. ______________
16. ______________
17. ______________
18. ______________
19. ______________

-er* and *-or

20. ______________

Look through this week's readings for more words that contain *r*-controlled vowel syllables. Record the words you find in your writer's notebook. Then read the words aloud.

Name ______________________________

A. Write the spelling words that contain the matching spelling pattern for the *r*-controlled vowel syllable. Then read the words aloud.

binocular	director	marvelous	splendor	governor
gentler	remainder	dimmer	peddler	vapor
scissors	semester	charter	professor	equator
founder	laborer	pillar	stagger	fonder

-ar

1. ______________
2. ______________
3. ______________

-er

4. ______________
5. ______________
6. ______________
7. ______________
8. ______________
9. ______________
10. ______________
11. ______________

-or

12. ______________
13. ______________
14. ______________
15. ______________
16. ______________
17. ______________
18. ______________

-or* and *-er

19. ______________

-ar* and *-er

20. ______________

B. Compare the words *director* and *semester*. How are they alike? How are they different?

____

____

____

____

Look through this week's readings for more words that contain *r*-controlled vowel syllables. Record the words you find in your writer's notebook. Then read the words aloud.

Name ______________________________

perform	director	margin	splendor	governor
gentler	danger	error	peddler	vapor
scissors	saucer	crater	professor	equator
founder	labor	pillar	shatter	fonder

A. Write the spelling word that contains the same base word as the other words in each group below.

1. dangerous, dangerously, ____________
2. fond, fondly, ____________
3. splendid, splendidly, ____________
4. peddle, peddling, ____________
5. laborer, laboring, ____________
6. found, foundation, ____________
7. err, erring, ____________
8. performer, performance, ____________

B. Write the spelling word that best completes each sentence.

9. Please write your name in the left-hand ____________.
10. Did the mirror ____________ when you dropped it?
11. Workers stood on ladders to paint each ____________ of the building.
12. We could see a ____________ on the moon through the telescope.
13. I grabbed ____________ and cut the ribbon.
14. A ____________ will catch any liquid that drips from your cup.
15. Can you name two countries that lie near the ____________?
16. The ____________ of our state was elected again.
17. Water ____________ from the boiling kettle steamed up the window.
18. My father is a ____________ at a state university.
19. I need a ____________ tissue for my sore, stuffy nose.
20. The movie ____________ made two popular films this year.

Name ____________________

Underline the six misspelled words below. Using the spelling patterns for *r*-controlled vowel syllables, write the words correctly on the lines.

I'm fondor of sweet drinks than of sugarless ones. And although I'm not a professer of nutrition, I don't think sodas and sports drinks are so bad for you. That doesn't mean we should drink them all the time. An occasional sweet drink, however, isn't going to shattur anyone's plans to stay healthy.

1. ____________ **2.** ____________ **3.** ____________

Young people drink far too many sodas. It's not an errer to say that these drinks are bad for your health. What's wrong with just plain water? It's gentlor on the stomach, has fewer calories, and is good for you. We need to recognize the splendar of plain water—and drink more of it!

4. ____________ **5.** ____________ **6.** ____________

Writing Connection

Write an opinion about something else that is said to be good or bad for your health. Tell how you feel about it. Use at least four spelling words in your writing.

____

____

____

____

____

____

____

____

____

____

____

Name ____________________

Remember

When a vowel is followed by the letter *r,* the two combine to form a special ***r*-controlled vowel** sound. Both the vowel and the *r* must remain in the same syllable. As you read the following words aloud, listen carefully to the vowel sound in each underlined syllable.

favor, /fā/ /vər/; ***marble,*** /mär/ /bəl/; ***feather,*** /feth/ /ər/; ***pursuit,*** /pər/ /süt/

perform	director	margin	splendor	governor
gentler	danger	error	peddler	vapor
scissors	saucer	crater	professor	equator
founder	labor	pillar	shatter	fonder

A. Fill in the missing letters of each word to form a spelling word. Write the spelling word on the line. Then read each word aloud.

1. pil __ __ __ ____________
2. cra __ __ __ ____________
3. profes __ __ __ ____________
4. splen __ __ __ ____________
5. shat __ __ __ ____________
6. equa __ __ __ ____________
7. sau __ __ __ ____________
8. la __ __ __ ____________
9. direc __ __ __ ____________
10. gover __ __ __ ____________
11. va __ __ __ ____________
12. er __ __ __ ____________
13. scis __ __ __ __ ____________
14. fon __ __ __ ____________
15. gen __ __ __ __ ____________

B. Write these spelling words on the lines in alphabetical order. Alphabetize them to the third letter. ***margin, danger, perform, peddler, founder***

16. ____________
17. ____________
18. ____________
19. ____________
20. ____________

Name ______________________________

Content words are words that are specific to a field of study. For example, words like *gravity, hypothesis,* and *energy* are science content words.

Authors use content words to explain a concept or idea. Sometimes you can figure out what a content word means by using context clues. You can also use a print or digital dictionary to help you find the meaning of unfamiliar content words.

Go on a word hunt with a partner. Find as many content words related to archeology as you can. Write them in the chart.

Science Words

CONNECT TO CONTENT

"Machu Picchu: Ancient City" shares two different views about the purpose of the city to the ancient Incans. The authors use details to support their positions.

Circle two words that you were able to figure out the meaning of using context clues. Write the words and what they mean on the lines.

____

____

____

____

Name ____

Read each sentence from "How Did King Tut Die?" Underline the context clues in the sentence that help you figure out the meaning of each word in bold. Then write a new sentence using the word in bold.

1. Since then, no one has been able to solve the mystery of how the young **pharaoh**, or king, died.

____

____

2. One strong **hypothesis**, or theory, is that Tut died after being injured in a chariot accident.

____

____

3. Then, when Carter's team removed it from its **sarcophagus**, or coffin, they also broke many of the bones.

____

____

4. King Tut likely died of an illness made deadly by **genetic** disorders inherited from his parents.

____

____

Name ______________________________

- A **pronoun** takes the place of a noun or nouns and may be singular or plural. Singular pronouns are *I, you, he, she, it, me, him,* and *her.* Plural pronouns are *we, you, they, them,* and *us.*
- An **antecedent** is the noun (or nouns) to which the pronoun refers.

  My mother will be home late. She is busy at work.
- An **indefinite pronoun** does not refer to a particular person, place, or thing. Examples of indefinite pronouns include *some, everyone, nowhere, everything,* and *anything.*

  Everyone is having fun at the picnic.

Read each sentence. Circle each pronoun. Then draw a line under the antecedent. (Note: If the pronoun is indefinite, there may be no antecedent.)

1. The girl saw the bike she had always wanted.
2. The bike had lights, bells, and streamers on it.
3. The girl's brother asked if he could get a bike, too.
4. "Everything here is too expensive," the mother said.
5. The parents told the children, "You may have to wait."
6. "We don't mind," said the boy and the girl.
7. "I have an idea," the father said to the children.
8. By looking at less fancy bikes, the family could afford two of them.

In your writer's notebook, write a short passage about something that you or someone you know wants. Select a genre, such as a personal narrative, a speech, a story, or a free verse poem. Include at least five pronouns (one indefinite pronoun). Then circle each pronoun and underline any antecedents. Check to make sure that each pronoun is used correctly.

Name ______________________________

- **Pronouns** and **antecedents** must agree in both number, case, and gender. A singular pronoun refers to a singular antecedent: *Maria is my best friend, and she lives one block away.* A plural pronoun refers to a plural antecedent: *Two squirrels chased each other. They were having fun.*
- Antecedents may or may not appear in the same sentence as their related nouns or pronouns: *We wanted to see Susan's play. We are very proud of her.*
- The **case** of a pronoun depends on whether the pronoun is a subject, object, or possessive: *He went to the store. We reminded him. He forgot his wallet.*

Read each sentence. Choose the pronoun in parentheses that best completes the sentence. Write it on the line provided.

1. Our neighbors told us about a trip (he, they) are taking. ____________
2. They asked my sister if (he, she) would like to join them. ____________
3. My brother was upset that they did not ask (him, them). ____________
4. My father suggested that (I, we) could go as a family. ____________

Read the excerpt from "A Warrior for Women's Rights." Circle two pronouns and underline their antecedents. Then write two sentences in your writer's notebook about someone you admire. Include one pronoun. Edit your work for pronoun usage and agreement.

In October 1917, [Alice] Paul was arrested for organizing the protests. She and the other suffragists were mistreated in jail. Newspapers printed stories about the women's treatment, earning them the public's sympathy.

Name ______________________________

- **Pronouns** and **antecedents** must agree in both number and gender. A singular pronoun refers to a singular antecedent: *Ruth practices every day because she wants to win the competition.* A plural pronoun refers to a plural antecedent: *Earthworms do not have eyes, but they can sense light.*
- Antecedents may or may not appear in the same sentence as their related pronouns.

  The pine tree looks beautiful in winter. It stays green all year.

Read each sentence. Change any repeated word or words into the correct pronoun and rewrite the sentence on the line provided.

1. The animals can't find food, and the animals are becoming very hungry.

   ____

2. A lack of rainfall on the prairie has made the prairie very dry.

   ____

3. Clouds form every day, but no rain falls from the clouds.

   ____

4. Mrs. Dibble, a local ecologist, says that Mrs. Dibble is concerned.

   ____

5. She came to our class today and told our class about the problem.

   ____

Look back through your writer's notebook for a paragraph that includes pronouns. Check that each pronoun agrees with its antecedent. Also check for any spelling mistakes. You may use a dictionary to help you.

Name ______________________________

- **Pronouns** and **antecedents** must agree in number, case, and gender. A singular pronoun refers to a singular antecedent. A plural pronoun refers to a plural antecedent.
- Singular pronouns are *I, you, he, she, it, me, him,* and *her.* Plural pronouns are *we, you, they, them,* and *us.*

Proofread the paragraph. On the lines below, correct mistakes in pronoun usage and agreement. Make sure that the tenses are correct.

I see the new movie and wanted to write about them. My favorite actress had the lead role, and he did an excellent job. Most of the special effects were good, but some of it looked fake. My friends said that he didn't like the film much. We saw it together, and none of you care for the music. My father will see a different movie when they goes to the theater with Mom tonight.

COMMON ERRORS

If you use a pronoun, make sure it has a clear antecedent. Otherwise, readers might not know the noun to which it refers.

____

____

____

____

____

____

____

____

____

____

____

____

Name ______________________________

Read the student draft and look for any corrections that need to be made. Then choose the best answer to each question.

(1) We put on the ice skates Mom brought for me. (2) Once we were finished, she put on his own skates. (3) She taught us how to skate backwards. (4) Dad saw us and said that Dad was impressed. (5) We skated until they got tired and hungry. (6) They had a great time out on the pond!

1. What change needs to be made in sentence 1?
   - **A** Change ***We*** to **Us**
   - **B** Change ***We*** to **Them**
   - **C** Change ***me*** to **we**
   - **D** Change ***me*** to **us**

2. What change needs to be made in sentence 2?
   - **F** Change ***we*** to **us**
   - **G** Change ***we*** to **Mom**
   - **H** Change ***his*** to **her**
   - **J** Change ***his*** to **their**

3. What change, if any, should be made in sentence 3?
   - **A** Change ***She*** to **We**
   - **B** Change ***us*** to **them**
   - **C** Change ***us*** to **him**
   - **D** Make no change

4. What is the correct way to write sentence 4?
   - **F** Dad saw we and said that Dad was impressed.
   - **G** Dad saw them and said that Dad was impressed.
   - **H** Dad saw us and said that he was impressed.
   - **J** Dad saw us and said that they was impressed.

5. What is the correct way to write sentence 5?
   - **A** We skated until them got tired and hungry.
   - **B** We skated until we got tired and hungry.
   - **C** We skated until us got tired and hungry.
   - **D** We skated until she got tired and hungry.

6. What is the correct way to write sentence 6?
   - **F** Someone had a great time out on the pond!
   - **G** Everything had a great time out on the pond!
   - **H** Some had a great time out on the pond!
   - **J** Everyone had a great time out on the pond!

Name ______________________________

Fold back the paper along the dotted line. Use the blanks to write each word as it is read aloud. When you finish the test, unfold the paper. Use the list at the right to correct any spelling mistakes.

	1. ______	1. slogan
	2. ______	2. woolen
	3. ______	3. listen
	4. ______	4. heron
	5. ______	5. frighten
	6. ______	6. lengthen
	7. ______	7. captain
	8. ______	8. mountain
	9. ______	9. sandal
	10. ______	10. signal
	11. ______	11. global
	12. ______	12. bushel
	13. ______	13. marvel
	14. ______	14. barrel
	15. ______	15. practical
	16. ______	16. pretzel
	17. ______	17. fable
	18. ______	18. chuckle
	19. ______	19. angle
	20. ______	20. nozzle
Review Words	21. ______	21. scissors
	22. ______	22. pillar
	23. ______	23. governor
Challenge Words	24. ______	24. dungeon
	25. ______	25. salmon

Name ______________________________

Many words end with /əl/ or /ən/. Final syllables that include these sounds are unaccented and use the schwa vowel sound, /ə/. Final /əl/ and /ən/ can have a number of different spelling patterns.

/əl/: ***handle*** ***caramel*** ***technical***

/ən/: ***taken*** ***melon*** ***human*** ***fountain***

Read the words aloud. Listen to the final syllable.

DECODING WORDS

The word *table* has an open syllable and an unaccented final stable syllable that includes /əl/. Blend the sounds in the syllables together: /tā/ /bəl/.

Write the words that contain the matching sound and spelling pattern.

slogan	frighten	sandal	marvel	fable
woolen	lengthen	signal	barrel	chuckle
listen	captain	global	practical	angle
heron	mountain	bushel	pretzel	nozzle

/əl/ spelled *al*

1. ____________
2. ____________
3. ____________
4. ____________

/əl/ spelled *el*

5. ____________
6. ____________
7. ____________
8. ____________

/əl/ spelled *le*

9. ____________
10. ____________
11. ____________
12. ____________

/ən/ spelled *an*

13. ____________

/ən/ spelled *en*

14. ____________
15. ____________
16. ____________
17. ____________

/ən/ spelled *on*

18. ____________

/ən/ spelled *ain*

19. ____________
20. ____________

Use the spelling patterns above to write a short rhyming poem. Include four spelling words. One of these words should have a final stable syllable. Edit your work for spelling. Then read your poem aloud.

Name ______________________________

Many words end with /əl/ or /ən/. Final syllables that include these sounds are unaccented and use the schwa vowel sound, /ə/. Final /əl/ and /ən/ can have a number of different spelling patterns.

/əl/: ***handle*** ***caramel*** ***technical***

/ən/: ***taken*** ***melon*** ***human*** ***fountain***

Read the words aloud. Listen to the final syllable.

DECODING WORDS

The word *table* has an open syllable and an unaccented final syllable that includes /əl/. Blend the sounds in the syllables together: /tā/ /bəl/.

Write the spelling words that contain the matching sound and spelling pattern.

slogan	frighten	sandal	marvel	fable
woolen	soften	signal	barrel	simple
listen	captain	global	practical	angle
bacon	mountain	nickel	pretzel	ankle

/əl/ spelled *al*

1. ____________
2. ____________
3. ____________
4. ____________

/əl/ spelled *el*

5. ____________
6. ____________
7. ____________
8. ____________

/əl/ spelled *le*

9. ____________
10. ____________
11. ____________
12. ____________

/ən/ spelled *an*

13. ____________

/ən/ spelled *en*

14. ____________
15. ____________
16. ____________
17. ____________

/ən/ spelled *on*

18. ____________

/ən/ spelled *ain*

19. ____________
20. ____________

Use the spelling patterns above to write a short rhyming poem. Include four spelling words. Then edit and proofread your work for spelling.

Name ______________________________

A. Write the spelling words that contain the matching sound and spelling pattern.

slogan	frighten	financially	marveled	morsel
hasten	lengthen	identical	barrel	chuckled
broaden	salmon	global	practically	ample
abandon	mountain	chisel	parallel	nozzle

/əl/ spelled *al*

1. ______________
2. ______________
3. ______________
4. ______________

/əl/ spelled *el*

5. ______________
6. ______________
7. ______________
8. ______________
9. ______________

/əl/ spelled *le*

10. ______________
11. ______________
12. ______________

/ən/ spelled *an*

13. ______________

/ən/ spelled *en*

14. ______________
15. ______________
16. ______________
17. ______________

/ən/ spelled *on*

18. ______________
19. ______________

/ən/ spelled *ain*

20. ______________

B. Compare the words *financially* and *frighten*. How are they alike? How are they different?

____

____

____

____

Use the spelling patterns above to write a short rhyming poem. Include four spelling words. Then edit and proofread your work for spelling.

Name ______________________________

slogan	frighten	sandal	marvel	fable
woolen	lengthen	signal	barrel	chuckle
listen	captain	global	practical	angle
heron	mountain	bushel	pretzel	nozzle

A. Write the spelling word that has the same, or almost the same, meaning.

1. worldwide ____________
2. motto ____________
3. tale ____________
4. to scare ____________
5. to laugh ____________
6. spout ____________
7. to extend ____________
8. useful ____________

B. Write the spelling word that best completes each sentence.

9. A large, salty ____________ makes a tasty snack.
10. I lost a leather ____________ at the beach.
11. The ____________ of the ship welcomed us aboard.
12. Do you know how much a ____________ of apples costs?
13. The city put up a new traffic ____________ near the school.
14. A thick ____________ hat will keep your head warm.
15. The gardener collects rainwater in a ____________.
16. I spotted a ____________ flying above the marsh.
17. We climbed to the peak of the highest ____________.
18. ____________ to the birds singing in the trees!
19. The ____________ of the sun told us it was late afternoon.
20. I ____________ at how quickly my nephew has grown.

Name ____

Underline the six misspelled words in the paragraphs below. Write the words correctly on the lines.

Everyone knew Sailor Peg. She was capton of the biggest ship in port. In fact, everything Peg did was big! Just one sneeze from Peg would frightain seagulls for miles away, and shipwrecked sailors once used her sandel as a raft.

Peg's woolan cap was huge, too. When a hurricane blew through town, ten families hid in it. After the storm, Peg cleaned up the town in one sweep. Then she sailed away. Peg wasn't seen again, but people in town say you can still hear her chuckal if you stand by the shore and liston carefully.

1. ____________________ 4. ____________________

2. ____________________ 5. ____________________

3. ____________________ 6. ____________________

Writing Connection

Write a passage for another tall tale. Use at least four spelling words in your writing. Edit and proofread your work using knowledge of the spelling patterns for the final /əl/ and /ən/.

____

____

____

____

____

____

____

____

____

____

____

Name ____________________

Remember

Each spelling word ends with /əl/ or /ən/. These two sounds include the unaccented schwa sound, /ə/. Each sound can be spelled in different ways.

/əl/: ***bundle*** ***cancel*** ***festival*** /ən/: ***seven*** ***season*** ***certain***

The word *season* has an open syllable and an unaccented final syllable. The final syllable has /ən/. Blend the sounds in the syllables together: /sē/ /zən/.

slogan	frighten	sandal	marvel	fable
woolen	lengthen	signal	barrel	chuckle
listen	captain	global	practical	angle
heron	mountain	bushel	pretzel	nozzle

A. Fill in the missing letters to form a spelling word. Then write it on the line.

1. her __ __ ____________
2. length __ __ ____________
3. an __ __ __ ____________
4. mar __ __ __ ____________
5. wool __ __ ____________
6. bush __ __ ____________
7. sig __ __ __ ____________
8. noz __ __ __ ____________
9. bar __ __ __ ____________
10. fright __ __ ____________
11. slo __ __ __ ____________
12. fa __ __ __ ____________
13. glob __ __ ____________
14. san __ __ __ ____________
15. chuck __ __ ____________

B. Write these spelling words on the lines in reverse alphabetical order: *practical, captain, mountain, listen, pretzel.*

16. ____________
17. ____________
18. ____________
19. ____________
20. ____________

Name ______________________________

Content words are words that are specific to a field of study. For example, words like *government, politics,* and *amendments* are social studies content words.

Authors use content words to explain a concept or idea. Sometimes you can figure out what a content word means by using context clues. You can also use a dictionary to help you find the meaning of unfamiliar content words.

Go on a word hunt with a partner. Find content words related to Rosa Parks's and Frederick Douglass's efforts to achieve equal rights. Write them in the chart.

Social Studies Words

______ ______ ______

______ ______ ______

______ ______ ______

CONNECT TO CONTENT

Rosa Parks fought for her rights by refusing to give up her seat on a bus. Many in the African American community joined her protest. They too refused to ride city buses in order to fight for equal rights.

Circle two words above that you were able to figure out the meaning to using context clues. Write the words and what they mean on the lines.

____

____

____

____

____

____

Name ____

Write the vocabulary words next to their meanings in parentheses on the sign about a new discovery. Use context clues to help you.

archaeologist	assuring	fragments	historian	intact	preserved
reconstruct	remnants	era	savings	cultural	appreciation

ATTENTION, LA SALLE VILLAGE RESIDENTS:

Local ______________ **(person who digs up and studies remains of ancient towns and cities)** Dr. Naomi Walcott recently discovered some green ceramic ______________ **(small broken pieces)** in our neighborhood. As she began to dig down into the ground, she found even more ______________ **(small pieces of something that are left over).** Unearthing so many pieces in one area allowed her to ______________ **(put separated parts back together)** a ceramic dish from a past ______________ **(a period of time or history).** The plate has been sent to a museum so that it can be studied and ______________ **(protected so that it does not get damaged).**

Dr. Walcott believes that there is more earthenware—perhaps even one that is fully ______________ **(whole)** beneath our park. In order to expand the search, the playground and soccer field areas will be closed until further notice. Dr. Walcott is ______________ **(making someone feel sure about something)** us that the park will be restored to its original state before summer. She has even offered to use her own ______________ **(money set aside for the future)** to ensure her project is completed in a timely fashion.

In light of this exciting news, we have invited ______________ **(a person who knows a great deal about history)** Shaun Blackwell to speak to our residents about the earliest French colony this Thursday evening. Please contact our office to reserve a seat.

It is our hope that Dr. Walcott's incredible ______________ **(relating to customs, beliefs, and traditions)** discovery will give us a better understanding of the people who lived here long ago.

With sincere ______________ **(understanding the value of something)** for your cooperation and support during this time,

La Salle Village Management

Name ______________________________

- A **subject pronoun**—*I, you, he, she, it, we, they*—takes the place of a noun used as a subject.
- An **object pronoun**—*me, you, him, her, it, us, them*—takes the place of a noun used as an object. It comes after a preposition or an action verb.
- A **relative pronoun**—*that, which, who, whom, whose*—is used at the beginning of a dependent clause: *We chose the pears that felt softest.*
- A **reflexive pronoun** is used when the object of a sentence is the same as the subject: *He helped himself to a slice of pie.*

Read each sentence. Underline each pronoun. Then write on the line what type of pronoun you have underlined.

1. Lara taught herself how to play the guitar. ______________
2. She also knows how to play the piano and the flute. ______________
3. Ian likes the drums and plays them in a band. ______________
4. Ian invited her to try out for the band. ______________
5. Lara has learned the songs that the band will play. ______________
6. The band members then talked among themselves. ______________
7. Ian was the member who cast the final vote. ______________
8. In the end, they decided to have Lara join the band. ______________

In your writer's notebook, write about a skill you learned or want to learn. Include at least one relative pronoun and one reflexive pronoun. Underline the relative pronouns and circle the reflexive pronouns.

Name ______________________________

- Use a **subject pronoun** as the subject: *I, you, he, she, it, we, they.*

  Are you coming to the game? We are leaving at noon.

- Use an **object pronoun** after an action verb or a preposition: *me, you, him, her, it, us, them.*

  Dana told Jon and me to go without her. She will meet us later.

Read each sentence. Choose the correct pronoun and write it on the line.

1. We set out seeds for the birds, and (they, them) flew over. ____________

2. I took a picture of (they, them) with my camera. ____________

3. My sister and (I, me) tried to identify them. ____________

4. My father loaned (we, us) a field guide for birds. ____________

5. (He, Him) also had a pair of binoculars. ____________

Reading/Writing Connection

Read the excerpt from "Our Voices, Our Votes." Underline the subject pronouns and circle the object pronouns. Then write two sentences about Abigail Adams. Include a subject pronoun and a object pronoun. Edit your work for pronoun usage.

During the early 1800s, many women's groups joined with abolitionists to demand equal rights. Abolitionists were people who wanted to end slavery. They believed that freedom was a natural right. Women marched with them in protest. Some of them helped enslaved people escape to places where they could be free.

____

____

Name ______________________________

- Use **quotation marks** before and after direct quotations.
- Use a **comma** or **commas** to separate a phrase, such as *she said,* from the quotation itself.
- Place a comma or period inside closing quotation marks.
- There is no space between an opening quotation mark and the following word or a closing quotation mark and the preceding word.

"Mom, I had so much fun at the birthday party," Charlie said.

Rewrite the sentences correctly by adding commas and quotation marks.

1. I want to try that new video game he said.

____

2. She said It's a very hard game. It requires a great deal of skill.

____

3. That's no problem he said. I've played something like it before.

____

4. He told himself You'll do fine if you keep a positive attitude.

____

Connect to Community

Talk to a parent or another trusted adult about a special skill he or she has. Then write a paragraph about the conversation. Include at least one quotation. Check to make sure that you used quotation marks and commas correctly.

____

____

____

____

____

Name ______________________________

- A **subject pronoun** takes the place of a noun used as a subject. An **object pronoun** takes the place of a noun used as an object.
- Use **quotation marks** before and after direct quotations.
- Use a **comma** or **commas** to separate a phrase, such as *he said,* from the quotation itself. Place a comma or period inside closing quotation marks.

Rewrite the sentences below. Correct any mistakes in pronoun usage or in punctuating dialogue.

1. The teacher said. "We'll have special guests joining we tomorrow.

____

____

COMMON ERRORS

Place a question mark or exclamation mark inside the quotation marks when it is used as part of a quotation: *"Are you ready?" I asked. "Almost!" he replied.*

2. I'm not going to tell you who them are, "she added."

____

____

3. "I said, I love surprises. Me can hardly wait"!

____

4. The teacher, said Here's a clue. "See if you can figure them out."

____

5. I raised my hand. I hope that it's the astronauts I said.

____

Name ______________________________

Read the student draft and look for any corrections that need to be made. Then choose the best answer to each question.

(1) The scientist wrote themselves a note about the research. (2) She took the test tubes and placed it in the light. (3) After a few moments, the liquid in one of they turned bright red. (4) For a moment, the scientist stood in shock, but soon she called their colleague into the lab.

(5) "I never could have predicted these results!" she exclaimed.

(6) This is remarkable, "her colleague said," but we'll have to test it again to be sure.

1. What change needs to be made in sentence 1?

A Change ***themselves*** to **ourselves**

B Change ***themselves*** to **myself**

C Change ***themselves*** to **herself**

D Change ***themselves*** to **yourself**

2. How does sentence 2 need to be changed?

F Change ***it*** to **them**

G Change ***it*** to **they**

H Change ***it*** to **those**

J Change ***it*** to **their**

3. What change, if any, should be made in sentence 3?

A Change ***they*** to **it**

B Change ***they*** to **those**

C Change ***they*** to **them**

D Make no change

4. What change should be made in sentence 4?

F Change ***she*** to **her**

G Change ***she*** to **they**

H Change ***their*** to **her**

J Change ***their*** to **them**

5. What change, if any, needs to be made to sentence 5?

A Delete the quotation marks

B Delete the exclamation point and insert a comma

C Put quotation marks around "she exclaimed"

D Make no change

6. What is the correct way to write sentence 6?

F "This is remarkable," her colleague said, "but we'll have to test it again to be sure."

G "This is remarkable, her colleague said, but we'll have to test it again to be sure."

H "This is remarkable, her colleague said," but we'll have to test it again to be sure.

J "This is remarkable." Her colleague said. "But we'll have to test it again to be sure.

Name ______________________________

Fold back the paper along the dotted line. Use the blanks to write each word as it is read aloud. When you finish the test, unfold the paper. Use the list at the right to correct any spelling mistakes.

1. ____________ 1. unusual
2. ____________ 2. underwater
3. ____________ 3. regain
4. ____________ 4. repaired
5. ____________ 5. unaware
6. ____________ 6. unfriendly
7. ____________ 7. unfinished
8. ____________ 8. unimportant
9. ____________ 9. refreeze
10. ____________ 10. replenish
11. ____________ 11. reunite
12. ____________ 12. rediscover
13. ____________ 13. rewrap
14. ____________ 14. disconnect
15. ____________ 15. discourage
16. ____________ 16. dishonest
17. ____________ 17. nonspecific
18. ____________ 18. misguide
19. ____________ 19. overwhelm
20. ____________ 20. submerge

Review Words

21. ____________ 21. listen
22. ____________ 22. signal
23. ____________ 23. fable

Challenge Words

24. ____________ 24. impatiently
25. ____________ 25. inaccurate

Name ______________________________

A **prefix** is a word part added to the beginning of a word that changes its meaning. Here are some common prefixes.

un-,	"not"	***dis-***,	"not"
mis-,	"wrongly"	***non-***,	"not"
over-,	"too much"	***re-***,	"again"
under-,	"below," "too little"	***sub-***,	"under"

Read the prefixes and spelling words aloud.

DECODING WORDS

Look at the word *submerge*. It begins with the prefix *sub-*, which means "under." Use the prefix to read the word and figure out its meaning: /sub/ /mûrj/. *Submerge* means "sink below."

Write the spelling words that begin with each prefix.

unusual	unaware	refreeze	rewrap	nonspecific
underwater	unfriendly	replenish	disconnect	misguide
regain	unfinished	reunite	discourage	overwhelm
repaired	unimportant	rediscover	dishonest	submerge

un-

1. ______________
2. ______________
3. ______________
4. ______________
5. ______________

dis-

6. ______________
7. ______________
8. ______________

mis-

9. ______________

non-

10. ______________

re-

11. ______________
12. ______________
13. ______________
14. ______________
15. ______________
16. ______________
17. ______________

over-

18. ______________

under-

19. ______________

sub-

20. ______________

Look through this week's readings for more words to sort. Record them in your writer's notebook. Read the words aloud to a partner and discuss how the prefixes change the base words.

Name ____

A **prefix** is a word part added to the beginning of a word that changes its meaning. Here are some common prefixes.

un-, "not"	*dis-*, "not"
mis-, "wrongly"	*non-*, "not"
over-, "too much"	*re-*, "again"
under-, "below," "too little"	*sub-*, "under"

Read the prefixes and spelling words aloud.

DECODING WORDS

Look at the word *submerge*. It begins with the prefix *sub-*, which means "under." Use the prefix to read the word and figure out its meaning: /sub/ /mûrj/. *Submerge* means "sink below."

Write the spelling words that begin with each prefix.

unusual	unaware	refreeze	rewrap	nonslip
underwater	unfriendly	replenish	disconnect	misguide
regain	unfinished	reunite	dislike	overact
repaired	unimportant	rediscover	distrust	submerge

un-

1. ____________________
2. ____________________
3. ____________________
4. ____________________
5. ____________________

dis-

6. ____________________
7. ____________________
8. ____________________

mis-

9. ____________________

non-

10. ____________________

re-

11. ____________________
12. ____________________
13. ____________________
14. ____________________
15. ____________________
16. ____________________
17. ____________________

over-

18. ____________________

under-

19. ____________________

sub-

20. ____________________

Look through this week's readings for more words to sort. Record them in your writer's notebook. Read the words aloud to a partner and discuss how the prefixes change the base words.

Name ______________________________

A. Write the spelling words that begin with each prefix.

unusually	subaquatic	dishonesty	rewrap	nonspecific
underwater	unfriendly	replenished	rediscovering	misguided
regain	unfinished	reunited	discouraged	miscalculated
repaired	unimportant	overwhelm	disconnect	submerge

un-

1. ______________
2. ______________
3. ______________
4. ______________

dis-

5. ______________
6. ______________
7. ______________

mis-

8. ______________
9. ______________

non-

10. ______________

re-

11. ______________
12. ______________
13. ______________
14. ______________
15. ______________
16. ______________

over-

17. ______________

under-

18. ______________

sub-

19. ______________
20. ______________

B. Compare the words *repaired* and *unfinished*. How are they alike? How are they different?

____

____

____

Look through this week's readings for more words to sort. Record them in your writer's notebook. Read the words aloud to a partner and discuss how the prefixes change the base words.

Name ____

unusual	unaware	refreeze	rewrap	nonspecific
underwater	unfriendly	replenish	disconnect	misguide
regain	unfinished	reunite	discourage	overwhelm
repaired	unimportant	rediscover	dishonest	submerge

A. Write the spelling word that best completes each analogy.

1. *Busy* is to *idle* as *noteworthy* is to ________________.
2. *Drift* is to *float* as *plunge* is to ________________.
3. *Cheap* is to *valuable* as *common* is to ________________.
4. *Ignore* is to *notice* as ________________ is to *encourage*.
5. *Vanish* is to *disappear* as ________________ is to *recover.*
6. *Raw* is to *cooked* as ________________ is to *completed.*
7. *Clear* is to *uncertain* as *exact* is to ________________.
8. *Teach* is to *instruct* as ________________ is to *confuse*.
9. *Welcoming* is to ________________ as *cheerful* is to *gloomy.*
10. *Ready* is to *prepared* as *unmindful* is to ________________.

B. Write the spelling word that best completes each sentence.

11. My dog tore open the gift, so I had to ________________ it.
12. Please ________________ the hairdryer when you are done.
13. Is it ________________ to eat grocery food you haven't paid for yet?
14. Too many sounds can ________________ the senses.
15. We will ________________ with our cousins at the family picnic.
16. A sunken ship was one of their ________________ finds.
17. Dad can ________________ his old surfing skills at the beach.
18. Once the meat has thawed, you should not ________________ it.
19. We need to ________________ the shelves at the food pantry.
20. Can the old clock be ________________ so that it will chime again?

Name ______________________________

Underline the six misspelled words in the cast of characters and scene description below. Write the words correctly on the lines.

Cast of Characters

Chase Mendez, famous detective
Ben Rowe, owner of Rowe's Boats
Nick Sparks, nonimportant actor
Anna Penny, mishonest banker
Dr. Chen, local dentist
Mrs. Kent, disfriendly neighbor

Scene: Ben Rowe and Nick Sparks are returning to shore after an overwater diving trip. Anna Penny is waiting for them at the dock with Dr. Chen. Dr. Chen is holding a cracked vase that has been reepaired. Detective Mendez and Mrs. Kent are walking up the dock. They are all disaware of the dark storm clouds gathering.

1. ____________ **2.** ____________ **3.** ____________

4. ____________ **5.** ____________ **6.** ____________

Writing Connection

Write a cast of characters and a set description for another play. Map out your ideas first in your writer's notebook. Use at least four spelling words in your writing.

____

____

____

____

____

____

____

____

____

____

Name ______________________________

Remember

A prefix is a group of letters added to the beginning of a word that changes the word's meaning. These are some common prefixes.

un-, "not" ***dis-***, "not" ***mis-***, "wrongly" ***non-***, "not"

re-, "again" ***over-***, "too much" ***under-***, "below," "too little" ***sub-***, "under"

Unite means "bring together," so *reunite* means "bring together again." Use your knowledge of V/V and VC*e* syllables to read the word: /rē/ /ū/ /nīt/.

unusual	unaware	refreeze	rewrap	nonspecific
underwater	unfriendly	replenish	disconnect	misguide
regain	unfinished	reunite	discourage	overwhelm
repaired	unimportant	rediscover	dishonest	submerge

A. Add the prefix to each word to form a spelling word. Write the spelling word on the line. Then read it out loud.

1. un + friendly = ____________
2. re + discover = ____________
3. dis + connect = ____________
4. un + usual = ____________
5. re + gain = ____________
6. un + finished = ____________
7. mis + guide = ____________
8. dis + courage = ____________
9. re + paired = ____________
10. un + important = ____________
11. sub + merge = ____________
12. re + unite = ____________
13. non + specific = ____________
14. un + aware = ____________
15. dis + honest = ____________

B. Write these spelling words on the lines in alphabetical order. Alphabetize them to the third letter. ***rewrap, underwater, refreeze, overwhelm, replenish***

16. ____________
17. ____________
18. ____________
19. ____________
20. ____________

Name ____________________

A **hyperbole** is an exaggeration that is not meant to be taken literally. You can look at the words and phrases that show the writer is exaggerating and speaking figuratively to understand hyperbole.

Read this sentence: *It was so hot outside that Rose thought she was melting.* Rose did not actually think she was melting. The writer wants to emphasize how hot it was outside.

Read the messages below. Underline the words and phrases that help you identify hyperbole. Then write the meaning of each exaggeration on the lines provided.

Hey, I just got home. My backpack weighs a ton! I have a million things to do! I feel like this week is never going to end.

I just finished my work. It was the easiest assignment EVER! Do you want to meet for dinner later? I won't wait an eternity for you.

Yes! I'm so hungry, I could eat a horse!

Aa GIF

____

____

____

____

____

____

____

____

____

____

____

____

____

Name ______________________________

Prefixes are word parts added to the beginnings of words. Suffixes are word parts added to the ends of words. Prefixes and suffixes change the meaning of the base word. By learning the meaning of affixes, you can figure out the meaning of unfamiliar words and correctly use them in your writing. Circle any prefixes or suffixes in the word in bold in each sentence. Then write the meaning of the word on the line.

1. Passersby attacked the women and called them names, but the **demonstrators** continued their silent march.

   Word meaning:

   ____

2. She came from a Quaker family that believed in women's education and women's equality, **uncommon** beliefs for the time.

   Word meaning:

   ____

3. She earned degrees in **biology** and sociology before going to England to study social work.

   Word meaning:

   ____

4. Her stay in England **transformed** Paul.

   Word meaning:

   ____

5. Alice Paul had always been shy, but she was not afraid of **confrontation**.

   Word meaning:

   ____

6. She and the other suffragists were **mistreated** in jail.

   Word meaning:

   ____

Choose three of the words in bold from the activity above. In your writer's notebook, write three sentences using the words.

Name ____

- Add *-s* to most present-tense verbs when the subject is one of the singular pronouns *he, she,* or *it*. Do not add *-s* to present-tense verbs when the subject is *I, we, you,* or *they*.
- Some **indefinite pronouns** are singular: *Somebody is knocking on the door.* Others are plural: *Many agree with me*. Others can be plural or singular: *Some is still left in the fridge. Some are still finishing their project.* When an indefinite pronoun is used as a subject, the verb must agree with it.
- A prepositional phrase after an indefinite pronoun can indicate whether the pronoun is singular or plural: *Some of the book is challenging. Some of the pages are challenging*. However, a prepositional phrase does not affect pronouns that are always singular or always plural: *Each of the rooms is occupied*.

Read each sentence. Underline the subject of the sentence. Then write the correct present-tense form of the verb in parentheses on the line provided.

1. We (own) dozens of books about space exploration. ______________
2. As a matter of fact, they (have) their own shelves. ____________
3. Some (interest) me more than others. ______________
4. One of my favorites (tell) the story of a young astronaut. __________
5. She (write) about her many years of preparation. ______________
6. Everyone (know) how difficult that program can be. ______________
7. Sometimes it (take) many years to complete the training. ______________
8. My sister and I (hope) to see a rocket launch some day. ______________

In your writer's notebook, tell about a genre of writing that you enjoy. Use five pronouns in your response. Include at least one indefinite pronoun and one prepositional phrase. Then edit your work for subject-verb agreement.

Name ______________________________

- A **contraction** is a shortened form of two words.
- Subject pronouns can be combined with some verbs to form contractions. An **apostrophe** (') shows that a letter or letters have been left out.

  we're = we are; she's = she is; they've = they have
  he's = he is; I'm = I am; there's = there is; I'll = I will

Read the excerpt from "Where's Brownie?" Underline the pronoun-verb contractions. On the lines below, write the pronoun and verb used to form each contraction.

Sam: He's just a lizard, Alex. I mean chameleon. It's not exactly "absence makes the heart grow fonder."

Evan: Listen to this! Chameleons change color to match their environments when they're confused or afraid.

Alex: Of course! Nicky, any GREEN lizards over there?

Nicky: (*points into the tree*) There's just that one.

Alex: It's Brownie!

____

Reading/Writing Connection

Write a short dialogue with pronoun-verb contractions about a time you were running late. Select a genre, such as a drama or personal narrative. Plan a first draft by freewriting in your writer's notebook. Edit your work for pronoun-verb agreement.

____

____

____

____

____

____

Name ____

- An **abbreviation** is a shortened form of a word. Most abbreviations begin with a capital letter and end with a period: *Dr., Mr., Ms., Mrs., Jr., Rd., Blvd.*
- Postal abbreviations for states, such as *MN* or *TX,* use all capital letters with no periods.

Read each sentence. Underline each word that can be abbreviated. Then write the correct abbreviation on the line provided.

1. Mister Howard Riley will visit the dentist today. ____________
2. He is one of Doctor Merrick's new patients. ____________
3. The office is on Spring Street in Medfield. ____________
4. Most visitors drive along Harbor Avenue to find parking. ____________
5. The new garage on Cliff Road opened last week. ____________
6. The dentist has a second office in Concord, New Hampshire. ____________
7. A study by Professor Bea Wilby compared several dentists. ____________
8. She included doctors from the New York-New Jersey area. ____________

Write a paragraph about a visit to the post office. Include five abbreviations. Then check your work to make sure that you used proper capitalization and punctuation.

____

____

____

____

____

Name ______________________________

- Pronouns and verbs must agree in number and gender.
- Subject pronouns can be combined with some verbs to form contractions. An **apostrophe** (’) shows that a letter or letters have been left out.
- An **abbreviation** is a shortened form of a word. Most abbreviations begin with a capital letter and end with a period. Postal abbreviations for states use all capital letters with no periods.

Proofread the paragraph. On the lines below, correct mistakes in pronoun usage, pronoun-verb agreement, and abbreviations.

The Oxville Fair took place at the fairgrounds on Lakeside Ave last weekend. Wer’e pleased to announce the winners of the raffle. Theyll each receive gift certificates, which we’ill mail out next week. The first-place prize goes to Mr Lutz of Deerfield, Wa. Second place goes to ms. Kujali of Elmfield, OR. And the third place winner is Dctr. Sanders of Kentsville CAL. The fair’s director, Mrs Triplett, said that she’re very pleased with this year’s event.

HANDWRITING CONNECTION

Be sure to write your answer legibly in cursive. Remember to leave appropriate spaces between words.

____

____

____

____

____

____

____

____

____

____

Name ____

Read the student draft and look for any corrections that need to be made. Then choose the best answer to each question.

(1) You're enjoy the water park. (2) Some say it features the longest slide in the country. (3) My family and I plans to go again this weekend. (4) It's located right over the state line in Bloomington, m.n. (5) If you wants to join us, let me know. (6) I'm ask my parents if there is room in mrs Logan's car.

1. What change, if any, needs to be made in sentence 1?

A Change ***You're*** to **Your**

B Change ***You're*** to **You'll**

C Change ***You're*** to **You are**

D Make no change

2. What change, if any, should be made in sentence 2?

F Change ***say*** to **says**

G Change ***it*** to **they**

H Change ***features*** to **feature**

J Make no change

3. What change, if any, should be made in sentence 3?

A Change ***My family and I*** to **us**

B Change ***I*** to **me**

C Change ***plans*** to **plan**

D Make no change

4. What is the correct way to write sentence 4?

F It's located right over the state line in Bloomington, m.n.

G It's located right over the state line in Bloomington, M.N.

H It's located right over the state line in Bloomington, MN.

J It's located right over the state line in Bloomington, MIN.

5. What change, if any, needs to be made to sentence 5?

A Change ***you*** to **you'll**

B Change ***wants*** to **want**

C Change ***want*** to **were**

D Change ***us*** to ***them***

6. What is the correct way to write sentence 6?

F I'm asks my parents if there is room in Mrs Logan's car.

G I'll asks my parents if there is room in mrs. Logan's car.

H I'm ask my parents if there is room in Mrs. Logan's car.

J I'll ask my parents if there is room in Mrs. Logan's car.

Name ______________________________

Fold back the paper along the dotted line. Use the blanks to write each word as it is read aloud. When you finish the test, unfold the paper. Use the list at the right to correct any spelling mistakes.

1.	____________	**1.** contest
2.	____________	**2.** content
3.	____________	**3.** protest
4.	____________	**4.** combat
5.	____________	**5.** permits
6.	____________	**6.** rebel
7.	____________	**7.** present
8.	____________	**8.** insert
9.	____________	**9.** desert
10.	____________	**10.** subject
11.	____________	**11.** minute
12.	____________	**12.** compact
13.	____________	**13.** conduct
14.	____________	**14.** contract
15.	____________	**15.** refuse
16.	____________	**16.** conflict
17.	____________	**17.** research
18.	____________	**18.** excuse
19.	____________	**19.** entrance
20.	____________	**20.** extract
Review Words 21.	____________	**21.** unusual
22.	____________	**22.** rewrap
23.	____________	**23.** dishonest
Challenge Words 24.	____________	**24.** effect
25.	____________	**25.** affect

Name ____________________

Homographs are words that are spelled alike but that have different meanings. They may also be different parts of speech.

Many homographs have different pronunciations. Often, two-syllable homographs are accented on different syllables.

- **pro<u>duce</u>** (verb, "create"): *The company will produce fifty more T-shirts.*
- **<u>pro</u>duce** (noun, "farm products; fruits and vegetables"): *The market sells fresh produce.*

Say the two pronunciations of each spelling word.

SPELLING TIP

To know how to pronounce a homograph, look for context clues. How would you pronounce the word *digest* in this sentence? *I need more time to digest the information.*

Write the spelling words in alphabetical order within each group.

contest	permits	desert	conduct	research
content	rebel	subject	contract	excuse
protest	present	minute	refuse	entrance
combat	insert	compact	conflict	extract

words beginning with *c* or *d*

1. ____________
2. ____________
3. ____________
4. ____________
5. ____________
6. ____________
7. ____________
8. ____________

words beginning with *e* or *i*

9. ____________
10. ____________
11. ____________
12. ____________

words beginning with *m, p,* or *pr*

13. ____________
14. ____________
15. ____________
16. ____________

words beginning with *r* or *s*

17. ____________
18. ____________
19. ____________
20. ____________

Name ______________________________

Homographs are words that are spelled alike but that have different meanings. They may also be different parts of speech.

Many homographs have different pronunciations. Often, two-syllable homographs are accented on different syllables.

- **pro<u>duce</u>** (verb, "create"): *The company will produce fifty more T-shirts.*
- **<u>pro</u>duce** (noun, "farm products; fruits and vegetables"): *The market sells fresh produce.*

Say the two pronunciations of each spelling word.

SPELLING TIP

To know how to pronounce a homograph, look for context clues. How would you pronounce the word *digest* in this sentence? *I need more time to digest the information.*

Write the spelling in alphabetical order within each group.

contest	permits	desert	object	research
content	rebel	record	contract	excuse
protest	present	minute	refuse	buffet
combat	insert	produce	conflict	extract

words beginning with *b, c,* or *d*

1. ____________
2. ____________
3. ____________
4. ____________
5. ____________
6. ____________
7. ____________

words beginning with *e* or *i*

8. ____________
9. ____________
10. ____________

words beginning with *m* or *o*

11. ____________
12. ____________

words beginning with *p* or *pr*

13. ____________
14. ____________
15. ____________
16. ____________

words beginning with *r*

17. ____________
18. ____________
19. ____________
20. ____________

Name ______________________________

A. Write the spelling words in alphabetical order within each group.

incense	permits	desert	conduct	research
content	rebel	subject	coordinate	excuse
protest	contract	predicate	refuse	entrance
combat	insert	compact	conflict	extract

words beginning with *c* or *d*

1. ______________
2. ______________
3. ______________
4. ______________
5. ______________
6. ______________
7. ______________
8. ______________

words beginning with *e* or *i*

9. ______________
10. ______________
11. ______________
12. ______________
13. ______________

words beginning with *p* or *pr*

14. ______________
15. ______________
16. ______________

words beginning with *r* or *s*

17. ______________
18. ______________
19. ______________
20. ______________

B. Why is *contract* a homograph? Explain your answer on the lines below. You may use a dictionary to help you.

____

____

____

____

Look through this weeks readings for more homographs. Record the words in your writer's notebook. You may use a dictionary to help you.

Name ______________________________

contest	permits	desert	conduct	research
content	rebel	subject	contract	excuse
protest	present	minute	refuse	entrance
combat	insert	compact	conflict	extract

Write the spelling word that best completes each sentence. Underline the syllable that is stressed in each word that you write.

1. We held a ________________ to complain about airport noise.
2. A wide variety of cactus plants grow in the ________________.
3. The ________________ began with a silly argument.
4. We will ________________ our findings at the meeting.
5. Washing your hands takes only a ________________.
6. Teachers praised the student's good ________________.
7. I ________________ to go to bed at eight o'clock.
8. What is your favorite ________________ in school?
9. The winner of the ________________ will get a new bike.
10. Does the ________________ state when we will be paid?
11. I don't like to ________________ against my parents.
12. The ________________ to the zoo is clearly marked.
13. What is the best way to ________________ a cold?
14. ________________ a coin into the slot.
15. Are you ________________ in your hotel room?
16. The dentist will ________________ my wisdom teeth.
17. A library card ________________ you to borrow books.
18. Dad's car is a small yellow ________________.
19. What is your ________________ for missing class?
20. Scientists are working to ________________ the disease.

Name ____

Underline the six misspelled words in the paragraphs below. Write the words correctly on the lines.

Aunt Sarah was the first woman in our family to drive a car. When she was young she would speed down the deesert road near her home, a cloud of dust behind her. People in town said Sarah would rebbel against anything, but I know she just enjoyed life. She wasn't conntent unless she was trying new things.

As years went by, Sarah's conduck didn't change. She would jump on a train or plane in a minut. She loved traveling and used any excuze to pack her suitcase and explore the world.

1. ______________________ 4. ______________________

2. ______________________ 5. ______________________

3. ______________________ 6. ______________________

Writing Connection

Write about someone you admire. Use at least four spelling words in your writing.

____

____

____

____

____

____

____

____

____

____

____

____

Name ______________________________

Homographs are words that are spelled alike but have different meanings. They may be different parts of speech and have different pronunciations.

- **tear** (noun meaning "a salty liquid released from a person's eye"): *A tear ran down my cheek.*
- **tear** (verb meaning "to rip"): *If you tear the shirt, you will not be able to return it.*

Read each sentence aloud. Listen for the different pronunciations of *tear*.

contest	permits	desert	conduct	research
content	rebel	subject	contract	excuse
protest	present	minute	refuse	entrance
combat	insert	compact	conflict	extract

Fill in the missing letter or letters to form each spelling word. Then write the word on the line.

1. c __ ntract ____________
2. reb __ l ____________
3. pr __ test ____________
4. c __ mpact ____________
5. pres __ nt ____________
6. c __ nduct ____________
7. s __ bject ____________
8. c __ nflict ____________
9. extr __ ct ____________
10. comb __ t ____________
11. cont __ nt ____________
12. perm __ ts ____________
13. c __ ntest ____________
14. d __ sert ____________
15. m __ nute ____________
16. __ ntrance ____________
17. ins __ __ t ____________
18. exc __ __ __ ____________
19. ref __ __ __ ____________
20. res __ __ __ ch ____________

Name ______________________________

Expand your vocabulary by adding or removing inflectional endings, prefixes, or suffixes to a base word to create different forms of a word.

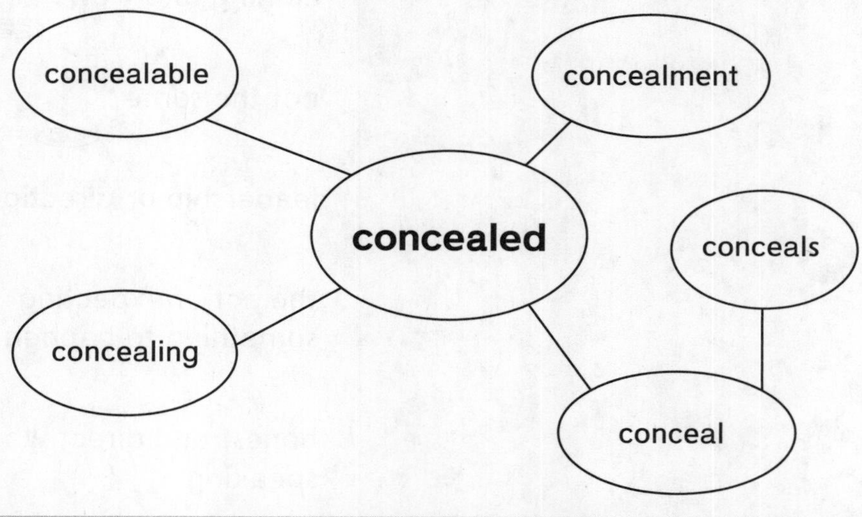

Write as many related words to *precise* as you can on the lines below. Use an electronic or print dictionary to help you.

______________________ ______________________

______________________ ______________________

______________________ ______________________

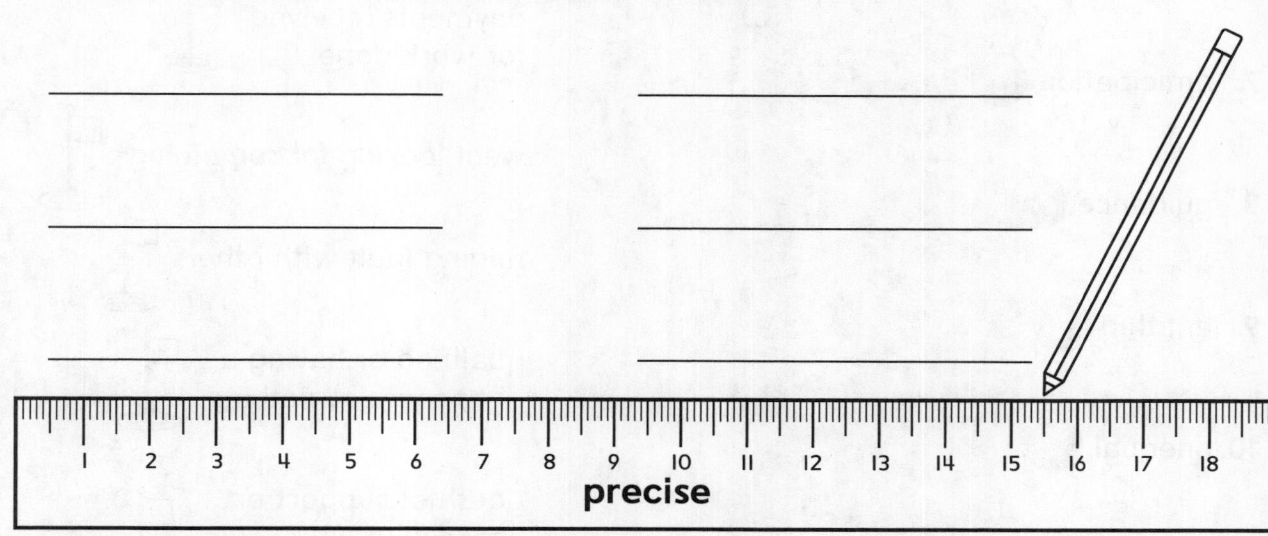

Name ______________________________

Hole in one! Match the definitions on the left with the vocabulary words on the right. Use a dictionary if you get stuck.

1. wages
2. defy
3. emerging
4. neutral
5. reserved
6. critical
7. anticipation
8. guidance
9. entitled
10. unequal
11. outspoken
12. sought

coming into view

not the same

leadership or direction

the act of expecting something to happen

honest and direct when speaking

to refuse to obey

payments received for work done

went looking for something

finding fault with others

qualified or having a right to do something

does not support or agree with either side of an argument

saved for a purpose or special person

Name ______________________________

- A **pronoun** takes the place of a noun in a sentence.
- A **possessive pronoun** takes the place of a possessive noun. It shows who or what has or owns something: *Ron's bike is green. His bike is green.*
- Some possessive pronouns are used before nouns. *That used to be our apartment.* Others can stand alone in a sentence: *That used to be ours.*

Read each rule on the park sign. Underline the possessive pronouns.

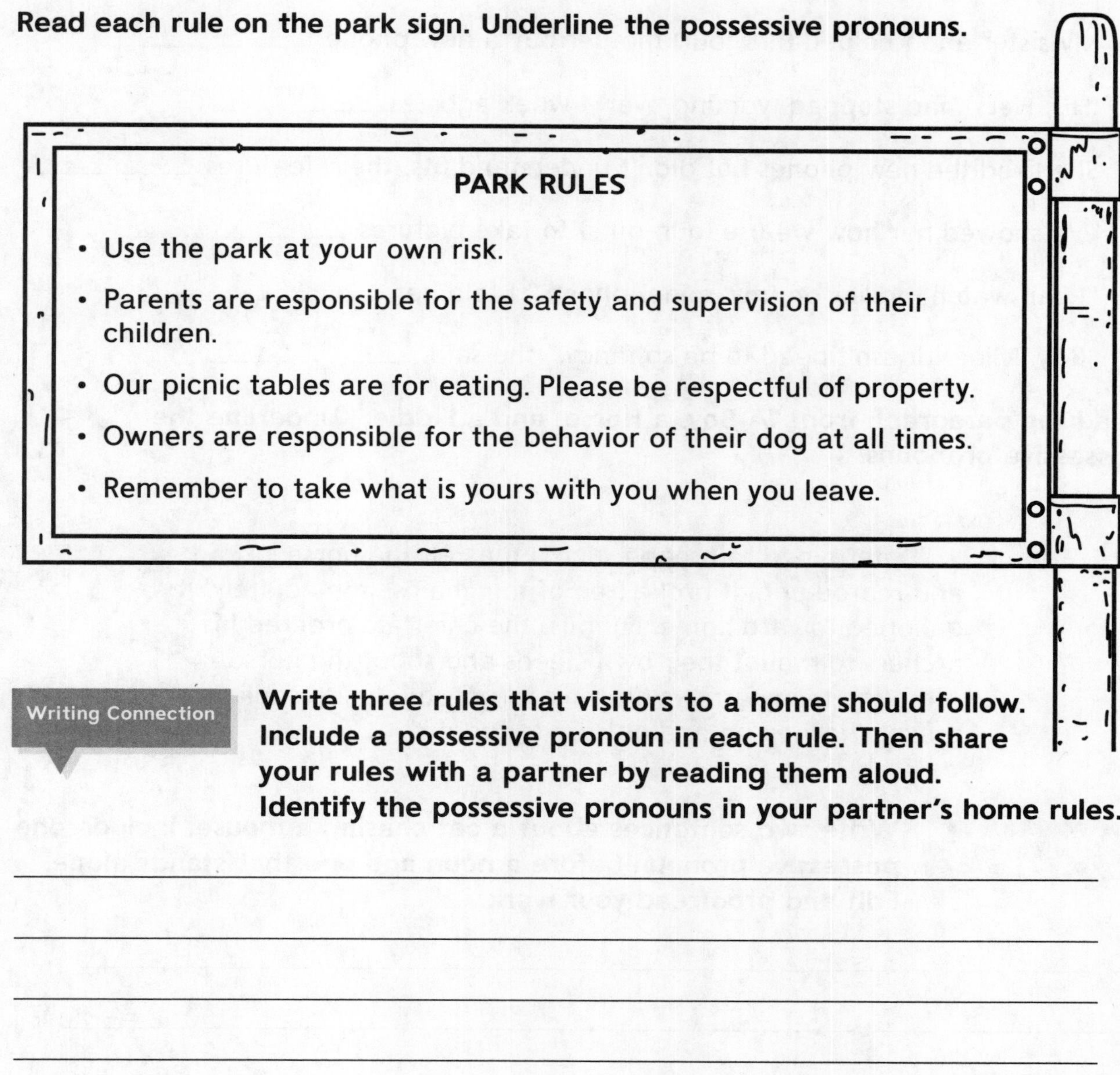

Writing Connection

Write three rules that visitors to a home should follow. Include a possessive pronoun in each rule. Then share your rules with a partner by reading them aloud. Identify the possessive pronouns in your partner's home rules.

____

____

____

____

____

Name ______________________________

- These **possessive pronouns** are used before nouns: *my, his, her, its, our, your,* and *their.*
- These possessive pronouns can stand alone: *mine, yours, his, hers, its, ours, yours,* and *theirs.*

Write the word in parentheses that best completes each sentence.

1. My sister and I helped (her, our) mother buy a new phone. ______________
2. (His, Hers) had stopped working over a week ago. ______________
3. She liked the new phones but didn't understand (its, their) features. ______________
4. We showed her how we use (our, ours) to take pictures. ______________
5. "I can watch movies on (my, mine) phone," I told her. ______________
6. "(My, Mine) doesn't need to be so fancy," she said. ______________

Read the paragraph from "A Boy, a Horse, and a Fiddle." Underline the possessive pronouns.

Determined to escape such a master, the horse kicked and reared until it broke free of the chains. Immediately, it galloped toward home. Furious, the chieftain ordered his archers to mount their own steeds and shoot the horse. Although many arrows hit their target, the white stallion bravely dashed on and outran its captors.

Write two sentences about a cat chasing a mouse. Include one possessive pronoun before a noun and one that stands alone. Edit and proofread your work.

____

____

____

Name ____________________

- An **apostrophe** takes the place of a letter or letters left out of a contraction.
- **Possessive pronouns** never use apostrophes.
- **Reflexive pronouns** are used as objects and refer back to the subject. The ending *-self* is used with singular pronouns: *She wrote the song by herself.* The ending *-selves* is used with plural pronouns: *We helped ourselves to slices of pizza.*

Read each sentence. Choose the word in parentheses that best completes the sentence. Write it on the line provided.

1. The doctors will speak about (their, they're) latest research. ____________
2. (Their, They're) scheduled to talk in an hour. ____________
3. (It's, Its) important to learn about new treatments. ____________
4. "(Your, You're) going to be surprised," one doctor told me. ____________
5. The other said, "This will affect how you live (your, you're) life." ____________
6. I will write (me, myself) notes during the presentation. ____________
7. They asked (himself, themselves) questions before they began. ____________
8. "If (your, you're) concerned about staying healthy, what can you do?" ____________
9. "You should all treat (yourself, yourselves) well by eating good foods." ____________
10. I'll be sure to follow (their, they're) advice. ____________

In your writer's notebook, write a dialogue between you and a friend about your favorite food. Include at least two possessive pronouns, two reflexive pronouns, and two contractions. Edit and proofread your dialogue for spelling, punctuation, and grammar.

Name ______________________________

- A **possessive pronoun** takes the place of a possessive noun. It shows who or what has or owns something. These possessive pronouns are used before nouns: *my, his, her, its, our, your,* and *their.* These possessive pronouns can stand alone: *mine, yours, his, hers, its, ours, yours,* and *theirs.*
- An **apostrophe** takes the place of a letter or letters left out of a contraction.

Proofread the paragraph. On the lines below, correct mistakes in pronoun usage and apostrophe placement.

Ours town's carpentry club will have it's open house tomorrow. Members will show displays of they're most recent creations. One of them's projects will win a prize. The club has also decided to change their name. Its now going to be called The Hammerhead Club. If you'ld like to join them, bring you're application to their next meeting. Next year's winning display could be your!

COMMON ERRORS

Some possessive pronouns sound the same as contractions: *its/it's, your/you're,* and *their/they're.* Remember that possessive pronouns never use apostrophes.

____

____

____

____

____

____

____

____

____

____

____

Name ____

Read the student draft and look for any corrections that need to be made. Then choose the best answer to each question.

(1) We heard some baby birds in they're nest waiting for the mother bird to return with food. (2) Them nest was in a tree in ours backyard. (3) They were chirping and entertaining theirself. (4) The baby birds were chirping so loudly in their nest that I had to cover your ears. (5) Mom used she video camera to record each of the birds. (6) Finally, the mother bird flew back to their nest to give each baby bird it's lunch!

1. What change needs to be made in sentence 1?
   - **A** Change ***We*** to **Us**
   - **B** Change ***We*** to **Them**
   - **C** Change ***they're*** to **their**
   - **D** Change ***they're*** to **its**

2. What is the correct way to write sentence 2?
   - **F** Their nest was in a tree in our backyard.
   - **G** Their nest was in a tree in ours backyard.
   - **H** Them's nest was in a tree in our backyard.
   - **J** Them nest was in a tree in your backyard.

3. What is the correct way to write sentence 3?
   - **A** They were chirping and entertaining theirselves.
   - **B** They were chirping and entertaining theirs.
   - **C** They were chirping and entertaining itselves.
   - **D** They were chirping and entertaining themselves.

4. What is the correct way to write sentence 4?
   - **F** The baby birds were chirping so loudly in their nest that I had to cover my ears.
   - **G** The baby birds were chirping so loudly in they nest that I had to cover your ears.
   - **H** The baby birds were chirping so loudly in their nest that I had to cover her ears.
   - **J** The baby birds were chirping so loudly in their nest that I had to cover its ears.

5. What change needs to be made to sentence 5?
   - **A** Change ***Mom*** to **She**
   - **B** Change ***she*** to **her**
   - **C** Change ***each*** to **every**
   - **D** Change ***the*** to **them**

6. How does sentence 6 need to be changed?
   - **F** Change ***their*** to **they're**
   - **G** Change ***their*** to **theirs**
   - **H** Change ***it's*** to **our**
   - **J** Change ***it's*** to **its**

Name ______________________________

Fold back the paper along the dotted line. Use the blanks to write each word as it is read aloud. When you finish the test, unfold the paper. Use the list at the right to correct any spelling mistakes.

	1. ________	1. rancher
	2. ________	2. searcher
	3. ________	3. pressure
	4. ________	4. future
	5. ________	5. butcher
	6. ________	6. measure
	7. ________	7. pleasure
	8. ________	8. mixture
	9. ________	9. treasure
	10. ________	10. feature
	11. ________	11. pasture
	12. ________	12. creature
	13. ________	13. lecture
	14. ________	14. gesture
	15. ________	15. nature
	16. ________	16. fracture
	17. ________	17. moisture
	18. ________	18. stretcher
	19. ________	19. legislature
	20. ________	20. azure
Review Words	21. ________	21. contest
	22. ________	22. desert
	23. ________	23. entrance
Challenge Words	24. ________	24. miniature
	25. ________	25. disclosure

Name ______________________________

- When a multisyllabic word ends with the syllable *ture* or *cher,* the syllable is usually unaccented and has the sound /chər/. Examples include *lecture* and *teacher.*
- When a multisyllabic word ends with the syllable *sure* or *zure,* the syllable is usually unaccented and has the sound /zhər/. Examples include *treasure* and *azure.*

The final syllable of each spelling word uses the schwa vowel sound, /ə/.

DECODING WORDS

Divide the word *leisure* into syllables: *lei/sure.* The first syllable is open and includes the digraph *ei.* The second syllable is unaccented and uses a schwa. Say the syllables together to decode the word: /lē/ /zhər/.

Write the spelling words that contain the matching sound and spelling pattern.

rancher	butcher	moisture	searcher	treasure
lecture	measure	feature	gesture	pasture
pressure	pleasure	stretcher	nature	creature
azure	mixture	legislature	fracture	future

/chər/ spelled *ture*

1. ____________
2. ____________
3. ____________
4. ____________
5. ____________
6. ____________
7. ____________
8. ____________
9. ____________
10. ____________
11. ____________

/chər/ spelled *cher*

12. ____________
13. ____________
14. ____________
15. ____________

/zhər/ spelled *sure*

16. ____________
17. ____________
18. ____________
19. ____________

/zhər/ spelled *zure*

20. ____________

Write a short fictional passage about finding treasure. Include four multisyllabic words that end in *ture, cher,* or *sure*. You may use a dictionary to help you. Then edit and proofread your work.

Name ______________________________

- When a multisyllabic word ends with the syllable *ture* or *cher,* the syllable is usually unaccented and has the sound /chər/. Examples include *lecture* and *teacher.*
- When a multisyllabic word ends with the syllable *sure* or *zure,* the syllable is usually unaccented and has the sound /zhər/. Examples include *treasure* and *azure.*

The final syllable of each spelling word uses the schwa vowel sound, /ə/.

DECODING WORDS

Divide the word *leisure* into syllables: *lei/sure.* The first syllable is open and includes the digraph *ei.* The second syllable is unaccented and uses a schwa. Say the syllables together to decode the word: /lē/ /zhər/.

Write the spelling words that contain the matching sound and spelling pattern.

rancher	butcher	moisture	searcher	treasure
lecture	measure	feature	gesture	pasture
picture	pleasure	capture	nature	creature
archer	mixture	seizure	catcher	future

/chər/ spelled *ture*

1. ____________
2. ____________
3. ____________
4. ____________
5. ____________
6. ____________
7. ____________
8. ____________
9. ____________
10. ____________
11. ____________

/chər/ spelled *cher*

12. ____________
13. ____________
14. ____________
15. ____________
16. ____________

/zhər/ spelled *sure*

17. ____________
18. ____________
19. ____________

/zhər/ spelled *zure*

20. ____________

Write a short fictional passage about finding treasure. Include four multisyllabic words that end in *ture, cher,* or *sure*. You may use a dictionary to help you. Then edit and proofread your work.

Name ______________________________

A. Write the spelling words that contain the matching sound and spelling pattern.

stature	leisurely	moisturize	searcher	manufacture
lecture	exposure	feature	gesture	pasture
pressured	pleasure	stretcher	architecture	posture
azure	mixture	legislature	fractured	enchanter

/chər/ spelled *ture* or *tur*

1. ____________
2. ____________
3. ____________
4. ____________
5. ____________
6. ____________
7. ____________
8. ____________
9. ____________
10. ____________
11. ____________
12. ____________

/chər/ spelled *cher*

13. ____________
14. ____________

/zhər/ spelled *sure*

15. ____________
16. ____________
17. ____________
18. ____________

/zhər/ spelled *zure*

19. ____________

word without /chər/ or /zhər/

20. ____________

B. Compare the words *moisture* and *stretcher*. How are they alike? How are they different?

____

____

____

____

Write a short fictional passage about finding treasure. Include four multisyllabic words that end in *ture, cher,* or *sure*. You may use a dictionary to help you. Then edit and proofread your work.

Name ______________________________

rancher	butcher	treasure	lecture	moisture
searcher	measure	feature	gesture	stretcher
pressure	pleasure	pasture	nature	legislature
future	mixture	creature	fracture	azure

A. Write the spelling word that has the same, or almost the same, meaning.

1. stretch, stretched, ______________

2. search, searching, ______________

3. moist, moisten, ______________

4. mix, mixed, ______________

5. press, pressing, ______________

6. please, pleasing, ______________

7. lecturer, lectern, ______________

8. treasurer, treasury, ______________

B. Write the spelling word that best completes each sentence.

9. The grass in the ______________ is long and green.

10. He plans to open a clothing store in the near ______________.

11. Please make a ______________ with your hand when you are ready.

12. The ______________ has many different cuts of meat on sale.

13. Will you please ______________ the width of the desk?

14. The huge ______________ in the movie frightened my little brother.

15. The best ______________ of this computer is its screen.

16. Do you think the ______________ will enact the proposed law?

17. The ______________ has a beautiful stream running through his land.

18. The stone in her ring is a bright ______________ color.

19. We like to take hikes and enjoy ______________ on the weekends.

20. The doctor said that my ______________ should heal nicely.

Name ______________________________

Underline the six misspelled words in the paragraphs below. Write the words correctly on the lines.

Late afternoon at the seashore is a pleazure. The air begins to cool. A salt breeze blows moistcher onto your face. If you are a good searchur, this is a good time to walk along the beach to look for shells.

Then the sun begins to set. Natchur is at its best. The azsure sky turns pink and a huge sun looms on the horizon. A gull circles, making noises like no other creachere. Everything is lovely! But have you ever wondered what makes the sky change color or why the sun looks so large? Is there a scientific explanation?

1. ______________________ 4. ______________________

2. ______________________ 5. ______________________

3. ______________________ 6. ______________________

Writing Connection

Write information about another event in nature that interests you. Use four spelling words in your writing. As you edit and proofread your work, remember the *ture, cher,* and *sure* spelling patterns.

____

____

____

____

____

____

____

____

____

____

____

Name ______________________________

Remember

- When a multisyllabic word ends with the syllable *ture* or *cher*, the syllable is usually unaccented and pronounced as /chər/: *structure, bleacher.*
- When a multisyllabic word ends with the syllable *sure* or *zure*, the syllable is usually unaccented and pronounced as /zhər/: *exposure, seizure.*

Read the four examples above aloud. Listen carefully to the difference between /chər/ and /zhər/.

rancher	butcher	treasure	lecture	moisture
searcher	measure	feature	gesture	stretcher
pressure	pleasure	pasture	nature	legislature
future	mixture	creature	fracture	azure

A. Fill in the missing letters of each word to form a spelling word. Then write the spelling word on the line.

1. mix __ __ __ __ ____________
2. trea __ __ __ __ ____________
3. fu __ __ __ __ ____________
4. plea __ __ __ __ ____________
5. legisla __ __ __ __ ____________
6. fea __ __ __ __ ____________
7. pas __ __ __ __ ____________
8. crea __ __ __ __ ____________
9. mea __ __ __ __ ____________
10. ges __ __ __ __ ____________
11. na __ __ __ __ ____________
12. pres __ __ __ __ ____________
13. mois __ __ __ __ ____________
14. lec __ __ __ __ ____________
15. frac __ __ __ __ ____________

B. Write these spelling words on the lines in reverse alphabetical order: *rancher, searcher, butcher, stretcher, azure.*

16. ____________
17. ____________
18. ____________
19. ____________
20. ____________

Name ______________________________

You can use **synonyms** and **antonyms** to figure out the meaning of a word. Synonyms have the same or similar meanings, such as *precise* and *accurate*. Antonyms are words that have opposite meanings, such as *exhausted* and *energized*. Consider what you know about the connotations, or feelings, associated with each synonym or antonym you find.

Read the advertisement below. Use context clues to circle the synonym or antonym for each word in bold. Then write the meaning of the bold word. Note whether each word has a positive, negative, or neutral connotation.

ATTENTION STUDENTS:

Are you tired of **boring** indoor activities?
Looking for an intriguing outdoor **pastime**?

Join Sonny's Summer Scouting Adventures
for some exciting nature fun in the sun!

Don't just **trek** the hardest trails or
hike the tallest mountains—conquer them!
Don't be **timid**—boost your self-confidence
through our program!

Be a part of the **original** scout troop
and forget about the imitation **squads**.

Ready to join? Give us a shout!

Name ____

An **adage** is an old saying that expresses a common observation or piece of wisdom about life. The adage "Don't forget to stop and smell the roses" means to relax and appreciate the small things in life.

Similarly, a **proverb** is a short popular saying that expresses a common truth. For example, the proverb "If the shoe fits, wear it" means "if a criticism about you is true, learn to accept it."

The two terms are often used interchangeably.

Read each passage from "A Penny Saved." Underline each adage or proverb. Then write its meaning on the lines.

1. JORGE: Well, we all know that a penny saved is a penny earned, and we've stashed away lots of spare change over the months. We were planning on using that money for our summer adventure.

____

____

2. MOM: Hold on a moment, Mia. You should look before you leap. We need to consider Jorge's evidence first.

____

____

3. MOM (*stands up*): There is another explanation. After all, there are two sides to every coin. Jorge, as it turns out, I guess I'm your so-called "thief."

____

____

4. MOM: Jorge, they say that a fool and his money are soon parted. With that in mind, a smart boy like you will never go broke!

____

____

Write a short dialogue between two friends. Include one of the adages above in the dialogue.

Name ______________________________

- **Homophones** are words that sound the same but have different spellings and meanings. Some examples of homophone pairs include *read/reed, write/right, their/there, sight/site,* and *break/brake.*

Read each sentence. Choose the homophone in parentheses that best completes the sentence. Write it on the line provided.

1. "(Lets, Let's) go to the zoo this afternoon," I suggested. ____________
2. I was interested in seeing Paula the polar (bear, bare). ____________
3. "(We'd, Weed) have to leave right now," Mom said. ____________
4. "The zoo will be closed in about an (our, hour)." ____________
5. We didn't have much time to (waste, waist). ____________
6. "(Who's, Whose) coming with us?" Mom asked. ____________
7. My sister said she wanted to come, (to, too). ____________
8. "(There's, Theirs) a new fawn that I want to see," she said. ____________
9. When we arrived, she headed straight for the (dear, deer). ____________
10. I made my way (through, threw) the crowds to see Paula. ____________

Writing Connection

Write a paragraph about a place you want to visit. Include and underline at least five homophones. Make sure you use the correct spelling of each homophone.

____

____

____

____

____

____

Name ____

- Some pronouns and pronoun/verb contractions are **homophones**.
- Don't confuse these homophones: *there/they're/their, there's/theirs, its/it's,* and *your/you're*. These are also **high-frequency words**. Try to memorize the spelling and usage of each word.

Read each sentence. Choose the word in parentheses that best completes the sentence. Write it on the line provided.

1. "Watch (your, you're) step," the tour guide warned. ______________
2. "(Your, You're) about to enter the main cavern." ______________
3. The students avoided the rocks and stones in (there, their) path. ___________
4. "Careful. (Theirs, There's) a lot of moisture," the guide said. ______________
5. I asked, "What are those things up (there, their) called?" ______________
6. "(They're, Their) called stalactites," the guide answered. ______________
7. "(Your, You're) looking at structures that took centuries to form." ____________
8. The teacher took a picture with her camera, and the students took photos with (there's, theirs). ______________

Read this stanza from "Climbing a Hill." Underline the homophone. Then explain whether the word is a possessive pronoun or a contraction.

Hiking is like a roller coaster.
It's not just one long climb
and then the ride is over.

____

Write two lines of poetry about an activity you enjoy. Include a homophone of the word you identified above.

____

____

Name ______________________________

- Use **capital letters** at the beginning of complete thoughts. Be consistent if you also use capital letters at the beginning of each line.
- **Dashes** can be used to show examples or sudden breaks in thought. *I will see you at the picnic—that is, if I finish my project in time.*
- **Hyphens** are used in compound words (*forty-six, mother-in-law*) or to connect double-adjectives (*a well-respected professor*). They are also used to break up words between lines.
- Use **quotation marks** around dialogue or speech.
- Use **commas** to separate units of meaning.

Rewrite each line of the poem by putting capital letters and punctuation marks where they belong.

1. once in a while maybe twice in a while—

____

2. i think of fun things thoughts that get me to smile.

____

3. my mom used to say in a manner most grace

____

4. ful, A smile on your face brings light to a place.

____

5. thanks, Mom. You're right as is always the case!

____

In your writer's notebook, write a short poem about a family member. Include at least one hyphen, one dash, and one quotation. Edit and proofread your poem for capitalization, punctuation, and spelling.

Name ____________________

- Don't confuse words that are **homophones**.
- In poetry, usually use **capital letters** at the beginning of complete thoughts and, if desired, at the beginning of each line. **Dashes** can set off examples or sudden breaks in thought. **Hyphens** can break a word between lines. Use **quotation marks** around dialogue or speech. Use **commas** to separate units of meaning.

Proofread the poem. On the lines below, correct errors or inconsistencies in the use of pronouns, capitalization, and punctuation.

Bright stars—your shining in the highest sky
Asking earthbound soles like me, Why? Why? Why?"
Theirs won part of my heart eager to know
and another part thats afraid to show
it's self tonight to shine at any height.
I'll do whats write trust my heart's inner light.

____

____

____

____

____

____

Name ______________________________

Read the student draft and look for any corrections that need to be made. Then choose the best answer to each question.

(1) "Look at all the storm clouds over their!" Dad exclaimed. (2) "Who's idea was it to go to the beach today?" he asked.

(3) "Your getting upset over nothing," Mom said.

(4) "They're just clouds, Dad-nothing to worry about!" said Terrance.

(5) "Trust me, Dad said. (6) Its going to rain any minute now."

(7) "Those clouds will never make there way over here," she replied. (8) "Let's go!"

1. What change, if any, should be made in sentence 1?

A Change ***their*** to **there**

B Change ***their*** to **they're**

C Change ***their*** to **there's**

D Make no change

2. How does sentence 2 need to be changed?

F Change ***Who's*** to **Who**

G Change ***Who's*** to **Whose**

H Change ***it*** to **its**

J Change ***it*** to **it's**

3. What change, if any, should be made in sentence 3?

A Change ***Your*** to **You**

B Change ***Your*** to **You're**

C Change ***Your*** to **You've**

D Make no change

4. What change, if any, should be made in sentence 4?

F Change ***They're*** to **There**

G Change the hyphen to a dash

H Delete the quotation marks

J Make no change

5. What is the correct way to write sentences 5 and 6?

A "Trust me," Dad said. It going to rain any minute now.

B "Trust me," Dad said. "It's going to rain any minute now."

C "Trust me," Dad said. "Its going to rain any minute now."

D "Trust me, Dad said. "Its' going to rain any minute now.

6. How does sentence 7 need to be changed?

F Change ***there*** to **they're**

G Change ***there*** to **the**

H Change ***there*** to **their**

J Change ***there*** to **they**

Name ______________________________

Fold back the paper along the dotted line. Use the blanks to write each word as it is read aloud. When you finish the test, unfold the paper. Use the list at the right to correct any spelling mistakes.

	1. ______	1. distance
	2. ______	2. importance
	3. ______	3. balance
	4. ______	4. attendance
	5. ______	5. absence
	6. ______	6. performance
	7. ______	7. dependence
	8. ______	8. substance
	9. ______	9. disturbance
	10. ______	10. appearance
	11. ______	11. assistance
	12. ______	12. ignorance
	13. ______	13. brilliance
	14. ______	14. ambulance
	15. ______	15. residence
	16. ______	16. radiance
	17. ______	17. resistance
	18. ______	18. reluctance
	19. ______	19. persistence
	20. ______	20. hesitance
Review Words	21. ______	21. creature
	22. ______	22. measure
	23. ______	23. rancher
Challenge Words	24. ______	24. vigilance
	25. ______	25. inference

Name ______________________________

The suffixes *-ance* and *-ence* mean "an action or act" or "the state of." Adding these suffixes to a base word or root creates a noun: *assist* + *ance* = *assistance*.

Many words that end in *-ance* or *-ence* are related to adjectives that end with *-ant* or *-ent*: *assistance* is related to *assistant*.

Sometimes adding *-ance* or *-ence* changes the base word: *ignore* —> *ignorance* (drop *e*).

DECODING WORDS

Adding suffixes can change the consonant sound in a word. For example, the /t/ in *radiant* changes to /s/ when adding *-ance* to form *radiance*. In the word *select*, the /t/ changes to /sh/ when adding the suffix *-ion* to form *selection*. Use knowledge of adding suffixes to sound out each word.

Write the words that contain the matching syllable and spelling pattern.

distance	absence	disturbance	brilliance	resistance
importance	performance	appearance	ambulance	reluctance
balance	dependence	assistance	residence	persistence
attendance	substance	ignorance	radiance	hesitance

two syllables ending in *-ence*

1. ____________

two syllables ending in *-ance*

2. ____________
3. ____________
4. ____________
5. ____________

three syllables ending in *-ence*

6. ____________
7. ____________
8. ____________

three syllables ending in *-ance*

9. ____________
10. ____________
11. ____________

12. ____________
13. ____________
14. ____________
15. ____________
16. ____________
17. ____________
18. ____________
19. ____________
20. ____________

Look for more words with the suffix *-ance* or *-ence*. Record each word and a related word in your writer's notebook. Note any consonant sound changes. Then read the words aloud.

Name ______________________________

The suffixes *-ance* and *-ence* mean "an action or act" or "the state of." Adding these suffixes to a base word or root creates a noun: *assist* + *ance* = *assistance.*

Many words that end in *-ance* or *-ence* are related to adjectives that end with *-ant* or *-ent*: *assistance* is related to *assistant.*

Sometimes adding *-ance* or *-ence* changes the base word: *ignore* —> *ignorance* (drop *e*).

DECODING WORDS

Adding suffixes can change the consonant sound in a word. For example, the /t/ in *radiant* changes to /s/ when adding *-ance* to form *radiance.* In the word *select,* the /t/ changes to /sh/ when adding the suffix *-ion* to form *selection.* Use knowledge of adding suffixes to sound out each word.

Write the words that contain the matching syllable and spelling pattern.

distance	absence	disturbance	glance	resistance
importance	evidence	entrance	romance	chance
balance	dependence	dance	residence	presence
attendance	substance	clearance	radiance	hesitance

one syllable ending in *-ance*

1. ______________
2. ______________
3. ______________

two syllables ending in *-ence*

4. ______________
5. ______________

two syllables ending in *-ance*

6. ______________
7. ______________
8. ______________
9. ______________
10. ______________
11. ______________

three syllables ending in *-ence*

12. ______________
13. ______________
14. ______________

three syllables ending in *-ance*

15. ______________
16. ______________
17. ______________
18. ______________
19. ______________
20. ______________

Look for more words with the suffix *-ance* or *-ence*. Record each word and a related word in your writer's notebook. Note any consonant sound changes. Then read the words aloud.

Name ______________________________

A. Write the spelling words that contain the matching syllable and spelling pattern.

tolerance	absence	disturbance	brilliance	resistance
perseverance	prevalence	appearance	ambulance	reluctance
acceptance	dependence	assistance	residence	persistence
attendance	substance	ignorance	radiance	hesitance

two syllables ending in *-ence*

1. ____________

two syllables ending in *-ance*

2. ____________
3. ____________

three syllables ending in *-ence*

4. ____________
5. ____________
6. ____________
7. ____________

three syllables ending in *-ance*

8. ____________
9. ____________
10. ____________
11. ____________
12. ____________
13. ____________
14. ____________
15. ____________
16. ____________
17. ____________
18. ____________
19. ____________

four syllables ending in *-ance*

20. ____________

B. Compare the words *dependence* and *disturbance*. How are they alike? How are they different?

____

____

____

Look for more words with the suffix *-ance* or *-ence*. Record each word and a related word in your writer's notebook. Note any consonant sound changes. Then read the words aloud.

Name ______________________________

distance	absence	disturbance	brilliance	resistance
importance	performance	appearance	ambulance	reluctance
balance	dependence	assistance	residence	persistence
attendance	substance	ignorance	radiance	hesitance

A. Write the spelling word that has the same, or almost the same, meaning.

1. need ______________
2. commotion ______________
3. glow ______________
4. material ______________
5. refusal ______________
6. home ______________
7. brightness ______________
8. steadiness ______________
9. look ______________
10. uncertainty ______________
11. unwillingness ______________
12. determination ______________

B. Write the spelling word that belongs with each word family below.

13. ignore, ignorant, ______________
14. assist, assistant, ______________
15. import, important, ______________
16. perform, performer, ______________
17. distant, distantly, ______________
18. absent, absently, ______________
19. attend, attendant, ______________
20. ambulate, perambulator, ______________

Name ____

Underline the six misspelled words in the paragraphs below. Using your knowledge of spelling patterns, write the words correctly on the lines.

When the forest fire began to spread, Ranger Flynn drove a distence of ten miles to reach the nearby town of Pineville. Once he was there, he went straight to the residance of the mayor to warn her of the danger. He wanted to make sure the mayor was aware of the importence of preparing the town for the blaze.

1. ____________ **2.** ____________ **3.** ____________

The mayor asked Ranger Flynn for assistence. There was no hesitence in his agreement. He spoke at a town meeting to clear up any ignorence of the approaching fire and to discuss how to combat it.

4. ____________ **5.** ____________ **6.** ____________

Writing Connection

Write a passage for a story about a town that faces a challenge. Use at least four spelling words in your writing.

____

____

____

____

____

____

____

____

____

____

____

____

____

Name ______________________________

Remember

Adding the suffixes *-ance* and *-ence* to a base word or root creates a noun. For example: *perform* + *-ance* = *performance* (the act of performing).

Sometimes adding *-ance* or *-ence* will change the base word: *apply* —> *appliance* (change *y* to *i*).

Adding a suffix can change a consonant sound in a word. The /t/ in *resident* changes to /s/ when *-ence* is added (*residence*), whereas the /t/ in *select* changes to /sh/ when the suffix *-ion* is added (*selection*).

What sound does the /t/ in *reluctant* change to when *-ance* is added to form *reluctance*? Blend the sounds in the word together: /ri/ /luk/ /təns/.

distance	absence	disturbance	brilliance	resistance
importance	performance	appearance	ambulance	reluctance
balance	dependence	assistance	residence	persistence
attendance	substance	ignorance	radiance	hesitance

A. Fill in the missing letter to form a spelling word. Write the word on the line.

1. ambul __ nce ______________
2. resid __ nce ______________
3. bal __ nce ______________
4. subst __ nce ______________
5. persist __ nce ______________
6. brilli __ nce ______________
7. hesit __ nce ______________
8. disturb __ nce ______________
9. appear __ nce ______________
10. import __ nce ______________
11. dist __ nce ______________
12. ignor __ nce ______________
13. depend __ nce ______________
14. perform __ nce ______________

B. Write these spelling words in alphabetical order. Alphabetize them to the third letter. ***reluctance, attendance, resistance, absence, assistance, radiance***

16. ______________
17. ______________
18. ______________
19. ______________
19. ______________
20. ______________

Name ____

Expand your vocabulary by generating synonyms, or words with the same or similar meanings, to show shades of meaning of the word.

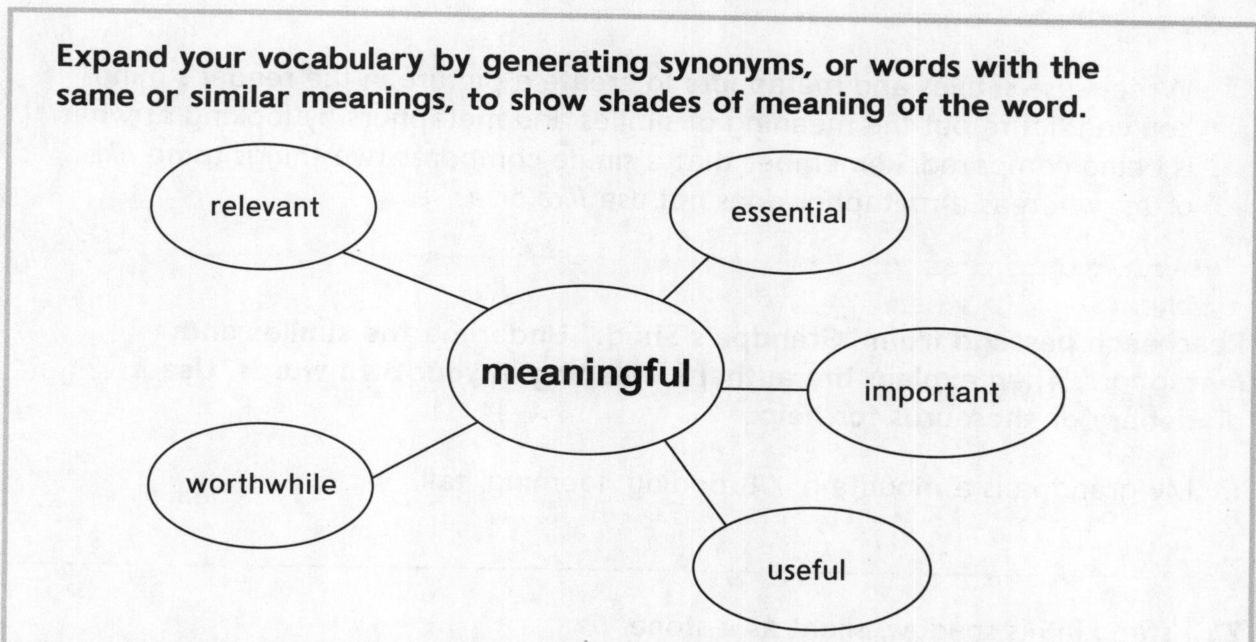

Add rocks to the landscape below to write as many synonyms of *barren* as you can. Use a dictionary or thesaurus to help you.

Name ____

Writers use similes and metaphors to create a picture in the reader's mind. You can figure out the meaning of similes and metaphors by looking at what is being compared. Remember that a simile compares two things using *like* or *as*, whereas a metaphor does not use *like* or *as*.

Read each passage from "Grandpa's Shed." Underline the similes and metaphors. Then explain the author's meaning in your own words. Use a dictionary or thesaurus for help.

1. My grandpa is a mountain, / Brooding, looming, tall.

____

2. I stand in his shadow, silent as a stone.

____

3. That shed's a squat gray mushroom,

____

4. The old man's hands are vises, / Prying open paint cans lightning fast.

____

5. My words explode like fireworks.

____

6. Anticipating anger, my mouth shuts like a trap.

____

7. We share that shed like one vast canvas,

____

Name ______________________________

- A **clause** is a group of words that has a subject and a predicate.
- An **independent,** or **main, clause** has one complete subject and one complete predicate. It can stand alone as a sentence.

  I painted the room last weekend.

- A **dependent,** or **subordinate, clause** cannot stand alone as a sentence. It is introduced by a **subordinating conjunction**, such as *after, although, before, because, if, since, until, when, where,* and *while.*

  I took a shower <u>after I painted the room</u>.

Read each sentence. Write whether the underlined words are an *independent* clause or a *dependent* clause.

1. <u>I spent Saturday afternoon at the craft fair.</u> ______________________
2. I got in free <u>because I am a student</u>. ______________________
3. If I bought something, <u>I would receive a discount</u>. ______________________
4. <u>Since my mom is a painter</u>, she had a booth there. ______________________
5. People liked her paintings, and <u>she sold quite a few</u>. ______________________
6. I stayed at the booth <u>while she went to get lunch</u>. ______________________
7. <u>Several people stopped by</u>, but no one bought anything. ______________________
8. <u>When Mom got back</u>, I told her about the visitors. ______________________
9. She shared some of the food <u>that she had bought</u>. ______________________
10. After we ate, <u>I checked out the rest of the fair</u>. ______________________

In your writer's notebook, write a short passage about a fair you have attended or parade you have seen. Include at least five dependent clauses. Vary your sentence structure. Check your work to make sure that a subordinating conjunction introduces each dependent clause.

Name ____________________

- A **complex sentence** contains an independent, or main, clause and a dependent, or subordinate, clause.
- Use a comma after an **introductory dependent clause**.

  Whenever I can't fall sleep, I reread an old book.

Use the subordinating conjunction in parentheses to combine the two clauses into one complex sentence. Write the new sentence on the line provided.

1. it was hot/we drank lots of water (because)

   ____

2. night approached/it became harder to see (as)

   ____

Reading/Writing Connection

Read this paragraph from "Changing Views of Earth." Underline two dependent clauses. Then write three sentences about an invention that would make your life easier. Include two dependent clauses. Check to make sure that you use commas and subordinating conjunctions correctly.

> Long ago, humans based their knowledge on what they experienced with their eyes and ears. If people could heighten their senses, they might not feel so mystified by the events confronting them daily. For example, something as simple as the rising sun perplexed people for centuries. They believed that the Earth stayed in place while the Sun moved around it. This was called the geocentric model.

____

____

____

____

Name ______________________________

- An **appositive** is a noun, noun phrase, or noun clause that explains or describes a nearby noun or pronoun.
- An appositive may come before or after a noun or a pronoun. Commas are used to set off many appositives.

  Zoe, our class president, gave an excellent speech.

Combine the two sentences into one by creating an appositive out of the second sentence. Write the new sentence on the line provided.

1. Ms. Thayer visited our class today. Ms. Thayer is our town's police chief.

   ____

2. She spoke about KOPS. KOPS is the "Keep Our Parks Safe" program.

   ____

3. She asked a student to help her. That student was Jodee Oskamp.

   ____

4. Our town's paper ran an article about the visit. The Flyer is our town's paper.

   ____

Write instructions explaining how to find a specific location in your school. Include at least two appositives. Then read the instructions to a partner. Ask your partner to restate them. Are the instructions clear enough to follow? If not, revise them to include additional appositives.

____

____

____

____

____

____

Name ______________________________

- Use a comma after an **introductory dependent,** or **subordinate, clause**.
- An **appositive** may come before or after a noun or a pronoun. Commas are used to set off many appositives.

Proofread the paragraph. On the lines below, correct mistakes in the use of clauses, appositives, and commas.

Baseball legend Billy "Bib" Barker will be signing photos after today's game. If you have a chance come by to say hello to him. Current members of the team which won last year's state championship will join Bib. Before Bib leaves the stadium Suki Yee our mayor will present him with a special award the key to the city. Channel 3 our local news station will broadcast the event live.

COMMON ERRORS

An appositive requires commas when it contains extra information. However, if the information is essential to the sentence, a comma is not used. Example: *The author Mark Twain was known for his humorous writing.* "Mark Twain" is necessary to identify who the author is.

____

____

____

____

____

____

____

____

____

Name ________________________________

Read the student draft and look for any corrections that need to be made. Then choose the best answer to each question.

(1) Mom had to walk to work while she missed the bus. (2) She arrived at the store as the clock struck nine. (3) Unless Robert the store manager wasn't there yet she opened the store herself. (4) Until an hour had passed, she called the manager at home. (5) Her manager laughed whenever it was a holiday. (6) Although my mom heard that the store was closed for the day, she laughed, too. (7) She had never been more embarrassed!

1. What change needs to be made in sentence 1?

A Change ***had*** to **have**

B Change ***she*** to **she'll**

C Add a comma after ***work***

D Change ***while*** to **because**

2. What change, if any, should be made in sentence 2?

F Change ***She*** to **Her**

G Change ***at*** to **after**

H Change ***as*** to **because**

J Make no change

3. What is the correct way to write sentence 3?

A Since Robert, the store manager, wasn't there yet, she opened the store herself.

B Once Robert the store manager, wasn't there yet she opened the store herself.

C If Robert the store manager wasn't there yet she opened the store, herself.

D Unless Robert the store manager wasn't there yet she opened the store herself.

4. How does sentence 4 need to be changed?

F Change ***Until*** to **Although**

G Change ***Until*** to **Even though**

H Change ***Until*** to **After**

J Change ***Until*** to **Unless**

5. What change, if any, needs to be made to sentence 5?

A Change ***whenever*** to **because**

B Change ***whenever*** to **before**

C Change ***whenever*** to **wherever**

D Make no change

6. What is the correct way to write sentence 6?

F If my mom heard that the store was closed for the day, she laughed, too.

G While my mom heard that the store was closed for the day, she laughed, too.

H Whether my mom heard that the store was closed for the day, she laughed, too.

J When my mom heard that the store was closed for the day, she laughed, too.

Name ____________________

Fold back the paper along the dotted line. Use the blanks to write each word as it is read aloud. When you finish the test, unfold the paper. Use the list at the right to correct any spelling mistakes.

1. ____________ 1. serious
2. ____________ 2. furious
3. ____________ 3. eruption
4. ____________ 4. usually
5. ____________ 5. direction
6. ____________ 6. position
7. ____________ 7. forgetful
8. ____________ 8. comfortable
9. ____________ 9. finally
10. ____________ 10. destruction
11. ____________ 11. apparently
12. ____________ 12. completely
13. ____________ 13. eventually
14. ____________ 14. carefully
15. ____________ 15. microscopic
16. ____________ 16. allergic
17. ____________ 17. scientific
18. ____________ 18. safety
19. ____________ 19. activity
20. ____________ 20. sickness

Review Words

21. ____________ 21. distance
22. ____________ 22. ambulance
23. ____________ 23. substance

Challenge Words

24. ____________ 24. aquatic
25. ____________ 25. mathematics

Name ______________________________

A suffix is one or more letters added to a base word or root. It changes the meaning and part of speech of the base word. For example:

-ful, means "full of"; forms an adjective
-ion, -tion, -ation, -ition, mean "act or process of"; forms a noun

Many adverbs end in ***-ly***: *helpfully, busily.* Some adjectives that end in *e,* such as *comfortable,* drop the *e* when *-ly* is added: *comfortably.* Adjectives that end in *l* double the final consonant when *-ly* is added: *finally.*

DECODING WORDS

Adding a suffix can change the final consonant sound in a base word. The /t/ in *direct* changes to /sh/ when *-ion* is added (*direction*). The /k/ in *music* changes to /sh/ when *-ian* is added (*musician*). Use knowledge of suffixes to sound out each word.

Write the spelling words that match the parts of speech. Then read each word aloud, with and without its suffix.

serious	direction	finally	eventually	scientific
furious	position	destruction	carefully	safety
eruption	forgetful	apparently	microscopic	activity
usually	comfortable	completely	allergic	sickness

nouns	adverbs	adjectives
1. ______	8. ______	14. ______
2. ______	9. ______	15. ______
3. ______	10. ______	16. ______
4. ______	11. ______	17. ______
5. ______	12. ______	18. ______
6. ______	13. ______	19. ______
7. ______		20. ______

Look for more words with suffixes, such as *-ic, -tion,* or *-ian.* Record each word and its base word word in your writer's notebook. Note any /k/ to /sh/ or /t/ to /sh/ changes. Read the words aloud. How does each suffix affect each base word?

Name ______________________________

A suffix is one or more letters added to a base word or root. It changes the meaning and part of speech of the base word. For example:

-ful, means "full of"; forms an adjective
-ion, -tion, -ation, -ition, mean "act or process of"; forms a noun

Many adverbs end in ***-ly***: *helpfully, busily.* Some adjectives that end in *e*, such as *comfortable*, drop the *e* when *-ly* is added: *comfortably.* Adjectives that end in *l* double the final consonant when *-ly* is added: *finally.*

DECODING WORDS

Adding a suffix can change the final consonant sound in a base word. The /t/ in *direct* changes to /sh/ when *-ion* is added (*direction*). The /k/ in *music* changes to /sh/ when *-ian* is added (*musician*). Use knowledge of suffixes to sound out each word.

Write the spelling words that match the parts of speech. Then read each word aloud, with and without its suffix.

serious	direction	finally	eventually	pacific
furious	position	usually	carefully	safety
eruption	forgetful	destruction	electric	activity
happily	comfortable	sadly	allergic	sickness

nouns	adverbs	adjectives
1. ____________	8. ____________	14. ____________
2. ____________	9. ____________	15. ____________
3. ____________	10. ____________	16. ____________
4. ____________	11. ____________	17. ____________
5. ____________	12. ____________	18. ____________
6. ____________	13. ____________	19. ____________
7. ____________		20. ____________

Look for more words with suffixes, such as *-ic, -tion,* or *-ian.* Record each word and its base word word in your writer's notebook. Note any /k/ to /sh/ or /t/ to /sh/ changes. Read the words aloud. How does each suffix affect each base word?

Name ______________________________

A. Write the spelling words that match the parts of speech. Then read each word aloud, with and without its suffix.

seriously	sensible	subconscious	mathematics	enjoyable
furiously	eventually	destruction	improvement	charitable
aquatic	forgetful	unforgettable	allergic	microscopic
eruption	comfortably	questionable	scientific	argument

nouns

1. ______________
2. ______________
3. ______________
4. ______________
5. ______________
6. ______________

adverbs

7. ______________
8. ______________
9. ______________
10. ______________

adjectives

11. ______________
12. ______________
13. ______________
14. ______________
15. ______________
16. ______________
17. ______________
18. ______________
19. ______________
20. ______________

B. Circle the suffix in each word. Then write a definition of the word based on the suffix.

comfortable ______________________________

destruction ______________________________

forgetful ______________________________

Adding a suffix can change the final consonant sound in a base word. For example, the /t/ in *reject* changes to /sh/ when *-ion* is added (*rejection*): /ri/ /jek/ /shən/. The /k/ in *music* changes to /sh/ when *-ian* is added (*musician*): /mū/ /zish/ /ən/.

Record the words *invent* and *electric* in your writer's notebook. Then write a related word using the suffix *-tion* or *-ian*. Read each word aloud. Note whether the word has a /t/ to /sh/ or /k/ to /sh/ change.

Name ______________________________

serious	direction	finally	eventually	scientific
furious	position	destruction	carefully	safety
eruption	forgetful	apparently	microscopic	activity
usually	comfortable	completely	allergic	sickness

A. Write the spelling word that matches each definition below.

1. very angry ______________

2. at last ______________

3. seemingly ______________

4. damage ______________

5. absent-minded ______________

6. freedom from harm or danger ______________

7. extremely tiny ______________

8. course of movement ______________

9. thoughtful, solemn ______________

10. with attention to detail ______________

B. Write the spelling word that best completes each sentence.

11. I moved the plant to a sunny ______________ on the windowsill.

12. We ______________ have soccer practice each day after school.

13. The effects of the volcanic ______________ were widespread.

14. I can't eat peanuts because I am ______________ to them.

15. The new seats in the theater are very ______________.

16. Finger painting is an ______________ many young children enjoy.

17. The ______________ made me feel tired and achy.

18. I found an article about global warming in a ______________ journal.

19. Our vacation will ______________ end, and we will return home.

20. The runner was ______________ exhausted after the race.

Name ____

Underline the six misspelled words in the paragraphs below. Using your knowledge of common suffixes, write the words correctly on the lines.

The hurricane threatened the seaside town. If the storm made landfall there, the destrucion would be widespread. Many homes would be completety destroyed. It was a serius situation, and officials urged residents to leave as soon as possible.

1. ____________ **2.** ____________ **3.** ____________

Kira and her mother watched the directsion of the storm. They feared that it would eventualy strengthen and turn toward the coast. Kira's mother packed up as many of their belongings as she could, and they fled to the safty of their cousin's inland home.

4. ____________ **5.** ____________ **6.** ____________

Writing Connection

Write a passage for a story about another event in nature that puts people at risk. Use at least four spelling words in your writing.

____

____

____

____

____

____

____

____

____

____

____

____

Name ____

A suffix is a letter or group of letters added to a base word or root. It changes the meaning and part of speech of the base word. For example:

-ness, means "quality or state"; forms a noun (*the calmness of the lake*)
-ist, means "person who"; forms a noun (*the family dentist*)

Adding a suffix can change the final consonant sound in a word. For example, the /t/ in *elect* changes to /sh/ when *-ion* is added (*election*): /i/ /lek/ /shən/. The /k/ in *optic* changes to /sh/ when *-ian* is added (*optician*): /op/ /tish/ /ən/.

serious	direction	finally	eventually	scientific
furious	position	destruction	carefully	safety
eruption	forgetful	apparently	microscopic	activity
usually	comfortable	completely	allergic	sickness

A. Add the suffix to form each spelling word. Write the word on the line. Then read the words aloud and listen for any consonant sound changes.

1. direct + ion = ____________________
2. final + ly = ____________________
3. posit + ion = ____________________
4. forget + ful = ____________________
5. comfort + able = ____________________
6. complete + ly = ____________________
7. furi + ous = ____________________
8. erupt + ion = ____________________
9. apparent + ly = ____________________
10. sick + ness = ____________________
11. eventual + ly = ____________________
12. destruct + ion = ____________________
13. usual + ly = ____________________
14. care + fully = ____________________
15. safe + ty = ____________________

B. Write these spelling words on the lines in reverse alphabetical order: *serious, microscopic, activity, scientific, allergic.*

16. ____________________
17. ____________________
18. ____________________
19. ____________________
20. ____________________

Name ______________________________

Content words are words that are specific to a field of study. For example, words like *astronomy, gravity,* and *asteroid* are science content words.

Authors use content words to explain a concept or idea. Sometimes you can figure out what a content word means by using context clues. You can also use a dictionary to help you find the meaning of unfamiliar content words.

Go on a word hunt with a partner. Find as many content words related to planets as you can. Write them in the chart.

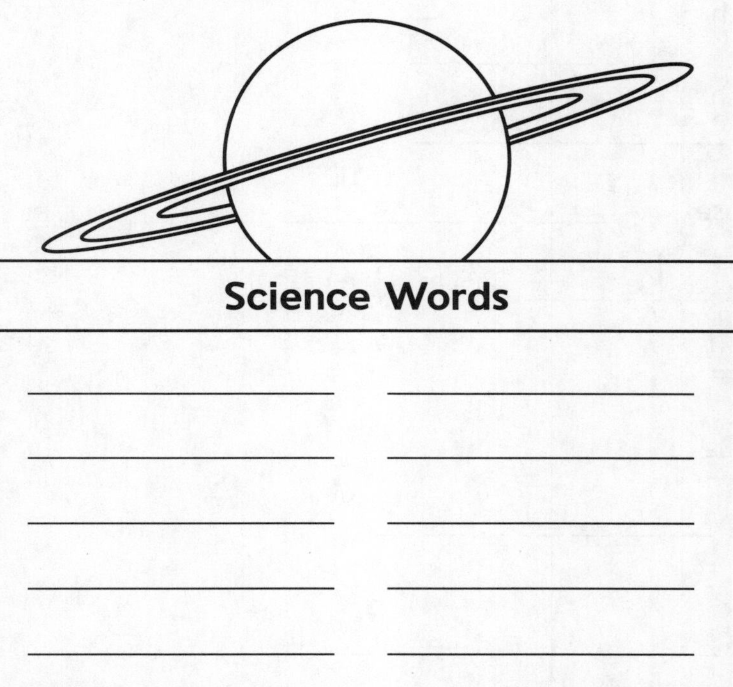

Science Words	
______________	______________
______________	______________
______________	______________
______________	______________
______________	______________

CONNECT TO CONTENT

The author of "When Is a Planet Not a Planet?" discusses why Pluto is no longer considered a planet. Modern technology has allowed scientists to discover new information about the planets in our solar system and beyond.

Circle two words that you were able to figure out the meaning of using context clues. Write the words and what they mean on the lines.

____

____

____

Name ______________________________

Read the clues. Complete the puzzle with your vocabulary words. Then use the letters in the boxes to solve the riddle. Use the dictionary if you get stuck.

barren	meaningful	neutral	interpret
mimic	function	encounter	expression
plumes	defy	precise	resolve

1. does not support or agree with either side of an argument _ _ _ _ _ [ ] _

2. to explain the meaning _ _ _ _ _ _ _ _ _

3. having importance or a purpose [ ] _ _ _ _ _ _ _ _ _

4. exact; accurate _ _ _ _ _ [ ] _ _

5. to imitate _ _ _ _ _ [ ]

6. lifeless _ _ [ ] _ _ _

7. to settle, explain, or solve _ _ _ _ [ ] _ _

8. putting thoughts and feelings into words and actions _ _ _ _ _ [ ] _ _ _ _

9. unexpected meeting _ _ [ ] _ _ _ _ _ _

10. use or purpose _ _ _ _ _ _ [ ] _

11. big, fluffy features [ ] _ _ _ _ _

12. to refuse to obey _ [ ] _ _

What has a slide but not a slope?

[ ] [ ] [ ] [ ] [ ] [ ] [ ] [ ] [ ] [ ] [ ]

Name ____

- A **complex sentence** contains an independent clause and a dependent clause.
- **Dependent clauses** are introduced by **subordinating conjunctions**, such as *while, because, if,* and *although*: *I jumped because I was happy.*
- Dependent clauses can also be introduced by **relative pronouns**, such as *who, whose, which, whom,* and *that,* and **relative adverbs**, such as *where, when,* and *why.*

  It is the only store that sells them. I will go when I have time.

Read each sentence. Underline the dependent clause. Then circle the introductory word in that clause. Finally, on the line provided, write whether the introductory word is a *subordinating conjunction, relative pronoun,* or *relative adverb*.

1. I volunteer at the animal shelter when I have free time. ____________________
2. I help care for pets that are awaiting adoption. ____________________
3. I walk them outside while their cages are being cleaned. ____________________
4. If I have time, I help prepare their meals. ____________________
5. The manager, who is also a veterinarian, is one of my heroes. ____________________
6. She runs the shelter because she loves animals. ____________________
7. I give special care to the animals whose needs are the greatest. ____________________
8. Although I have worked there for years, I still have much to learn.

   ____

In your writer's notebook, write a short passage about somewhere you would like to volunteer. Include at least three complex sentences. Circle any subordinating conjunctions, relative pronouns, or relative adverbs that introduce the dependent clauses. Edit and proofread your work.

Name ____

- A **dependent clause** in a complex sentence can come after an independent clause: *I will take some ice cream if there is any left.*
- A dependent clause can also come before an independent clause, separated by a comma: *If we leave now, we will arrive by noon.*

Use the word in parentheses to combine the two clauses into one complex sentence. Write the new sentence on the line provided.

1. I went shopping/I made a list (before)

____

2. I got to the store/I realized I had forgotten the list (when)

____

3. I tried to remember/I had written down (what)

____

4. I was thinking hard/you called on the phone and read me the list (while)

____

Writing Connection

Write a paragraph about a time you forgot something. Include one dependent clause that comes before an independent clause, and one that comes after. Then check your work to make sure you use commas correctly.

____

____

____

____

____

____

Name ______________________________

- An **essential clause** is necessary to identify a person or thing that is being described. It is not separated by commas: *The car that costs less is perfect.*
- A **nonessential clause** is not necessary to the meaning of the sentence. Commas are needed to set apart the clause: *Her new book, which I finished yesterday, is my favorite.*

Read the two clauses. Combine them into one sentence and write the new sentence on the line provided.

1. the day was a Saturday/that I was born

____

2. my parents were well prepared/who were living in Chicago

____

3. they had rented a house/that already had a nursery

____

4. the neighborhood had many children/which was near the lake

____

Read this excerpt from "The Crow and the Pitcher." Underline the clause. Then rewrite the sentence using a different essential or nonessential clause.

A crow, whose throat was parched and dry with thirst, saw a pitcher in the distance.

____

____

Write one sentence describing an animal. Include an essential or nonessential clause. Check for grammar and punctuation.

____

____

Name ________________________________

- When a **dependent clause** in a complex sentence comes before an independent clause, it is separated by a comma.
- An **essential clause** is necessary to identify a person or thing that is being described. It is not separated by commas.
- A **nonessential clause** is not necessary to the meaning of the sentence. Commas are needed to set apart the clause.

Proofread the paragraph. On the lines below, correct mistakes in complex sentence construction and comma usage.

The original settlers of our town who had arrived by boat came from Holland. The area, that they settled, was mostly forest at the time. After they chopped down the trees they created fields and pastures. Farming, which was difficult at first became their main source of food. Because they faced shortages in winter they began to hunt and fish as well. The fact that wildlife was plentiful, helped them survive.

COMMON ERRORS

Use the pronoun ***that*** in clauses that are essential to the meaning of the sentence: *The plays that Shakespeare wrote are classics.* Use the pronoun ***which*** in clauses that are nonessential: Charlotte's Webb, *which White wrote in 1952, is still read today.* The relative pronoun ***who*** can be used in either case.

____

____

____

____

____

____

____

____

Name ____

Read the student draft and look for any corrections that need to be made. Then choose the best answer to each question.

(1) The game whom I invented is similar to hockey. (2) While hockey uses hockey sticks broomball uses brooms. (3) We replaced pucks which are too hard to hit with, soccer balls. (4) Each team has four players and a goalie which doesn't wear skates. (5) The first team that scores three goals wins the game. (6) When I shared my idea for "broomball" with the coach. (7) She had it printed in the school newspaper, *The Tiger Times*!

1. What change needs to be made in sentence 1?

A Change ***whom*** to **while**

B Change ***whom*** to **who**

C Change ***whom*** to **that**

D Change ***whom*** to **whose**

2. What change, if any, should be made in sentence 2?

F Change ***While*** to **Because**

G Insert a comma after ***sticks***

H Insert a comma after ***broomball***

J Make no change

3. What change, if any, should be made in sentence 3?

A Insert a comma after ***pucks***

B Change ***which*** to **that**

C Delete the comma

D Make no change

4. How does sentence 4 need to be changed?

F Change ***and*** to **but**

G Insert a comma after ***players***

H Insert a comma after ***goalie***

J Change ***which*** to **who**

5. What change, if any, needs to be made to sentence 5?

A Insert a comma after ***team***

B Insert a comma after ***goals***

C Insert a comma after ***wins***

D Make no change

6. What is the correct way to write sentences 6 and 7?

F When I shared my idea for "broomball" with the coach, she had it printed in the school newspaper, *The Tiger Times!*

G When I shared my idea for "broomball" with the coach she had it printed in the school newspaper, *The Tiger Times!*

H When I shared my idea for "broomball" with the coach, she had it printed, in the school newspaper *The Tiger Times!*

J When I shared my idea for "broomball," with the coach, she had it printed in the school newspaper, *The Tiger Times!*

Name ____

Fold back the paper along the dotted line. Use the blanks to write each word as it is read aloud. When you finish the test, unfold the paper. Use the list at the right to correct any spelling mistakes.

	1. ______________	1. sweet
	2. ______________	2. suite
	3. ______________	3. pray
	4. ______________	4. prey
	5. ______________	5. poll
	6. ______________	6. pole
	7. ______________	7. waste
	8. ______________	8. waist
	9. ______________	9. manor
	10. ______________	10. manner
	11. ______________	11. pier
	12. ______________	12. peer
	13. ______________	13. currant
	14. ______________	14. current
	15. ______________	15. presence
	16. ______________	16. presents
	17. ______________	17. council
	18. ______________	18. counsel
	19. ______________	19. stationery
	20. ______________	20. stationary
Review Words	21. ______________	21. eruption
	22. ______________	22. forgetful
	23. ______________	23. allergic
Challenge Words	24. ______________	24. kernel
	25. ______________	25. colonel

Name ______________________________

Homophones are words that sound alike but are spelled differently and have different meanings, such as *ant* and *aunt*. Here is another example:

- ***break, brake***

I was careful not to ***break*** *the vase.*

When the light turned green, Mom took her foot off the ***brake****.*

SPELLING TIP

Memory tricks can help you spell some homophones.

- ***Stationery*** is used to write *letters*. Someone who is ***stationary*** is *standing* still.
- Your ***waist*** is above your *hips*. You throw ***waste*** in a garbage *basket*.

Create homophone pairs. Write a spelling word on a line in List 1. Match that word to another spelling word that has the same pronunciation but different spelling. Write the matching word in List 2.

sweet	poll	manor	currant	council
suite	pole	manner	current	counsel
pray	waste	pier	presence	stationery
prey	waist	peer	presents	stationary

List 1	**List 2**
1. ____________	1. ____________
2. ____________	2. ____________
3. ____________	3. ____________
4. ____________	4. ____________
5. ____________	5. ____________
6. ____________	6. ____________
7. ____________	7. ____________
8. ____________	8. ____________
9. ____________	9. ____________
10. ____________	10. ____________

Name ______________________________

Homophones are words that sound alike but are spelled differently and have different meanings, such as *ant* and *aunt*. Here is another example:

- ***break, brake***

*I was careful not to **break** the vase.*

*When the light turned green, Mom took her foot off the **brake**.*

SPELLING TIP

- Try this memory trick for *waist/waste*: Your ***waist*** is above your *hips*. You throw ***waste*** in a garbage *basket*.
- Remember that ***you're*** is a contraction for *you are*, whereas ***your*** shows possession.

Create homophone pairs. Write a spelling word on a line in List 1. Match that word to another spelling word that has the same pronunciation but different spelling. Write the matching word in List 2.

sweet	poll	manner	you're	choose
suite	pole	manor	your	chews
peel	waste	pier	presents	flower
peal	waist	peer	presence	flour

List 1

1. ______________
2. ______________
3. ______________
4. ______________
5. ______________
6. ______________
7. ______________
8. ______________
9. ______________
10. ______________

List 2

1. ______________
2. ______________
3. ______________
4. ______________
5. ______________
6. ______________
7. ______________
8. ______________
9. ______________
10. ______________

Name ______________________________

A. Create homophone pairs. Write a spelling word on a line in List 1. Match that word to another spelling word that has the same pronunciation but different spelling. Write the matching word in List 2.

sweet	bazaar	manner	pier	council
suite	bizarre	manor	peer	counsel
principal	allowed	current	presents	stationery
principle	aloud	currant	presence	stationary

List 1	List 2
1. ______	1. ______
2. ______	2. ______
3. ______	3. ______
4. ______	4. ______
5. ______	5. ______
6. ______	6. ______
7. ______	7. ______
8. ______	8. ______
9. ______	9. ______
10. ______	10. ______

B. Compare the words *presents* and *presence*. How are they alike? How are they different?

____

____

____

____

Name ____________________

sweet	poll	manor	currant	council
suite	pole	manner	current	counsel
pray	waste	pier	presence	stationery
prey	waist	peer	presents	stationary

A. Write the spelling word that goes with the words in each group below.

1. paper, envelopes, ____________________
2. unmoving, fixed, ____________________
3. survey, opinion, ____________________
4. post, flag, ____________________
5. river, flow, ____________________
6. fruit, berry, ____________________
7. style, way, ____________________
8. house, estate, ____________________

B. Write the spelling word that best completes each sentence.

9. An owl hunts for its ____________________ at night.
10. I ____________________ that the weather is good for our picnic.
11. It's a joy to be in the ____________________ of my friends.
12. My brother received many ____________________ for his birthday.
13. The ripe peaches were juicy and ____________________.
14. Our hotel ____________________ had two large bedrooms.
15. The city ____________________ voted to change the zoning law.
16. My sister and I often go to Grandfather for ____________________.
17. Jason is a ____________________ from my fifth-grade class.
18. We walked out on the ____________________ to watch the sailboats.
19. I don't think this old belt will fit around my ____________________.
20. It is a ____________________ of time to rake leaves on a windy day.

Name ______________________________

Underline the six misspelled words in the paragraphs below. Write the words correctly on the lines.

Alex walked up to the old manner house. The son of the owner was Alex's pier from school. Alex and the boy were in class together, but they were never close friends. The boy always seemed shy in Alex's presents.

1. ____________ **2.** ____________ **3.** ____________

The house was now closed up, and the family was gone for the summer. Alex thought it was a waist to leave such a beautiful house empty. Before the family left, the boy's father had told Alex he could fish in the stream on the property. Alex had his poll with him today, and he walked to a spot where the currant flowed gently.

4. ____________ **5.** ____________ **6.** ____________

Writing Connection

Write a passage for a story about two other peers. The story can be set in the past or the present. Use at least four spelling words in your writing.

Name ____

Remember

Homophones are words that have the same pronunciation but different spellings and meanings, as in the following examples.

• ***sea, see*** • ***peace, piece***

*The waves crashed in the **sea**.*

*It was so foggy that I could hardly **see** the moon.*

*We walked away from the noisy crowd, hoping to find some **peace**.*

*My friend offered me a **piece** of raspberry cake.*

sweet	poll	manor	currant	council
suite	pole	manner	current	counsel
pray	waste	pier	presence	stationery
prey	waist	peer	presents	stationary

Fill in the missing letters to form a spelling word. Then write the spelling word.

1. wai __ __ ____________________

2. was __ __ ____________________

3. prese __ __ s ____________________

4. pre __ e __ ce ____________________

5. stati __ __ ary ____________________

6. station __ __ __ ____________________

7. sw __ __ t ____________________

8. s __ __ te ____________________

9. pi __ __ ____________________

10. pe __ __ ____________________

11. cur __ en __ ____________________

12. curr __ __ t ____________________

13. man __ __ r ____________________

14. ma __ __ r ____________________

15. p __ __ e ____________________

16. p __ __ l ____________________

17. coun __ i __ ____________________

18. coun __ e __ ____________________

19. p __ a __ ____________________

20. __ __ ey ____________________

Name ____

A **thesaurus** is a print or digital reference that lists words and their synonyms, or words with similar meanings, and antonyms, or words with opposite meanings. A thesaurus can help you find alternative word choices to make your writing voice more powerful.

Use the online thesaurus entry below to help you revise and improve the student draft. Fill in the synonym or antonym that you think best replaces the word in parentheses.

nice [nahys]

Main Entry: nice

Part of Speech: adjective

Definition: likable, agreeable

Synonyms: admirable, amiable, attractive, charming, commendable, considerate, cordial, courteous, delightful, fair, favorable, friendly, genial, gentle, good, gracious, helpful, inviting, kind, lovely, pleasant, pleasurable, polite, seemly, swell, welcome, well-mannered, winning

Antonyms: bad, disagreeable, horrible, mean, nasty, repulsive, unfriendly, unlikable, unpleasant

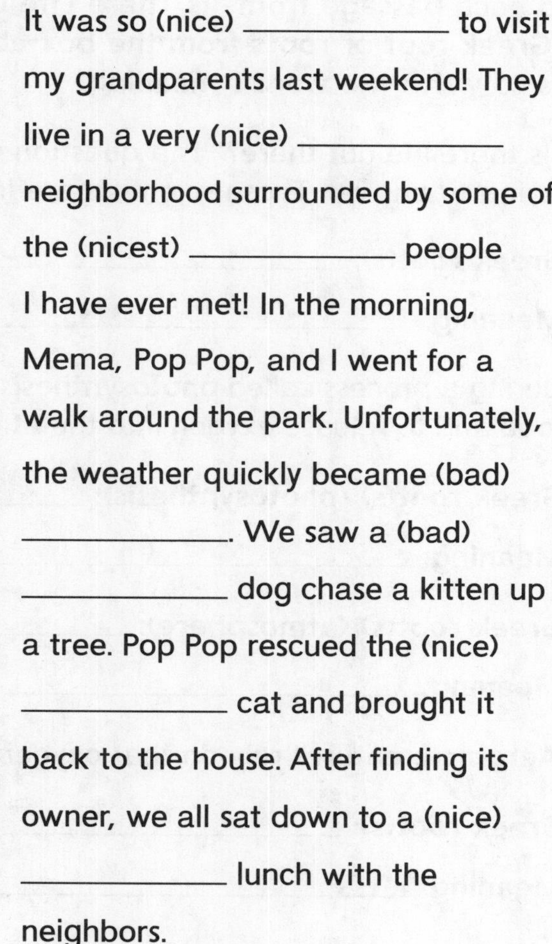

It was so (nice) ____________ to visit my grandparents last weekend! They live in a very (nice) ____________ neighborhood surrounded by some of the (nicest) ____________ people I have ever met! In the morning, Mema, Pop Pop, and I went for a walk around the park. Unfortunately, the weather quickly became (bad) ____________. We saw a (bad) ____________ dog chase a kitten up a tree. Pop Pop rescued the (nice) ____________ cat and brought it back to the house. After finding its owner, we all sat down to a (nice) ____________ lunch with the neighbors.

Name ______________________________

By learning the meaning of roots, you can figure out the meaning of unfamiliar words and use the words correctly in your writing.

aero = air	*chemo* = chemical	*sphaira* = globe, ball
atmos = vapor, steam	*hydro* = water	*syntithenai* = making or putting together
astro = star	*logy* = the study of	*therme* = heat
bio = life	*photo* = light	*geo* = of the earth

Read each passage from "Is There Life Out There?" For each word in bold, write the Greek root or roots from the box above. Use the Greek roots and context clues to write the word's meaning.

1. "Is there life out there?" is a question scientists who study **astrobiology** are trying to answer. These scientists are looking for life in space.

   Greek root(s): ______________________________

   Meaning: ______________________________

2. During a process called **photosynthesis**, plants use energy from sunlight to make food and to release oxygen into the **atmosphere**.

   Greek root(s) (photosynthesis): ______________________________

   Meaning: ______________________________

   Greek root(s) (atmosphere): ______________________________

   Meaning: ______________________________

3. **Aerobic** creatures rely on that oxygen to breathe.

   Greek root(s): ______________________________

   Meaning: ______________________________

4. The animals living around **hydrothermal** vents eat a form of bacteria that live on or below the ocean floor.

   Greek root(s): ______________________________

   Meaning: ______________________________

Name ____

- An **adjective** modifies a noun or a pronoun. Adjectives can tell what kind (*new, bright, tiny*), how many (*eight, few*), or how much (*some, all*). **Proper adjectives** should be capitalized: *Spanish language*.
- **Demonstrative adjectives** tell which one: *this, that, these, those*.
- The words *the, a,* and *an* are special adjectives called **articles**. Use *a* and *an* to refer to any one item in a group. Use *the* to refer to a specific item or more than one item.

Read each sentence. Underline each adjective. Circle any demonstrative adjectives or articles that you find.

1. Three horses approached the fence.
2. The Arabian horse had a long tail.
3. We held fresh grass up to his wet nose.
4. The white horse gave us a playful wink.
5. Two ranchers filled this large trough with cold water.
6. Those thirsty horses gathered to drink.
7. A warm breeze blew across the rolling prairie.
8. White clouds drifted along in the blue sky.
9. We headed back to the main house for an early dinner.
10. The third day of our vacation was nearing its end.

In your writer's notebook, write a short passage describing an outdoor scene. Underline each adjective, and circle each demonstrative adjective and article that you include. Check your work for correct grammar.

Name ____

- When more than one adjective is used to modify a noun, the adjectives must be listed in order. **Numbers** come first, followed by **opinion**, **size**, **age**, and **color**: *a delicious red cake*; *two beautiful old chairs*; *a large brown blanket*.
- **Commas** often separate two or more adjectives that describe the same noun: *Jorge played a quiet, sensitive song on the piano*. A comma does not normally follow a number in a description, however.

Read each sentence. Then include the adjectives in parentheses and rewrite the sentence on the line provided.

1. A truck drove down the road. (broken-down, noisy)

   ____

2. The driver wore a hat. (blue, silly, old)

   ____

3. He honked his horn. (brassy, annoying)

   ____

4. Dogs started barking inside the truck. (wet, three, frightened)

   ____

Read this sentence from "The Day the Rollets Got Their Moxie Back." Underline one adjective. Then rewrite the sentence using a second adjective to describe the noun.

For those short moments, the past didn't matter, and the future blossomed ahead of us like a beautiful flower.

____

____

Name ________________________________

- **Acronyms** are abbreviations usually formed with all capital letters and no periods, such as *TV, NASA,* and the *UN*.
- Underline or italicize **titles** from long works, such as books and magazines. Put quotation marks around the titles of shorter works, such as articles and chapters. Capitalize all major words in titles.

  I picked up a copy of Sunny Day magazine and turned to an article called "Hiking at Daybreak."

Read each sentence. Correct any errors in capitalization or punctuation and rewrite the sentence on the line provided.

1. We read about a program called Most, or "Make Our School Terrific."

____

____

2. It was featured in last month's issue of education ideas.

____

3. The article, Ten tips from top schools, offered many great suggestions.

____

____

4. For example, students could decorate a room like a nasa control center.

____

____

5. The author explained how in his first book, the intergalactic classroom.

____

In your writer's notebook, write a short passage describing a school program you would like to start. Include quotation marks and at least one acronym. Make sure to edit and proofread your work for punctuation and capitalization.

Name ____

- When more than one adjective is used to modify a noun, the adjectives must be listed in order. **Numbers** come first, followed by **opinion, size, age**, and **color**. Commas are often used to separate two or more adjectives related to the same noun.
- **Acronyms** are abbreviations that usually contain all capital letters and no periods.
- Underline or italicize titles from long works. Put quotation marks around the titles of shorter works. Capitalize the important words in titles.

Proofread the paragraph. On the lines below, correct mistakes in adjective usage, capitalization, and punctuation.

In short five days, our ecology club will talk about the Epa, or Environmental Protection Agency. I borrowed new three books about the subject, including The history of the E.P.A., from the library. These first chapter, entitled A day for The Earth, offers an lengthy fascinating timeline of events leading up to Earth Day. I will copy it onto a poster using the red big marker.

HANDWRITING CONNECTION

Be sure to write legibly in cursive. Leave appropriate spaces between words.

____

____

____

____

____

____

____

____

____

Name ______________________________

Read the student draft and look for any corrections that need to be made. Then choose the best answer to each question.

(1) We waited in a long line for the first showing of that new movie, Chasing the Storm. (2) Some images came from N.o.a.a., the agency that monitors weather. (3) Famous several actors and actresses walked by and waved. (4) The director spoke for five minutes in front of these excited audience. (5) After an director's speech, we rushed into the crowded theater. (6) My three friends agreed that this suspenseful movie debut was the amazing experience!

1. What change needs to be made in sentence 1?

A Insert a comma after ***long***

B Change ***that*** to **these**

C Italicize ***Chasing the Storm***

D No change is needed

2. What change, if any, should be made in sentence 2?

F Insert a comma after ***some***

G Delete the comma

H Change ***N.o.a.a.*** to **NOAA**

J Make no change

3. What change, if any, should be made in sentence 3?

A Change ***Famous several*** to **Several famous**

B Change ***Famous several*** to **Famous, several**

C Change ***Famous several*** to **Several, famous**

D Make no change

4. How does sentence 4 need to be changed?

F Change ***these*** to **the**

G Change ***these*** to **that**

H Change ***these*** to **a**

J Change ***these*** to **this**

5. What change, if any, needs to be made to sentence 5?

A Change ***an*** to **a**

B Change ***an*** to **that**

C Change ***an*** to **the**

D Make no change

6. What is the correct way to write sentence 6?

F My three friends agreed that this suspenseful movie debut was a amazing experience!

G My three friends agreed, that this suspenseful movie debut was the amazing experience!

H My three friends agreed that this, suspenseful movie debut, was the amazing experience!

J My three friends agreed that this suspenseful movie debut was an amazing experience!

Name ____________________

Fold back the paper along the dotted line. Use the blanks to write each word as it is read aloud. When you finish the test, unfold the paper. Use the list at the right to correct any spelling mistakes.

	1. ____________	**1.** prewash
	2. ____________	**2.** disable
	3. ____________	**3.** discolor
	4. ____________	**4.** mistaken
	5. ____________	**5.** preheats
	6. ____________	**6.** mistrust
	7. ____________	**7.** incorrect
	8. ____________	**8.** disconnect
	9. ____________	**9.** preview
	10. ____________	**10.** prejudge
	11. ____________	**11.** misjudge
	12. ____________	**12.** discomfort
	13. ____________	**13.** dismount
	14. ____________	**14.** misunderstand
	15. ____________	**15.** disobey
	16. ____________	**16.** dishonest
	17. ____________	**17.** injustice
	18. ____________	**18.** disapprove
	19. ____________	**19.** inexpensive
	20. ____________	**20.** indefinite
Review Words	**21.** ____________	**21.** presence
	22. ____________	**22.** stationary
	23. ____________	**23.** current
Challenge Words	**24.** ____________	**24.** prehistoric
	25. ____________	**25.** misbehave

Name ______________________________

A **prefix** is a group of letters added to the beginning of a word that changes the word's meaning. For example:

- ***dis-*** ("not" or "opposite of"): *distaste*
- ***in-*** ("not" or "opposite of"): *inaction*
- ***mis-*** ("wrong" or "badly"): *mislead*
- ***pre-*** ("before"): *prevent*

Read these words aloud.

DECODING WORDS

Look at the beginning part of the word *preview*. The prefix *pre-* means "before." Use the prefix to figure out the word's meaning. The word *preview* means "an earlier or advance view." Now read the word aloud: /prē/ /vyü/.

Write the spelling words that begin with each prefix. Then read the words aloud, with and without their prefixes.

prewash	preheats	preview	dismount	injustice
disable	mistrust	prejudge	misunderstand	disapprove
discolor	incorrect	misjudge	disobey	inexpensive
mistaken	disconnect	discomfort	dishonest	indefinite

dis-

1. ____________________
2. ____________________
3. ____________________
4. ____________________
5. ____________________
6. ____________________
7. ____________________
8. ____________________

in-

9. ____________________
10. ____________________
11. ____________________
12. ____________________

mis-

13. ____________________
14. ____________________
15. ____________________
16. ____________________

pre-

17. ____________________
18. ____________________
19. ____________________
20. ____________________

Look through this week's readings for more words with prefixes. Record the words you find in your writer's notebook. If you find new prefixes, use a dictionary to help determine their meaning.

Name ______________________________

A **prefix** is a group of letters added to the beginning of a word that changes the word's meaning. For example:

- ***dis-*** ("not" or "opposite of"): *distaste*
- ***in-*** ("not" or "opposite of"): *inaction*
- ***mis-*** ("wrong" or "badly"): *mislead*
- ***pre-*** ("before"): *prevent*

Read these words aloud.

DECODING WORDS

Look at the beginning part of the word *preview*. The prefix *pre-* means "before." Use the prefix to figure out the word's meaning. The word *preview* means "an earlier or advance view." Now read the word aloud: /prē/ /vyü/.

Write the spelling words that begin with each prefix. Then read the words aloud, with and without their prefixes.

prewash	preheats	preview	dismount	instep
disable	misplace	pretest	misunderstand	disagree
discolor	incorrect	mislead	disobey	indirect
mistaken	dislike	discomfort	dishonest	invisible

dis-

1. ______________
2. ______________
3. ______________
4. ______________
5. ______________
6. ______________
7. ______________
8. ______________

in-

9. ______________
10. ______________
11. ______________
12. ______________

mis-

13. ______________
14. ______________
15. ______________
16. ______________

pre-

17. ______________
18. ______________
19. ______________
20. ______________

Look through this week's readings for more words with prefixes. Record the words you find in your writer's notebook. If you find new prefixes, use a dictionary to help determine their meaning.

Name ________________________

A. Write the spelling words that begin with each prefix. Then read the words aloud, with and without their prefixes.

preview	dismount	disconnect	discomfort	injustice
disable	mistrust	inaccurate	misunderstand	disapprove
dismantle	prejudge	misjudge	discontent	inexpensive
mistaken	prerequisite	predisposition	dishearten	indefinite

dis-

1. ________
2. ________
3. ________
4. ________
5. ________
6. ________
7. ________
8. ________

in-

9. ________
10. ________
11. ________
12. ________

mis-

13. ________
14. ________
15. ________
16. ________

pre-

17. ________
18. ________
19. ________
20. ________

B. Compare the words *prejudge* and *misjudge*. How are they alike? How are they different?

____

____

____

____

Look through this week's readings for more words with prefixes. Record the words you find in your writer's notebook. If you find new prefixes, use a dictionary to help determine their meaning.

Name ____

prewash	preheats	preview	dismount	injustice
disable	mistrust	prejudge	misunderstand	disapprove
discolor	incorrect	misjudge	disobey	inexpensive
mistaken	disconnect	discomfort	dishonest	indefinite

A. Write the spelling word that matches each definition below.

1. untruthful ________________

2. detach ________________

3. judge wrongly ________________

4. unfair treatment ________________

5. see in advance ________________

6. not accurate ________________

7. unclear or unsure ________________

8. make a first cleaning ________________

9. not get the meaning ________________

10. decide before knowing ________________

11. wrong about something ________________

12. make unable to work ________________

B. Write the spelling word that best completes each analogy.

13. *Costly* is to *cheap* as *pricey* is to ________________.

14. *Allow* is to *permit* as *defy* is to ________________.

15. *Sorrow* is to *joy* as ________________ is to *ease.*

16. *Climb* is to *rise* as ________________ is to *descend.*

17. *Condemn* is to ________________ *as support* is to *favor.*

18. *Believe* is to ________________ as *trust* is to *doubt.*

19. ________________ is to *fade* as *unravel* is to *fray.*

20. ________________ is to *warms* as *freezes* is to *cools.*

Name ______________________________

Underline the six misspelled words in the paragraphs below. Using your knowledge of prefixes, write the words correctly on the lines.

If you feel miscomfort in a dirty, polluted environment but think you can't prevent it, you are pretaken. In fact, there are plenty of easy, nonexpensive ways to take action.

1. ____________ **2.** ____________ **3.** ____________

Some people unobey recycling rules, litter parks and streets, or pollute the water system. You can write letters to voice how you feel about this. Don't overjudge others, but tell people in charge that you misapprove of these actions. Then do your best to recycle, reuse, and clean up litter in your own neighborhood.

4. ____________ **5.** ____________ **6.** ____________

Writing Connection

Write information about what you can do to protect the environment in your community. Use at least four spelling words in your writing. Edit and proofread your work.

Name ______________________________

Remember

A **prefix** is a group of letters added to the beginning of a word. It changes the meaning of the base word. Read each prefix and italicized word aloud.

- ***dis-***, often means "not," "absence of," or "opposite of": *disown*
- ***in-***, often means "not" or "opposite of": *incorrect*
- ***mis-***, often means "wrong": *miscount*
- ***pre-***, often means "before": *precaution*

prewash	preheats	preview	dismount	injustice
disable	mistrust	prejudge	misunderstand	disapprove
discolor	incorrect	misjudge	disobey	inexpensive
mistaken	disconnect	discomfort	dishonest	indefinite

A. Add the prefix to each word to form a spelling word. Then write the word.

1. dis + obey = ______________

2. in + expensive = ______________

3. dis + connect = ______________

4. mis + trust = ______________

5. dis + approve = ______________

6. mis + taken = ______________

7. pre + judge = ______________

8. dis + color = ______________

9. in + definite = ______________

10. dis + comfort = ______________

11. pre + wash = ______________

12. mis + understand = ______________

13. dis + honest = ______________

14. pre + heats = ______________

15. dis + mount = ______________

B. Write these spelling words in alphabetical order. Alphabetize them to the third letter. ***incorrect, disable, preview, misjudge, injustice***

16. ______________ **18.** ______________ **20.** ______________

17. ______________ **19.** ______________

Name ______________________________

Expand your vocabulary by adding or removing inflectional endings, prefixes, or suffixes to a base word to create different forms of a word.

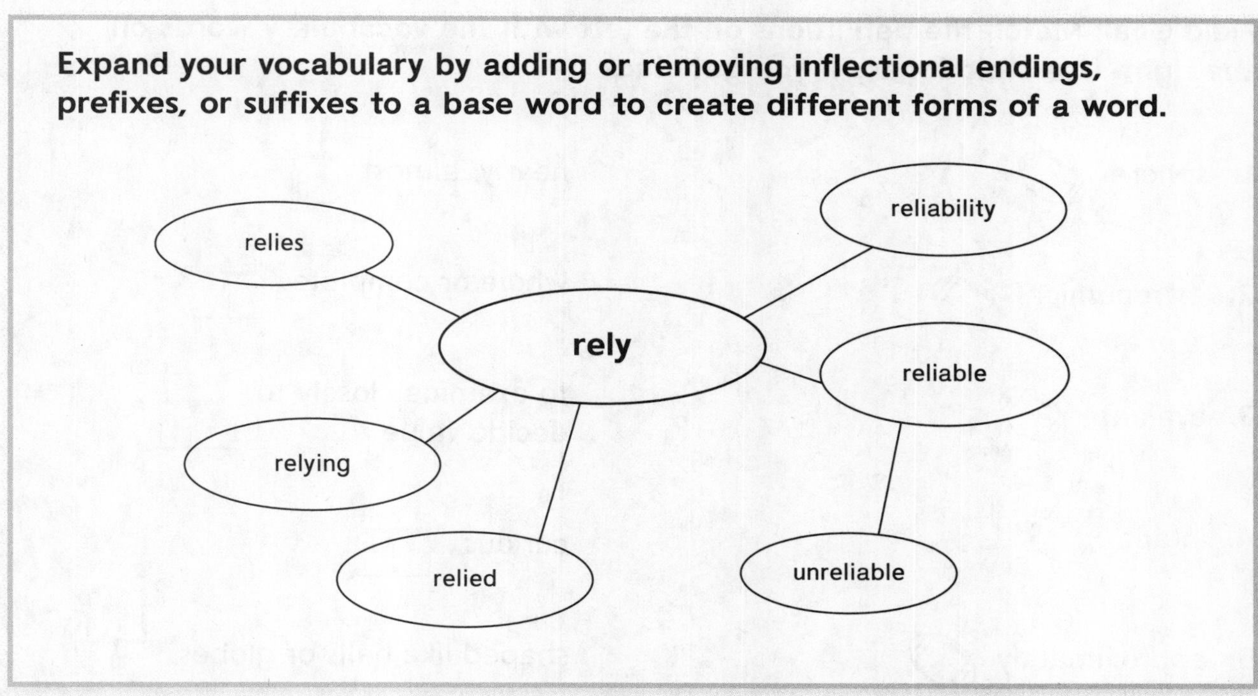

Add people to the human pyramid to write as many related words as you can. Use a dictionary to help you.

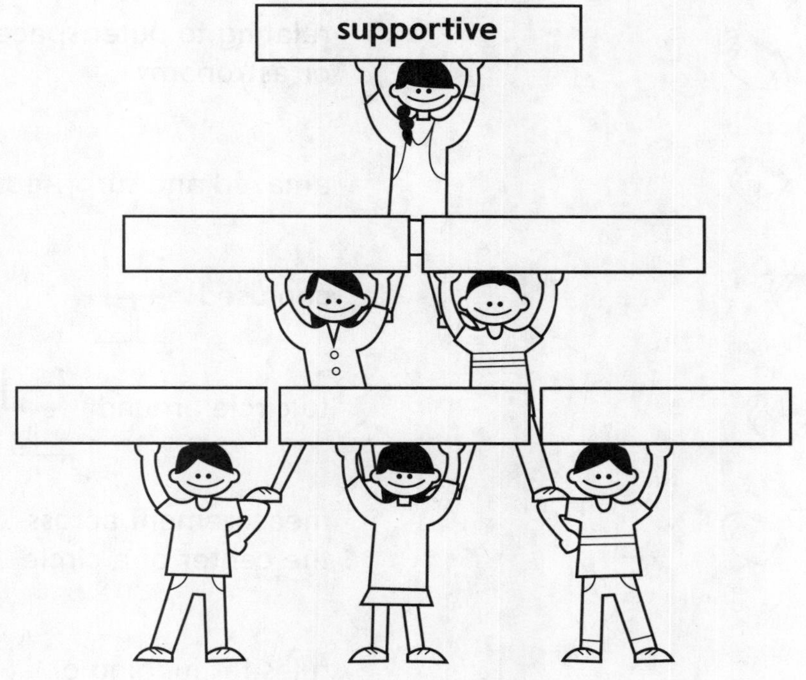

Name ______________________________

Field Goal! Match the definitions on the left with the vocabulary words on the right. Use a dictionary if you get stuck.

1. sphere 	nearly; almost
2. astronomical 	whole or complete
3. evaluate	to examine closely to decide value
4. intact 	curious
5. approximately	shaped like balls or globes
6. perplexed 	use math to find the answer
7. calculation	relating to outer space or astronomy 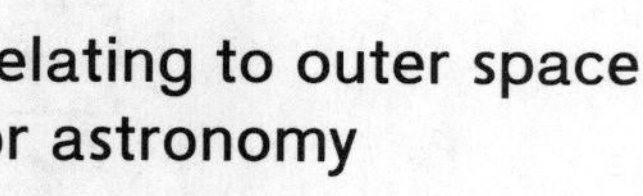
8. inquisitive	amazed and surprised
9. criteria 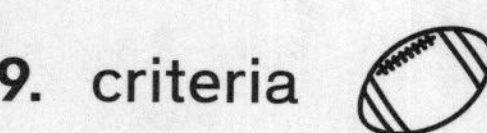	confused
10. diameter	to circle around
11. astounded	measurement across the center of a circle
12. orbit	rules for judging or making a decision

Name ______________________________

- **Comparative adjectives** compare two nouns or pronouns. Add *-er* to most adjectives to compare two items.
- **Superlative adjectives** compare more than two nouns or pronouns. Add *-est* to most adjectives to compare more than two items.
- Drop the *e* in adjectives such as *pale* before adding *-er* or *-est*: *palest*. Change the *y* to *i* in adjectives such as *sunny*: *sunnier*. For one-syllable adjectives such as *red,* double the final consonant: *reddest*.

Read each sentence. Write the proper form of the adjective in parentheses on the line provided.

1. My cousin is the (funny) person I know. ____________
2. She is also a (strong) swimmer than I am. ____________
3. She lives in a (large) town than ours. ____________
4. Her school has a (big) campus than we do. ____________
5. Our school has the (small) stadium in the state. ____________
6. We have (pretty) parks than her town, though. ____________
7. Our town's lake has one of the (sandy) beaches around. ____________
8. The water also tends to be the (cold) of all, too. ____________
9. This year, I spent a (short) amount of time with my cousin than last year.

   ____
10. We have already scheduled a (lengthy) visit than our last one. ____________

In your writer's notebook, write a short passage describing a family member or friend. Describe this person using two comparative adjectives and two superlative adjectives. Edit and proofread your work using the spelling rules for forming adjectives.

Name ______________________________

- Use **more** in front of most long adjectives to compare two items.

  This book is more interesting than the last one I read.

- Use **most** in front of most long adjectives to compare more than two items.

  This is the most interesting book I have ever read.

Read each sentence. Write the proper form of the adjective in parentheses on the line provided.

1. The mountain climbers' club was planning its (exciting) trip yet.

   ____

2. It would certainly be a (dangerous) outing than the last one. ____________________
3. Some climbers were (worried) than others. ____________________
4. The (concerned) club member of all asked many questions. ____________________
5. The mountain had some of the (icy) slopes the group had seen. ____________________
6. After hearing the answers, the member felt (confident) than before.

   ____

7. The climbers discussed which tools would be (useful) than others. ____________________
8. They agreed that safety was the (essential) thing to consider. ____________________
9. People were (talkative) during the latter half of the meeting. ____________________
10. For many, this would be the (adventurous) thing they had ever done!

    ____

In your writer's notebook, write a short fictional passage about an adventure you might go on with a club. Include at least five comparative or superlative adjectives. Make sure to follow the spelling rules for adjectives.

Name ______________________________

- Never use *more* and *-er* with the same adjective.
- Never use *most* and *-est* with the same adjective.

Read each sentence. Choose which word or words in parentheses best complete the sentence. Write your answer on the line provided.

1. Mom gathered the (most freshest, freshest) vegetables she could find.

   ____

2. She wanted to make the (more, most) delicious soup ever. ______________
3. First, she chose the (most ripe, ripest) tomatoes in the garden. ______________
4. Then she chopped up some of the (greenest, most green) peppers. ______________
5. It was a (healthier, more healthier) soup than the last one. ______________

Reading/Writing Connection

Read the paragraph from "Musical Impressions of the Great Depression." Underline the superlative adjective. Then write a paragraph about how music affects you. Use three comparative or superlative adjectives. Edit and proofread your work.

By the end of the 1930s, the hardest days of the Great Depression had passed. Times had been tough, but music had offered a way for people to share their fears and keep up their hopes. The music remains a legacy of this era that has inspired musicians to this day.

____

____

____

____

____

Name ______________________________

- **Comparative adjectives** compare two nouns or pronouns. Add *-er* to most adjectives to compare two items. **Superlative adjectives** compare more than two items. Add *-est* to most adjectives to compare more than two items.
- Use ***more*** in front of most long adjectives to compare two items. Use ***most*** in front of most long adjectives to compare more than two items.
- Never use *more* and *-er* with the same adjective. Never use *most* and *-est* with the same adjective.

Proofread the paragraph. On the lines below, correct mistakes in adjective usage and the formation of comparatives and superlatives.

After our ride, my bike was more dirty than a dog in a mud puddle. I thought about making it cleanest than it was before by hosing it down. My sister does that, but her bike is the most rustiest one in town. Dad usually has the usefulest suggestions in the family, so I asked his advice. He said that the hose was the quicker solution of all, but that a carefuller person than my sister would also wipe the bike dry afterward.

____

____

____

____

____

____

____

____

Name ______________________________

Read the student draft and look for any corrections that need to be made. Then choose the best answer to each question.

(1) For me, math is a hard subject than science. (2) Today's homework is even difficult than yesterday's. (3) Even the most smart student in the class had trouble! (4) Our teacher suggested an easyer way to do the assignment. (5) He always has the most intelligentest solution to every problem. (6) With his help, I finished my work fastest than anyone else in the class.

1. What change needs to be made in sentence 1?

A Change ***hard*** to **harder**

B Change ***hard*** to **hardest**

C Change ***a*** to **an**

D Change ***a*** to **the**

2. What change, if any, should be made in sentence 2?

F Change ***difficult*** to **difficulter**

G Change ***difficult*** to **most difficult**

H Change ***difficult*** to **more difficult**

J Make no change

3. What change, if any, should be made in sentence 3?

A Change ***most smart*** to **smartest**

B Change ***most smart*** to **smarter**

C Change ***most smart*** to **most smartest**

D Make no change

4. How does sentence 4 need to be changed?

F Change ***easyer*** to **easiest**

G Change ***easyer*** to **easier**

H Change ***easyer*** to **more easy**

J Change ***easyer*** to **most easy**

5. What is the correct way to write sentence 5?

A He always has the more intelligent solution to every problem.

B He always has the most intelligenter solution to every problem.

C He always has the intelligentest solution to every problem.

D He always has the most intelligent solution to every problem.

6. What is the correct way to write sentence 6?

F With his help, I finished my work faster than anyone else in the class.

G With his help, I finished my work more faster than anyone else in the class.

H With his help, I finished my work most fastest than anyone else in the class.

J With his help, I finished my work fastester than anyone else in the class.

Name ______________________________

Fold back the paper along the dotted line. Use the blanks to write each word as it is read aloud. When you finish the test, unfold the paper. Use the list at the right to correct any spelling mistakes.

	1. ______________	**1.** sadness
	2. ______________	**2.** gladness
	3. ______________	**3.** needless
	4. ______________	**4.** harmless
	5. ______________	**5.** darkness
	6. ______________	**6.** fullness
	7. ______________	**7.** stillness
	8. ______________	**8.** hopeless
	9. ______________	**9.** fearless
	10. ______________	**10.** weakness
	11. ______________	**11.** bottomless
	12. ______________	**12.** foolishness
	13. ______________	**13.** fondness
	14. ______________	**14.** effortless
	15. ______________	**15.** meaningless
	16. ______________	**16.** emptiness
	17. ______________	**17.** forgiveness
	18. ______________	**18.** motionless
	19. ______________	**19.** ceaseless
	20. ______________	**20.** fierceness
Review Words	**21.** ______________	**21.** disobey
	22. ______________	**22.** mistrust
	23. ______________	**23.** preview
Challenge Words	**24.** ______________	**24.** weightlessness
	25. ______________	**25.** thoughtlessness

Name ______________________________

A **suffix** is a group of letters added to the end of a word. It changes the word's meaning and part of speech. Two common suffixes are *-less* and *-ness*.

- ***-less*** ("without"): *wireless, endless*
- ***-ness*** ("state of being"): *willingness*

Read each spelling word aloud.

DECODING WORDS

Many words that end in *-y* change spelling when adding *-ness* or *-less*. In the word *mercy,* change the *y* to an *i*: *merciless*. Read *merciless* aloud and use the suffix to determine its meaning.

Write the spelling words that match the syllable pattern and suffix.

sadness	darkness	fearless	fondness	forgiveness
gladness	fullness	weakness	effortless	motionless
needless	stillness	bottomless	meaningless	ceaseless
harmless	hopeless	foolishness	emptiness	fierceness

two-syllable words with *-less*

1. ____________
2. ____________
3. ____________
4. ____________
5. ____________

two-syllable words with *-ness*

6. ____________
7. ____________
8. ____________
9. ____________
10. ____________
11. ____________
12. ____________
13. ____________

three-syllable words with *-less*

14. ____________
15. ____________
16. ____________
17. ____________

three-syllable words with *-ness*

18. ____________
19. ____________
20. ____________

Look through this week's readings for more words with suffixes. Record the words you find in your writer's notebook. Then use your knowledge of suffixes to determine their meaning.

Name ______________________________

A **suffix** is a group of letters added to the end of a word. It changes the word's meaning and part of speech. Two common suffixes are *-less* and *-ness*.

- ***-less*** ("without"): *wireless, endless*
- ***-ness*** ("state of being"): *willingness*

Read each spelling word aloud.

DECODING WORDS

Many words that end in *-y* change spelling when adding *-ness* or *-less*. In the word *mercy,* change the *y* to an *i*: *merciless.* Read *merciless* aloud and use the suffix to determine its meaning.

Write the spelling words that match the syllable pattern and suffix.

sadness	darkness	fearless	fondness	forgiveness
gladness	fullness	weakness	effortless	motionless
needless	stillness	bottomless	restless	tireless
harmless	hopeless	foolishness	happiness	goodness

two-syllable words with *-less*

1. ______________
2. ______________
3. ______________
4. ______________
5. ______________
6. ______________

two-syllable words with *-ness*

7. ______________
8. ______________
9. ______________
10. ______________
11. ______________
12. ______________
13. ______________
14. ______________

three-syllable words with *-less*

15. ______________
16. ______________
17. ______________

three-syllable words with *-ness*

18. ______________
19. ______________
20. ______________

Look through this week's readings for more words with suffixes. Record the words you find in your writer's notebook. Then use your knowledge of suffixes to determine their meaning.

Name ______________________________

A. Write the spelling words that match the syllable pattern and suffix.

vastness	peacefulness	sleeveless	fondness	forgiveness
eariness	numbness	weakness	effortless	motionless
breathless	stillness	bottomless	meaningless	ceaseless
harmless	merciless	foolishness	emptiness	fierceness

two-syllable words with *-less*

1. ______________
2. ______________
3. ______________
4. ______________

three-syllable words with *-less*

5. ______________
6. ______________
7. ______________
8. ______________
9. ______________

two-syllable words with *-ness*

10. ______________
11. ______________
12. ______________
13. ______________
14. ______________
15. ______________

three-syllable words with *-ness*

16. ______________
17. ______________
18. ______________
19. ______________
20. ______________

B. Compare the words *foolishness* and *meaningless*. How are they alike? How are they different?

____

____

____

Look through this week's readings for more words with suffixes. Record the words you find in your writer's notebook. Then use your knowledge of suffixes to determine their meaning.

Name ____

sadness	darkness	fearless	fondness	forgiveness
gladness	fullness	weakness	effortless	motionless
needless	stillness	bottomless	meaningless	ceaseless
harmless	hopeless	foolishness	emptiness	fierceness

A. Write the spelling word that matches each definition below.

1. sorrow; unhappiness ____________
2. without stopping ____________
3. desperate; doomed ____________
4. quietness; calm ____________
5. safe; innocent ____________
6. easy; without force ____________
7. deep; unlimited ____________
8. happiness; pleasure ____________
9. not moving ____________
10. brave; not afraid ____________

B. Write the spelling word that best completes each sentence.

11. Our voices echoed in the ____________ of the large room.
12. The child drew ____________ scribbles on paper.
13. It was ____________ to ask the question more than once.
14. We laughed at the circus clown's ____________.
15. She enjoys reading and has a ____________ for science fiction.
16. He was sorry and asked for ____________.
17. It was hard to find our way in the inky ____________.
18. My arm still has some ____________ because of the injury.
19. The cat arched its back and hissed with ____________.
20. After a few hours, the balloons lost some of their ____________.

Name ____

Underline the six misspelled words in the paragraphs below. Using your knowledge of suffixes, write the words correctly on the lines.

Imagine you are camping with your family in Great Smoky Mountains National Park. You see a black bear cub in the woods. It looks cute and harmliss. What should you do? Should you approach it or stay motionles? What if its mother is nearby? Mother bears have a reputation for fiercenase!

1. ____________ **2.** ____________ **3.** ____________

In warm weather, bears are most active in the morning and as darknese begins to fall. You can avoid needlass danger by never approaching or feeding a bear. Don't let your fondnis for animals get you in trouble. Visit the park's web site to learn about bears before your trip, and then stay away from them!

4. ____________ **5.** ____________ **6.** ____________

Writing Connection

Write information about staying safe in another vacation spot. Use at least four spelling words in your writing.

____

____

____

____

____

____

____

____

____

____

____

Name ______________________________

Remember

A **suffix** is a group of letters added to the end of a word. It changes the base word's meaning and part of speech. Here are two common suffixes.

- ***-less***, means "without": *limitless, windowless*
- ***-ness***, means "state of being": *silkiness, freshness*

Read these words aloud. Then determine their meaning using your knowledge of suffixes.

sadness	darkness	fearless	fondness	forgiveness
gladness	fullness	weakness	effortless	motionless
needless	stillness	bottomless	meaningless	ceaseless
harmless	hopeless	foolishness	emptiness	fierceness

A. Add the suffix to form a spelling word. Write the spelling word.

1. meaning + less = ____________
2. glad + ness = ____________
3. full + ness = ____________
4. bottom + less = ____________
5. dark + ness = ____________
6. fond + ness = ____________
7. fear + less = ____________
8. weak + ness = ____________
9. cease + less = ____________
10. still + ness = ____________
11. fierce + ness = ____________
12. effort + less = ____________
13. sad + ness = ____________
14. harm + less = ____________
15. forgive + ness = ____________

B. Write these spelling words on the lines in reverse alphabetical order: *needless, hopeless, foolishness, emptiness, motionless.*

16. ____________
17. ____________
18. ____________
19. ____________
20. ____________

Name ____

A **pun** is a humorous way of using a word or phrase so that more than one meaning is suggested. Puns use words with multiple meanings or words that sound like other words. For example: *When a clock is hungry, it goes back four seconds.* The literal meaning is that a hungry clock will go back four seconds in time. The non-literal meaning is that a hungry clock will go back for seconds, or to get more to eat.

Read each pair of sentences below. Identify the sentence that contains a pun. In each sentence that you choose, circle the multiple-meaning word or words that sound like other words. Then explain what the pun really means (literal meaning) and what is implied (non-literal meaning).

- **Bakers may not be broke, but they often knead dough.**
- **A good cook understands how flavors work together.**

Literal Meaning	Non-Literal Meaning

- **The best way to overcome a fear is to face it.**
- **I used to have a fear of hurdles, but I got over it.**

Literal Meaning	Non-Literal Meaning

Hunt for more multiple-meaning words and homophones with a partner. Then work together to write a short dialogue that includes at least one pun. Write it in your writer's notebook.

Name ______________________________

An **idiom** is an expression that cannot be understood from the literal meanings of the words in it. To figure out the meaning of an unfamiliar idiom, you can look for clues in the sentence or surrounding sentences.

This sentence uses the idiom "don't make a mountain out of a molehill": *Sonya told Felix not to make a mountain out of a molehill when he threw a fit about stubbing his toe.* You can use the clue "stubbing his toe" to determine that the idiom means "Don't make a big deal out of a small thing." Stubbing a toe is a small thing to throw a big fit over.

Read each passage from "Nancy's First Interview." Underline the idiom in each one. Then, on the lines below the passage, restate the idiom in your own words.

1. "You're really putting me on the spot," he said to the person at the other end of the line. "I already have a commitment today, Jim."

____

____

2. After the stock market crash of 1929, his newspaper had laid off most of the reporters. Four years later, they still had only a skeleton crew. He was glad to have a job, but he was overworked and underpaid.

____

____

3. He explained that they had owned a farm in Oklahoma, but lost it when costs rose. "Upkeep cost an arm and a leg, and the drought killed our chances of a good crop."

____

____

4. Mr. Jenson grinned and ruffled Nancy's hair. "I taught her everything she knows," he said. "She's a chip off the old block."

____

____

Name ______________________________

- ***Good*** and ***bad*** have irregular comparative and superlative forms.
- Use ***better*** to compare two people, places, or things. Use ***best*** to compare more than two.

Read each sentence. Choose which word in parentheses best completes the sentence. Write your answer on the line provided.

1. Mom wanted a (better, best) storage system for her tools. ____________
2. Her carpenter called for using the (better, best) materials available. ____________
3. She felt that oak was a (better, best) choice of wood than pine. ____________
4. The carpenter had an even (better, best) suggestion. ____________
5. Some recycled materials were (better, best) options than new wood. ____________
6. The (better, best) thing of all was that they helped the environment. ____________
7. Mom studied the data in order to make a (good, best) decision. ____________
8. In the end, she had the (good, better, best) storage closet ever. ____________

Connect to Community

Talk to a parent or another trusted adult about something you can do in your community to help the environment. Then write a paragraph about the conversation. Include the words *good, bad, better,* and *best* in your response. Check to make sure that you use each adjective correctly.

____

____

____

____

____

____

____

Name ______________________________

- ***Good*** and ***bad*** have irregular comparative and superlative forms.
- Use ***worse*** to compare two people, places, or things: *This new design is worse than the last one.* Use ***worst*** to compare more than two people, places, or things: *That was the worst orange I've ever eaten.*

Read each sentence. Choose which word in parentheses best completes the sentence. Write your answer on the line provided.

1. "I've got some (bad, worst) news," my brother said. ________________
2. "Your favorite band just put out their (worse, worst) song ever." ____________
3. "It can't be (worse, worst) than 'Sippy-Sip-Sip,'" I replied. ____________
4. "Well, that is the (worse, worst) song title they ever wrote," he admitted. ________
5. He continued, "But at least it wasn't a (bad, worst) melody." ____________
6. "In the new song, the music is bad, and the lyrics are (worse, worst)." __________
7. The song is called "The (Worse, Worst) Hat I Ever Wore." ____________
8. "It even has a (bad, worse) title," I said. ______________
9. "The live version is (bad, worse) than the recorded version," he said. ____________
10. I couldn't imagine how the song could be (worse, worst). ____________

In your writer's notebook, write a short passage about a song you dislike. Use the irregular comparative and superlative forms of the word *bad* in your explanation. Edit and proofread your work.

Name ____

- In comparisons, *better* and *best* are the irregular forms of the adjective *good; worse* and *worst* are the forms of the adjective *bad.*
- The comparative form of *many* is *more;* the superlative form is *most.*
- The comparative form of *much* is *more;* the superlative form is *most.*
- Never add *-er, -est, more,* or *most* to an irregular comparative or superlative form.

Read each sentence. Write the proper comparative or superlative form of the adjective in parentheses on the line provided.

1. We waited for the (good) day possible to go on a sailing trip. ____________
2. There were (many) boats on the water today than yesterday. ____________
3. My father gives me (much) advice about sailing than my mother does. ____________
4. Dad is a (bad) swimmer than my mother, though. ____________
5. It was the (much) fun I've had in a long time! ____________

Read the excerpt from one author's argument in "What Is the Future of the Rain Forests?" Underline the irregular comparative adjective. Then write a few sentences explaining your opinion of the author's plan. Include two irregular comparative adjectives.

> The removal of rain forest trees has some negative consequences, but it is necessary for the survival of people and national economies. Therefore, it is not practical or desirable to try to stop the cutting of all rain forest trees. A better plan is to make economic use of rain forests.

____

____

____

Name ____

- In comparisons, *better* and *best* are the irregular forms of the adjective *good*; *worse* and *worst* are the forms of the adjective *bad*.
- The comparative form of *many* is *more*; the superlative form is *most*.
- The comparative form of *much* is *more*; the superlative form is *most*.
- Never add *-er, -est, more,* or *most* to an irregular comparative or superlative form.

Proofread the paragraph. On the lines below, correct mistakes in the use of adjectives and the irregular formation of comparatives and superlatives.

The mechanic needed most time than he had to fix the car. Our attempt to fix it ourselves had made the problem worst, not gooder. He could repair the brakes, but he felt that the most best option would be to install new ones. That, of course, would cost most money. Either way, the mechanic said he needed to order most parts. He assured us that he would do the goodest job possible in the most quickest amount of time.

____

____

____

____

____

____

____

____

____

Name ____

Read the student draft and look for any corrections that need to be made. Then choose the best answer to each question.

(1) Our new cat creates most problems than our old cat. (2) She has the worse temper I have ever seen! (3) She is a good "attack cat" than a "lap cat." (4) Mom has the more patience of anyone in the house. (5) Even she thinks that adopting the new cat was the worst decision the family has made in a long, long time! (6) We hope to find her a gooder home than ours soon.

1. What is the correct way to write sentence 1?

A Our new cat creates more problems than our old cat.

B Our new cat creates many problems than our old cat.

C Our new cat creates mostest problems than our old cat.

D Our new cat creates morer problems than our old cat.

2. What change, if any, should be made in sentence 2?

F Change ***worse*** to **bad**

G Change ***worse*** to **most worser**

H Change ***worse*** to **worst**

J Make no change

3. What is the correct way to write sentence 3?

A She is a gooder "attack cat" than a "lap cat."

B She is a best "attack cat" than a "lap cat."

C She is a better "attack cat" than a "lap cat."

D She is a much "attack cat" than a "lap cat."

4. How is the correct way to write sentence 4?

F Mom has the most patience of anyone in the house.

G Mom has much patience of anyone in the house.

H Mom has the more patience of anyone in the house.

J Mom has the better patience of anyone in the house.

5. What change, if any, needs to be made to sentence 5?

A Change ***worst*** to **worse**

B Change ***worst*** to **bad**

C Change ***worst*** to **best**

D Make no change

6. What is the correct way to write sentence 6?

F We hope to find her a best home than ours soon.

G We hope to find her a better home than ours soon.

H We hope to find her a more better home than ours soon.

J We hope to find her a most better home than ours soon.

Name ______________________________

Fold back the paper along the dotted line. Use the blanks to write each word as it is read aloud. When you finish the test, unfold the paper. Use the list at the right to correct any spelling mistakes.

	1. ________	1. impress
	2. ________	2. impression
	3. ________	3. elect
	4. ________	4. election
	5. ________	5. locate
	6. ________	6. location
	7. ________	7. confuse
	8. ________	8. confusion
	9. ________	9. correct
	10. ________	10. correction
	11. ________	11. discuss
	12. ________	12. discussion
	13. ________	13. concentrate
	14. ________	14. concentration
	15. ________	15. estimate
	16. ________	16. estimation
	17. ________	17. decorate
	18. ________	18. decoration
	19. ________	19. exhaust
	20. ________	20. exhaustion
Review Words	21. ________	21. hopeless
	22. ________	22. fearless
	23. ________	23. forgiveness
Challenge Words	24. ________	24. conclude
	25. ________	25. conclusion

Name ____________________

One common suffix, ***-ion***, is added to certain words to change them from verbs to nouns.

confuse	**restrict**	**impress**
confusion	**restriction**	**impression**

The consonant sound at the end of each verb changes when *-ion* is added. The /z/ in *confuse* changes to /zh/ in *confusion*; the /t/ in *restrict* changes to /sh/ in *restriction*; the /s/ in *impress* changes to /sh/ in *impression*.

When the letter *i* follows *c, s, ss, sc,* or *t* in the last part of a word, it is usually silent and the consonants represent /sh/ (*confession, vacation, magician*) or /zh/ (*revision*).

DECODING WORDS

- When the base word ends in *e*, as in *locate* and *estimate*, the *e* is dropped before the suffix *-ion* is added: *location, estimation*.
- The final stable syllable *-tion* is always pronounced /shən/. Read the word *option* aloud: /op/ /shən/.

Write the spelling words that do not end in *-ion* next to the matching spelling words that do end in *-ion*. Then read each word aloud.

impress	locate	correct	concentrate	decorate
impression	location	correction	concentration	decoration
elect	confuse	discuss	estimate	exhaust
election	confusion	discussion	estimation	exhaustion

words without *-ion*	**words with *-ion***	**words without *-ion***	**words with *-ion***
________	________	________	________
________	________	________	________
________	________	________	________
________	________	________	________
________	________	________	________

Look through this week's readings for words with the suffix *-ion*. Record each word and a related word in your writer's notebook. Note any consonant sound changes. Then read the words aloud.

Name ______________________________

One common suffix, *-ion*, is added to certain words to change them from verbs to nouns.

confuse	**restrict**	**impress**
confusion	**restriction**	**impression**

Notice how the consonant sound at the end of each verb changes when *-ion* is added. The /z/ in *confuse* changes to /zh/ in *confusion*; the /t/ in *restrict* changes to /sh/ in *restriction*; the /s/ in *impress* changes to /sh/ in *impression*.

When the letter *i* follows *c, s, ss, sc,* or *t* in the last part of a word, it is usually silent and the consonants represent /sh/ (*confession, vacation, magician*) or /zh/ (*revision*).

DECODING WORDS

- When the base word ends in *e*, as in *locate* and *estimate*, the *e* is dropped before the suffix *-ion* is added: *location, estimation*.
- The final stable syllable *-tion* is always pronounced /shən/. Read the word *option* aloud: /op/ /shən/.

Write the spelling words that do not end in *-ion* next to the matching spelling words that do end in *-ion*. Then read the words aloud.

impress	locate	correct	decorate	relate
impression	location	correction	decoration	relation
elect	confuse	discuss	estimate	direct
election	confusion	discussion	estimation	direction

words without *-ion*	**words with *-ion***	**words without *-ion***	**words with *-ion***
______	______	______	______
______	______	______	______
______	______	______	______
______	______	______	______
______	______	______	______

Look through this week's readings for words with the suffix *-ion*. Record each word and a related word in your writer's notebook. Note any consonant sound changes. Then read the words aloud.

Name ______________________________

A. Write the spelling words that do not end in *-ion*. Then write the matching spelling words that do end in *-ion*. Read each word aloud.

impress	discuss	inflect	motivate	concentrate
impression	discussion	inflection	motivation	concentration
predict	estimate	exhaust	appreciate	confuse
prediction	estimation	exhaustion	appreciation	confusion

words without *-ion*	**words with *-ion***
______________	______________
______________	______________
______________	______________
______________	______________
______________	______________
______________	______________
______________	______________
______________	______________
______________	______________
______________	______________

B. Compare the words *impression* and *inflection*. How are they alike? How are they different?

____

____

____

Look through this week's readings for words with the suffix *-ion*. Record each word and a related word in your writer's notebook. Note any consonant sound changes. Then read the words aloud.

Name ______________________________

impress	locate	correct	concentrate	decorate
impression	location	correction	concentration	decoration
elect	confuse	discuss	estimate	exhaust
election	confusion	discussion	estimation	exhaustion

A. Write the spelling word that matches each definition below. Use spelling words that do not end in *-ion*.

1. to tire out ______________
2. to make right ______________
3. to choose by voting ______________
4. a rough calculation ______________
5. to find ______________
6. to think; to focus ______________
7. to talk about ______________
8. to have a favorable effect ______________
9. to adorn, make pleasing ______________
10. to mix up ______________

B. Write the spelling word that best completes each sentence. Use spelling words that end in *-ion*.

11. We had a long ______________ about the popular movie.
12. Do you know the ______________ of the new restaurant?
13. The puzzle took ______________, but I finally solved it.
14. I thought it would take two hours, but my ______________ was wrong.
15. She dressed neatly to make a good ______________.
16. The basket of shells made a nice ______________ in the beach house.
17. A busy schedule and lack of sleep can lead to ______________.
18. There was ______________ because the directions were unclear.
19. Will the mayor run for office again in the next ______________?
20. I made a ______________ to my writing when I edited it.

Name ____

Underline the six misspelled words in the paragraphs below. Using your knowledge of the suffix *-ion,* write the words correctly on the lines.

I support Mayor Jackson in the upcoming electshun. There has been a lot of discusion about his policies, but I feel he has been a good mayor. Recently he has put aside other matters to concentrat on plans for a new city park. I applaud his dedication to this project!

1. ______________ **2.** ______________ **3.** ______________

Mayor Jackson gives me the impreshion that he isn't a good leader. When talking about the locashun for the new city park, his ideas seemed to confuus citizens. Is he really the best mayor for our community? I don't think so!

4. ______________ **5.** ______________ **6.** ______________

Writing Connection

Write an opinion about something related to your own school or community. Use at least four spelling words in your writing.

____

____

____

____

____

____

____

____

____

____

____

____

Name ______________________________

Remember

The suffix ***-ion*** is added to certain words to change them from verbs to nouns.

revise (verb)	**attract** (verb)	**transmit** (verb)
revision (noun)	**attraction** (noun)	**transmission** (noun)

The consonant sound at the end of each verb changes when *-ion* is added. The /z/ in *revise* changes to /zh/ in *revision*; the /t/ in *attract* changes to /sh/ in *attraction*; the /t/ in *transmit* changes to /sh/ in *transmission.*

When the base word ends in *e,* as in *concentrate,* the *e* is dropped before the suffix *-ion* is added: *concentration.* Read each of these words aloud.

impress	locate	correct	concentrate	decorate
impression	location	correction	concentration	decoration
elect	confuse	discuss	estimate	exhaust
election	confusion	discussion	estimation	exhaustion

Fill in the missing letters to form a spelling word. Write the spelling word.

1. decor __ t __ ____________
2. decora __ __ __ __ ____________
3. el __ ct ____________
4. elec __ __ __ __ ____________
5. impr __ ss ____________
6. impres __ __ __ __ ____________
7. concentr __ t __ ____________
8. concentra __ __ __ __ ____________
9. disc __ ss ____________
10. discus __ __ __ __ ____________
11. estim __ t __ ____________
12. estima __ __ __ __ ____________
13. loc __ t __ ____________
14. loca __ __ __ __ ____________
15. conf __ s __ ____________
16. confu __ __ __ __ ____________
17. corr __ ct ____________
18. correc __ __ __ __ ____________
19. exh __ __ st ____________
20. exhaus __ __ __ __ ____________

Name ______________________________

Expand your vocabulary by adding or removing inflectional endings, prefixes, or suffixes to a base word to create different forms of a word.

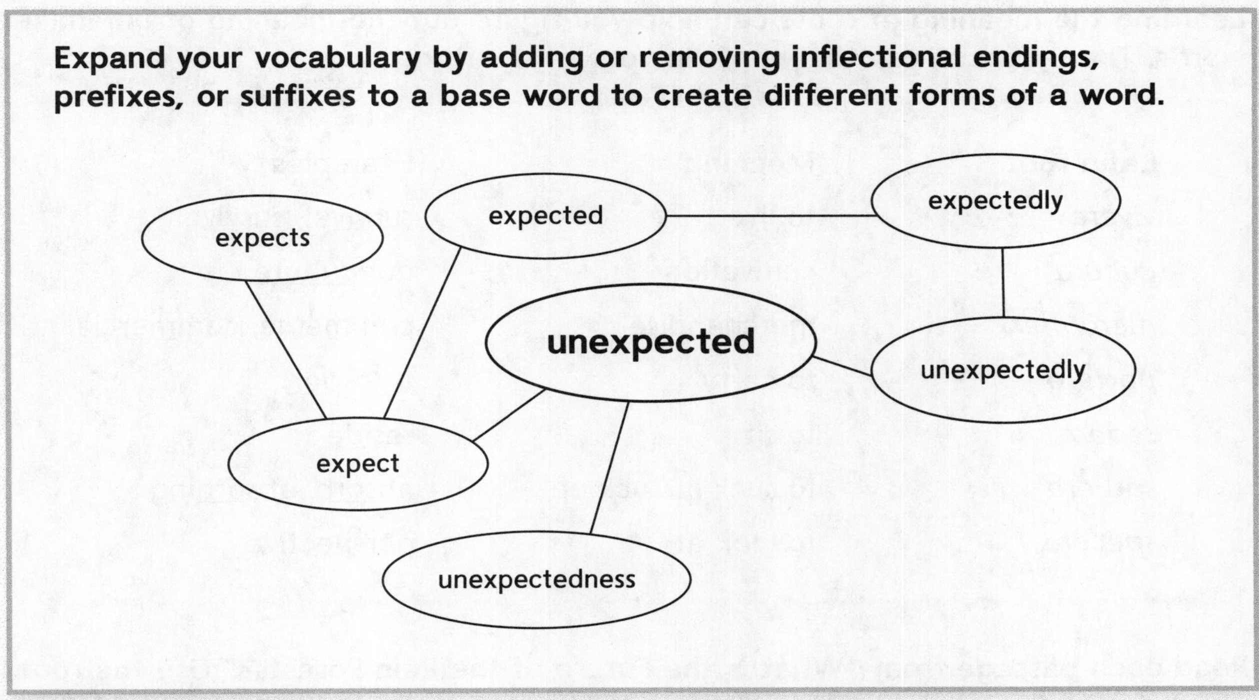

Write as many related words as you can on the lines below. Use a print or electronic dictionary to help you.

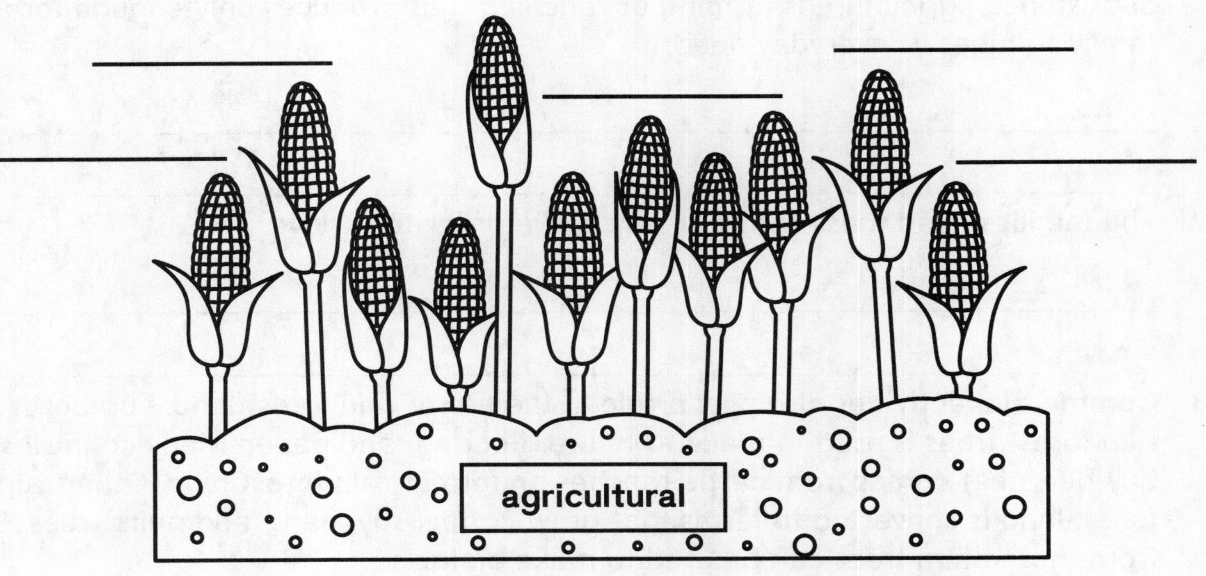

Name ______________________________

Learning the meaning of roots can help you figure out the meaning of unfamiliar words. Then you can use the words in your own writing.

Latin root	Meaning	Examples
vivere	to live	survival, survive
cultura	cultivation	agriculture
merc/merx	merchandise	commerce, commercial
portare	to carry	transport
sedere	to sit	reside
sorbere	to suck in/suck up	absorb, absorbing
specere	to look at	perspective

Read each passage from "What Is the Future of the Rain Forests?" Use the root words in the box and sentence clues to help you figure out the meaning of each word in bold. Write the word's meaning on the line. Then write your own sentence that uses the word in the same way.

1. When part of a rain forest is cut down, subsistence **agriculture** takes its place. Subsistence agriculture is farming or ranching that produces only enough for a family to meet its everyday needs.

____

____

2. The families need these farms or ranches in order to **survive**.

____

____

3. **Commercial** activities also play a role in the use of rain forest land. Lumber from rain forest trees is used to make furniture, flooring, and paper. Many countries buy beef that comes from cattle ranches on former rain forest land. Other rain forest land is converted to farms that grow coffee, soybeans, and palm trees. Oil from those palm trees can be used to make biofuels.

____

____

Name ______________________________

- An **adverb** can tell *how, when, where,* or *how often* an action happens. Many adverbs end in *-ly*: *I eat slowly.* (tells *how*)
- Some adverbs tell *how much* or *how intensely*: *I am absolutely certain.* (tells *how intensely*)
- **Conjunctive adverbs,** such as *therefore, meanwhile, however, similarly,* and *otherwise,* connect and clarify the relationship between two clauses: *I want a new bike; however, I need to save money first.*
- The **relative adverbs** *where, when,* and *why* can also introduce clauses: *That is the market where I buy fresh vegetables.*

Read each sentence. Underline each adverb. Circle any conjunctive or relative adverbs that you find.

1. I sat patiently on the park bench.
2. I hungrily ate my sandwich.
3. This is the time when I usually eat.
4. I carelessly dropped crumbs on the ground.
5. Tiny sparrows darted around frantically at my feet.
6. I tossed them in a spot where the birds could easily get them.
7. Soon they had eaten up all of the crumbs.
8. They quickly flew off but watched patiently from a nearby tree.
9. I visit the park frequently, but this had never happened before.
10. I had finished my lunch; therefore, I promptly returned to work.

In your writer's notebook, write a short passage about a place you visit often. Include at least one conjunctive adverb and one relative adverb. Edit and proofread your work.

Name ____

- An **adverb** can describe an adjective or another adverb.

  The weather today is *uncomfortably* *hot.* (describes the adjective *hot*)

  The performer arrived *very* *late.* (describes the adverb *late*)

Read each sentence. Underline each adverb. On the line(s) provided, write whether each adverb modifies a verb, an adjective, or another adverb.

1. The skier looked anxiously down the mountain. ____________________
2. Incredibly strong winds blew from the north. ____________________
3. The snow was accumulating quite quickly. ____________________
4. She could hardly see the bottom of the slope. ____________________
5. "I'm absolutely positive they'll cancel the race," he said. ____________________
6. A red light began flashing urgently near the start gate. ____________________
7. The skier felt somewhat relieved that the event was postponed. ____________________

Reading/Writing Connection

Read this paragraph from "Shipped Out." Underline at least two adverbs, and circle the verb that each adverb describes. Then rewrite one sentence so that an adverb modifies another adverb. Underline this new adverb.

> I remember how intently my parents read reports about the war, which I rarely understood. They often whispered to one another, and I'd shout out something like, "Speak up! I can't hear you!" They'd frown and leave me alone to talk in private.

____

____

____

Name ____________________

- **Capitalize** the first word and all proper nouns in a greeting.
- Capitalize only the first word in the closing.
- Capitalize these **abbreviations** commonly used in letters and formal e-mails: Mrs., Mr., Ms., Dr., Inc.

Read each part of the letter. On the lines provided, rewrite each part with the correct capitalization.

1. To whom it may concern:

   ____

2. I am writing on behalf of dr. Morton and mrs. rodriguez.

   ____

3. They are both employees of american meganews, inc.

   ____

4. Please let my assistant, ms. hart, know when we can all meet.

   ____

5. with all best wishes,

   ____

In your writer's notebook, write a short letter to a company about their customer service. Perhaps you want to make a suggestion or compliment an employee who helped you. Include at least two abbreviations. Edit and proofread your letter for capitalization and punctuation.

Name ______________________________

- Capitalize the first word and all proper nouns in a greeting. Capitalize only the first word in the closing.
- Capitalize these abbreviations commonly used in letters and formal e-mails: Mrs., Mr., Ms., Dr., Inc.
- When a **conjunctive adverb** appears at the start of a sentence, it is often followed by a comma: *I feel like relaxing at home tonight. However, we can go to the game if you want.* When a conjunctive adverb connects two ideas in one sentence, it is preceded by a semicolon and followed by a comma: *Mom was too busy at work to attend the dinner; moreover, she was not feeling well.*

Proofread the letter. On the lines below, correct mistakes in adverb usage and capitalization.

dear board members of Really-Fun games, inc.:

I have an idea for a game that is incredible exciting. It is called "Build the barrels." The game is normal played with two players; however you can easy add up to six more. My teacher, mr. Cooper, can quick send a recommendation if you need one. I sincere hope that you will take a look at this very exciting new idea.

One of Your Biggest Fans,

____

____

____

____

____

____

____

____

____

Name ____

Read the student draft and look for any corrections that need to be made. Then choose the best answer to each question.

(1) My mother sat quiet at the piano. (2) Suddenly, the orchestra began to play. (3) They performed an incredibly joyful symphony. (4) My mother played an uplifting piece very beautiful. (5) The audience was mesmerized by her performance, accordingly they immediate stood for a standing ovation. (6) I have never been so proud to have such an amazing talented mother. (7) Everybody calls her dr. Brown, but I get to call her "Mom."

1. What change, if any, should be made in sentence 1?
   - **A** Change ***quiet*** to **quietest**
   - **B** Change ***quiet*** to **quietly**
   - **C** Change ***quiet*** to **more quiet**
   - **D** Make no change

2. What change, if any, should be made in sentence 2?
   - **F** Change ***Suddenly*** to **Sudden**
   - **G** Change ***Suddenly*** to **Most suddenly**
   - **H** Change ***Suddenly*** to **More suddenly**
   - **J** Make no change

3. Which word does the adverb modify in sentence 3?
   - **A** performed
   - **B** incredibly
   - **C** joyful
   - **D** symphony

4. How does sentence 4 need to be changed?
   - **F** Change ***uplifting*** to **most uplifting**
   - **G** Change ***uplifting*** to **more uplifting**
   - **H** Change ***beautiful*** to **more beautiful**
   - **J** Change ***beautiful*** to **beautifully**

5. What is the correct way to write sentence 5?
   - **A** The audience was mesmerized, accordingly; they immediate stood for a standing ovation.
   - **B** The audience was mesmerized; accordingly they immediately stood for a standing ovation.
   - **C** The audience was mesmerized; accordingly, they immediately stood for a standing ovation.
   - **D** The audience was mesmerized, according they immediately stood for a standing ovation.

6. What change, if any, should be made in sentence 6?
   - **F** Change ***proud*** to **prouder**
   - **G** Change ***amazing*** to **amazingly**
   - **H** Change ***talented*** to **most talented**
   - **J** Make no change

7. How does sentence 7 need to be changed?
   - **A** Capitalize ***dr.***
   - **B** Delete the period after ***dr.***
   - **C** Lowercase ***Brown***
   - **D** Delete the comma after ***Brown***

Name ______________________________

Fold back the paper along the dotted line. Use the blanks to write each word as it is read aloud. When you finish the test, unfold the paper. Use the list at the right to correct any spelling mistakes.

1. ______________ 1. astronaut
2. ______________ 2. telephone
3. ______________ 3. automobile
4. ______________ 4. telescope
5. ______________ 5. mechanical
6. ______________ 6. myth
7. ______________ 7. television
8. ______________ 8. phonics
9. ______________ 9. astronomer
10. ______________ 10. photograph
11. ______________ 11. photography
12. ______________ 12. mythical
13. ______________ 13. homophone
14. ______________ 14. mechanic
15. ______________ 15. telegram
16. ______________ 16. telephoto
17. ______________ 17. autograph
18. ______________ 18. automatic
19. ______________ 19. disaster
20. ______________ 20. telegraph

Review Words

21. ______________ 21. correction
22. ______________ 22. discussion
23. ______________ 23. decoration

Challenge Words

24. ______________ 24. videophone
25. ______________ 25. photogenic

Name ______________________________

Many English words are of Greek origin. Recognizing Greek roots can help you remember a word's spelling and meaning.

Some common Greek roots include ***astro*** (star), ***auto*** (self), ***bio*** (life) ***graph*** (write), ***geo*** (earth), ***hydro*** (water), ***mech*** (machine), ***myth*** (beliefs), ***phon*** (sound), and ***photo*** (light).

Read each root aloud.

SPELLING TIP

Many Greek roots include the spelling pattern *ph,* which stands for /f/: *telephone, photograph, homophone, telephoto.* Can you think of any other words with this spelling pattern?

Write the spelling words that contain the matching Greek root. You will write some words more than once. Then read the words aloud.

astronaut	mechanical	automatic	telegraph	autograph
telephone	myth	photograph	mechanic	astronomer
automobile	television	telescope	telegram	disaster
photography	phonics	mythical	telephoto	homophone

astr/aster

1. ______________
2. ______________
3. ______________

tele

4. ______________
5. ______________
6. ______________
7. ______________
8. ______________
9. ______________

graph

10. ______________
11. ______________
12. ______________
13. ______________

photo

14. ______________
15. ______________
16. ______________

auto

17. ______________
18. ______________
19. ______________

phon

20. ______________
21. ______________
22. ______________

mech

23. ______________
24. ______________

myth

25. ______________
26. ______________

Name ____

Many English words are of Greek origin. Recognizing Greek roots can help you remember a word's spelling and meaning.

Some Greek roots include ***astro*** (star), auto (self), ***bio*** (life) ***graph*** (write), ***geo*** (earth), ***hydro*** (water), mech (machine), ***myth*** (beliefs), ***phon*** (sound), and ***photo*** (light).

Read each root aloud.

SPELLING TIP

Many Greek roots include the spelling pattern *ph,* which stands for /f/: *telephone, photograph, homophone, telephoto.* Can you think of any other words with this spelling pattern?

Write the spelling words that contain the matching Greek root. You will write some words more than once. Then read the words aloud.

astronaut	myth	photograph	telegram	videophone
telephone	television	telescope	telephoto	auto
photography	phonics	mythical	autograph	graph
mechanical	automatic	mechanic	disaster	homophone

astr/aster

1. ____________
2. ____________

tele

3. ____________
4. ____________
5. ____________
6. ____________
7. ____________

graph

8. ____________
9. ____________
10. ____________
11. ____________

photo

12. ____________
13. ____________
14. ____________

auto

15. ____________
16. ____________
17. ____________

phon

18. ____________
19. ____________
20. ____________
21. ____________

mech

23. ____________
24. ____________

myth

25. ____________
26. ____________

Name ______________________________

A. Write the spelling words that contain the matching Greek root. You will write some words more than once. Then read the words aloud.

astronaut	mechanical	automatic	telegraph	autograph
telephone	myth	photosynthesis	mechanic	astronomer
automobile	television	telescope	telegram	mechanized
photography	phonics	mythical	telephoto	homophone

astr

1. ____________
2. ____________

tele

3. ____________
4. ____________
5. ____________
6. ____________
7. ____________
8. ____________

graph

9. ____________
10. ____________
11. ____________

photo

12. ____________
13. ____________
14. ____________

auto

15. ____________
16. ____________
17. ____________

phon

18. ____________
19. ____________
20. ____________

mech

21. ____________
22. ____________
23. ____________

myth

24. ____________
25. ____________

syn

26. ____________

B. Read each sentence. Replace the underlined words with a spelling word and rewrite the sentence.

1. I understand <u>the science of sounds,</u> so I can read almost any word.

____

2. People who are <u>able to fix machines</u> will always be able to find a job.

____

Name ______________________________

astronaut	mechanical	automatic	telegraph	autograph
telephone	myth	photograph	mechanic	astronomer
automobile	television	telescope	telegram	disaster
photography	phonics	mythical	telephoto	homophone

A. Write the spelling word that has the same Greek root as each pair below.

1. disastrous, disastrously ______________
2. televise, televising ______________
3. telescoped, telescopic ______________
4. automaker, automotive ______________
5. telephoned, telephonically ______________
6. phonetics, phonically ______________

B. Write the spelling word that best completes each sentence.

7. In the ______________, a father and son wore wings so they could fly.
8. The actor scribbled his ______________ on a piece of paper.
9. A ______________ checked the brakes on our car.
10. Can you name the first ______________ to set foot on the moon?
11. Coded messages can be sent through wires by a ______________
12. The word *sweet* is a ______________ for the word *suite*.
13. The book shows a ______________ of President Lincoln.
14. The ______________ watched the sky from an observatory.
15. The old engine has many ______________ parts.
16. I want to take a class in ______________ so I can take better pictures.
17. A griffin is a ______________ beast that is part eagle and part lion.
18. This ______________ lens helps me take pictures from far away.
19. Dad's ______________ watch does not need winding.
20. A ______________ was once the best way to send important news.

Name ______________________________

Underline the six misspelled words in the paragraphs below. Using your knowledge of Greek roots, write the words correctly on the lines.

Years ago, Mr. and Mrs. Carter made a trip out west in their atomobile. They took many pictures of their trip, and one photagraph showed Mrs. Carter standing at the Grand Canyon at dusk with a small teliscope. When Kevin saw the picture, he asked Mr. Carter about it.

1. ____________ **2.** ____________ **3.** ____________

"We wanted to view the full moon," Mr. Carter said. "The Grand Canyon seemed like the perfect spot. It turned out to be a disester. We couldn't get the equipment set up, and then we had machanical trouble with the car. We finally made it back to our cabin and watched tellevision for the rest of the night!"

4. ____________ **5.** ____________ **6.** ____________

Writing Connection

Write a passage for a story about a mishap on another trip. The story can be set in the past or the present. Use at least four spelling words in your writing.

Name ____

Remember

Many English words come from the Greek language. Recognizing Greek roots can help you remember a word's spelling and meaning. For example, if you know the roots ***astro*** (star) and ***naut*** (ship), you should be able to determine the spelling and meaning of words like *astronaut, astronomer,* and *nautical.*

Read the spelling words aloud. Which words share the same Greek roots?

astronaut	mechanical	automatic	telegraph	autograph
telephone	myth	photograph	mechanic	astronomer
automobile	television	telescope	telegram	disaster
photography	phonics	mythical	telephoto	homophone

A. Fill in the missing letters of each word to form a spelling word. Then write the spelling word on the line.

1. tele ___ ___ oto ________________
2. my ___ ___ ical ________________
3. au ___ ___ mobile ________________
4. te ___ ___ vision ________________
5. autogra ___ ___ ________________
6. ___ ___ otograph ________________
7. as ___ ___ onomer ________________
8. ___ ___ chanical ________________
9. tele ___ ___ aph ________________
10. pho ___ ___ graphy ________________
11. tele ___ ___ one ________________
12. ___ ___ tomatic ________________
13. homoph ___ ___ e ________________
14. ___ ___ lescope ________________
15. ___ ___ tronaut ________________

B. Write these spelling words on the lines in reverse alphabetical order:
phonics, myth, telegram, disaster, mechanic

16. ________________
17. ________________
18. ________________
19. ________________
20. ________________

Name ____________________

Expand your vocabulary by adding or removing inflectional endings, prefixes, or suffixes to a base word to create different forms of a word.

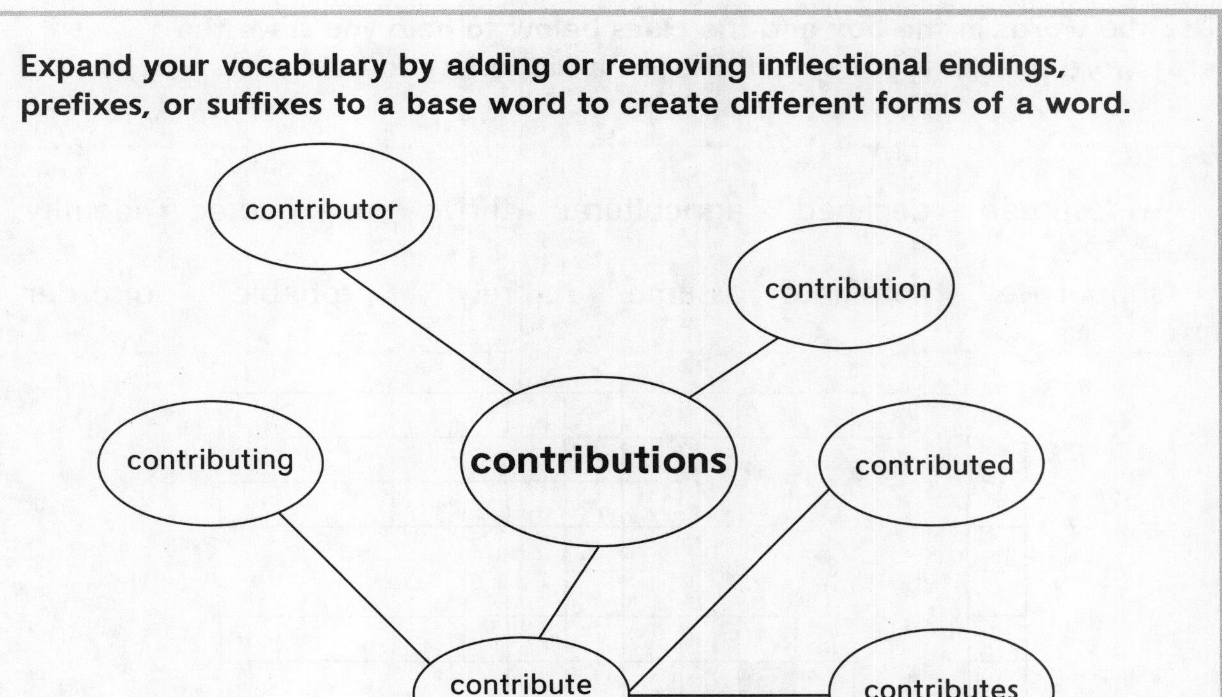

Add survival kit items to the backpack to write as many related words as you can. Use a dictionary to help you.

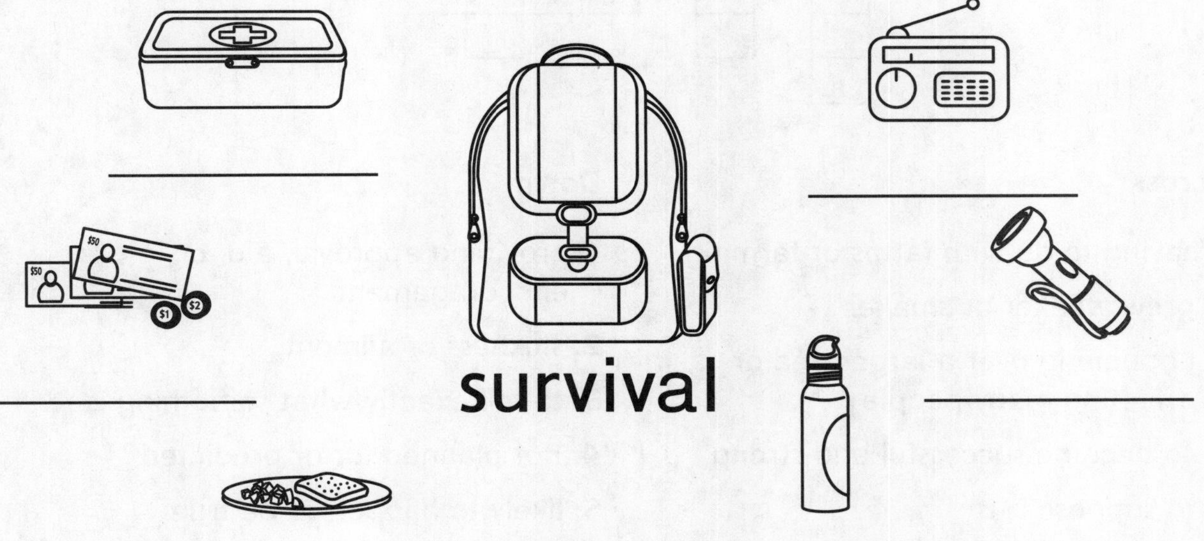

Name ______________________________

Use the words in the box and the clues below to help you solve the crossword puzzle. If you get stuck, use a dictionary to help you.

widespread	declined	agricultural	thrive	unexpected	identify
supportive	nominate	assume	rely	probable	disorder

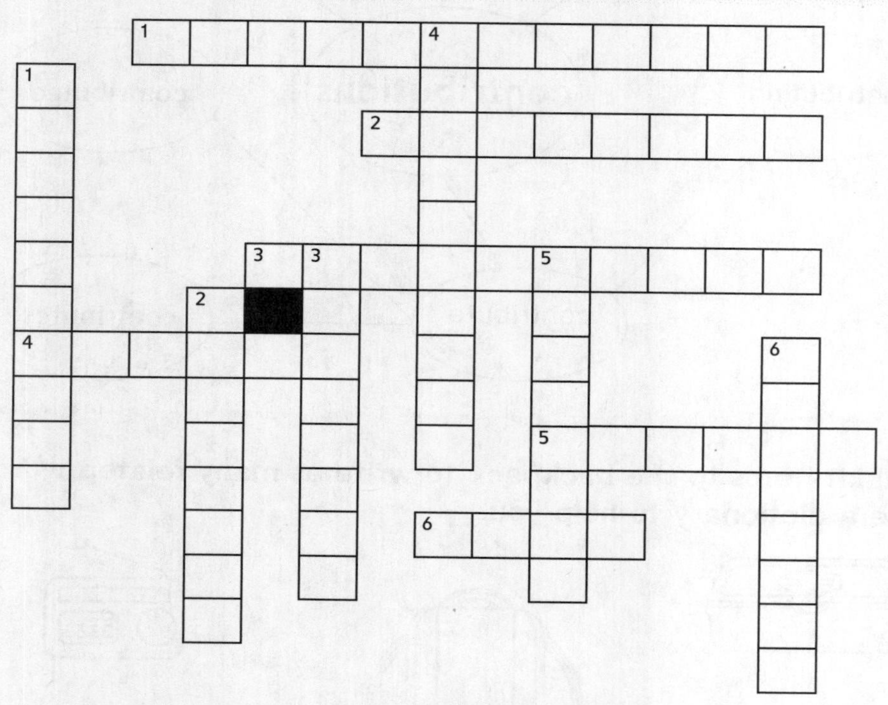

Across

1. having to do with farms or farming
2. grew weaker or smaller
3. happening over a large area or affecting many people
4. to become successful and strong
5. to suppose it is so
6. to depend on someone or something

Down

1. providing approval, aid, or encouragement
2. sickness or ailment
3. to tell exactly what something is
4. not planned for or predicted
5. likely to happen or be true
6. to propose that a person be chosen

Name ____

- An **adverb** can compare two or more actions. Adverbs that compare two actions use *-er* or *more*: *Amy jumped higher than Sam during the game.* Adverbs that compare three or more actions use *-est* or *most: Avery worked the hardest and most carefully of all.*

Read each sentence. Write the correct comparative form of the adverb in parentheses on the line provided.

1. I can run (fast) than my brother. ______________________
2. Our father runs (quickly) of all. ______________________
3. He trains (often) than my brother does. ______________________
4. He enjoys running (fully) than biking. ______________________
5. Even so, he practices swimming (seriously) of all. ______________________
6. I prefer team sports (strongly) than other sports. ______________________
7. I can throw (accurately) than our team's other pitcher. ______________________
8. In the entire league, she pitches (wildly) of all. ______________________
9. Our final game will be here (soon) than we expect. ______________________
10. The audience will cheer (loudly) of all during our final inning. ______________________

In your writer's notebook, write a short passage about a sport that you enjoy. Include at least three adverbs that compare two or more actions.

Name ______________________________

- Add *-er* or *-est* to most short adverbs to compare actions: *swam farther, swam the farthest.* Add *more* or *most* to adverbs that have two or more syllables or to adverbs that end in *-ly*: *more softly, most softly.*

Read each sentence. Write the correct comparative form of the adverb in parentheses on the line provided.

1. The sun shone (brightly) today than yesterday. ______________

2. The three of us raced to see who could pack (rapidly) for our trip.

____

3. I should have prepared (carefully) than I did. ______________

4. My bag was the (poorly) packed of all. ______________

5. Mom spoke to me (sternly) than usual. ______________

6. We might arrive (late) than expected at the airport. ______________

7. Luckily, the traffic was moving (smoothly) than normal. ______________

8. In fact, we checked in at the gate (early) of all. ______________

Read this sentence from "Allies in Action." Underline the adverb. Then rewrite the sentence using a comparative adverb.

He demonstrated how quickly the Navajo could encode and decipher messages.

____

____

Name ______________________________

- *Good* is often an adjective, and *well* is often an adverb that tells how. *Good* and *well* cannot be used interchangeably. *Well* is an adjective when it means *healthy*: *I was sick yesterday, but I am well now.*
- As with the adjective *good,* the comparative form of *well* is *better.* The superlative form is *best.*
- Never add *-er* and *more* or *-est* and *most* to the same adverb.

Read each sentence. Choose the word in parentheses that best completes each sentence and write it on the line provided.

1. The carpenter did a (good, well) job on our new porch. ____________
2. We paid him (good, well) for his hard work. ____________
3. The house looks (better, best) than before. ____________
4. The work was finished (sooner, more sooner) than we expected. ____________
5. We go outside more (frequent, frequently) than we used to. ____________
6. The porch is built of (good, well), strong wood. ____________
7. Our first dinner on the porch went very (good, well). ____________
8. Our second meal was even (better, best) than that. ____________
9. I always feel (good, well) after spending time outside. ____________
10. Nothing makes you feel (weller, better) than a sunny day! ____________

In your writer's notebook, write a short passage describing an experience that turned out better than you expected. Include at least five comparative adverbs. Make sure to use the correct comparative forms.

Name ______________________________

- Add *-er* or *-est* to most short adverbs to compare actions. Add *more* or *most* to adverbs that have two or more syllables or to adverbs that end in *-ly*.
- *Good* is often an adjective, and *well* is often an adverb that tells how. *Good* and *well* cannot be used interchangeably. *Well* is an adjective when it means *healthy*.

Proofread the paragraph. On the lines below, correct mistakes in grammar and mechanics.

I wasn't feeling good, so I went to the school nurse. She treated me carefully than the last time I visited. A new virus had recent been detected at school. It was spreading more faster than any disease she had ever seen. Luckily, the simple treatment she prescribed oftenest of all was also working more effectively of all. She said I should feel more well in a few days.

COMMON ERRORS

Never add *-er* and *more* or *-est* and *most* to the same adverb.

____

____

____

____

____

____

____

____

Name ____________________

Read the student draft and look for any corrections that need to be made. Then choose the best answer to each question.

(1) My parents were acting most strangely than ever. (2) My sister was behaving more suspiciously of all. (3) She was treating me more politely than usual. (4) Luckily, I am the smarter member of my family. (5) I easily fooled my sister into believing that I knew the secret. (6) Most finally I figured out why everyone was acting so strange—we got a new puppy!

1. What change needs to be made in sentence 1?

A Change ***most strangely*** to **more strangely**

B Change ***most strangely*** to **more stranger**

C Change ***strangely*** to **stranger**

D Change ***strangely*** to **strangelier**

2. What change, if any, should be made in sentence 2?

F Change ***suspiciously*** to **suspicious**

G Change ***more suspiciously*** to **most suspicious**

H Change ***more suspiciously*** to **most suspiciously**

J Make no change

3. What changes, if any, should be made in sentence 3?

A Change ***more*** to **most**

B Change ***more politely*** to **most polite**

C Change ***politely*** to **polite**

D Make no change

4. How does sentence 4 need to be changed?

F Change ***smarter*** to **smartest**

G Change ***smarter*** to **more smart**

H Change ***smarter*** to **most smart**

J Change ***smarter*** to **smartiest**

5. What change, if any, needs to be made to sentence 5?

A Change ***easily*** to **more easily**

B Change ***easily*** to **most easily**

C Change ***easily*** to **easier**

D Make no change

6. What is the correct way to write sentence 6?

F Most finally, I figured out why everyone was acting so strangely—we got a new puppy!

G Finally, I figured out why everyone was acting so strangely—we got a new puppy!

H Finally, I figured out why everyone was acting so stranger—we got a new puppy!

J More finally, I figured out why everyone was acting so strangest—we got a new puppy!

Name ____________________

Fold back the paper along the dotted line. Use the blanks to write each word as it is read aloud. When you finish the test, unfold the paper. Use the list at the right to correct any spelling mistakes.

	1. ________	1. subtraction
	2. ________	2. transportation
	3. ________	3. missile
	4. ________	4. portable
	5. ________	5. intermission
	6. ________	6. committee
	7. ________	7. respect
	8. ________	8. transport
	9. ________	9. tractor
	10. ________	10. spectator
	11. ________	11. attraction
	12. ________	12. export
	13. ________	13. inspector
	14. ________	14. distract
	15. ________	15. spectacle
	16. ________	16. inspect
	17. ________	17. mission
	18. ________	18. import
	19. ________	19. dismiss
	20. ________	20. suspect
Review Words	21. ________	21. telescope
	22. ________	22. astronaut
	23. ________	23. photograph
Challenge Words	24. ________	24. spectacular
	25. ________	25. protractor

Name ______________________________

Many English words are of Latin origin. Recognizing Latin roots can help you remember a word's spelling and meaning.

Some Latin roots include ***aud*** (to hear), ***miss/mit*** (to send), ***auto*** (self), ***dict*** (to say), ***port*** (to carry), ***scrib/script*** (write), ***spect*** (to look at), and ***tract*** (to pull).

Read each spelling word aloud. Do you notice any patterns?

DECODING WORDS

Many verbs end with the Latin root *spect* or *tract,* such as *inspect, attract,* and *distract.* When these words become nouns, the final consonant sound changes. For example, the /t/ in *attract* changes to /sh/ in *attraction.* Read this word aloud: /ə/ /trak/ /shən/.

Write the spelling words that contain the matching Latin root.

subtraction	export	tractor	inspector	mission
transportation	committee	spectator	distract	import
missile	respect	attraction	spectacle	intermission
portable	transport	dismiss	inspect	suspect

port

1. ____________
2. ____________
3. ____________
4. ____________
5. ____________

miss/mitt

6. ____________
7. ____________
8. ____________
9. ____________
10. ____________

spect

11. ____________
12. ____________
13. ____________
14. ____________
15. ____________
16. ____________

tract

17. ____________
18. ____________
19. ____________
20. ____________

Look through a dictionary for more words with Latin roots. Create a word sort for a partner in your writer's notebook. Then share your answers.

Name ______________________________

Many English words are of Latin origin. Recognizing Latin roots can help you remember a word's spelling and meaning.

Some Latin roots include ***aud*** (to hear), ***miss/mit*** (send), ***auto*** (self), ***dict*** (to say) ***port*** (to carry), ***scrib/script*** (write), ***spect*** (to look at), and ***tract*** (to pull).

Read each spelling word aloud. Do you notice any patterns?

DECODING WORDS

Many verbs end with the Latin root *spect* or *tract*, such as *inspect*, *attract*, and *distract*. When these words become nouns, the final consonant sound changes. For example, the /t/ in *attract* changes to /sh/ in *attraction*. Read this word aloud: /ə/ /trak/ /shən/.

Write the spelling words that contain the matching Latin root.

subtract	export	tractor	inspector	mission
port	commit	spectator	distract	import
missile	respect	traction	spectacle	intermission
portable	transport	dismiss	inspect	suspect

port

1. ____________
2. ____________
3. ____________
4. ____________
5. ____________

miss/mitt

6. ____________
7. ____________
8. ____________
9. ____________
10. ____________

spect

11. ____________
12. ____________
13. ____________
14. ____________
15. ____________
16. ____________

tract

17. ____________
18. ____________
19. ____________
20. ____________

Look through a dictionary for more words with Latin roots. Create a word sort for a partner in your writer's notebook. Then share your answers.

Name ______________________________

A. Write the spelling words that contain the matching Latin root.

subtraction	export	intractable	inspector	mission
transportation	committee	spectator	distract	import
missile	prospector	attraction	spectacle	intermission
portable	transport	dismissal	inspect	circumspect

port

1. ____________
2. ____________
3. ____________
4. ____________
5. ____________

miss/mitt

6. ____________
7. ____________
8. ____________
9. ____________
10. ____________

spect

11. ____________
12. ____________
13. ____________
14. ____________
15. ____________
16. ____________

tract

17. ____________
18. ____________
19. ____________
20. ____________

B. Compare the words *subtraction* and *transportation*. How are they alike? How are they different?

____

____

____

Look through a dictionary for more words with Latin roots. Create a word sort for a partner in your writer's notebook. Then share your answers.

Name ____________________

subtraction	export	tractor	inspector	mission
transportation	committee	spectator	distract	import
missile	respect	attraction	spectacle	intermission
portable	transport	dismiss	inspect	suspect

A. Write the spelling word that has the same, or almost the same, meaning.

1. examiner ____________

2. sight ____________

3. to check ____________

4. observer ____________

5. to move ____________

6. to release ____________

7. honor ____________

8. job ____________

9. to suppose ____________

10. break ____________

B. Write the spelling word that best completes each sentence.

11. The bus is my ____________ to and from school.

12. Which automobiles do we ____________ from other countries?

13. I used ____________ to figure out how much money was left.

14. The food court is a popular ____________ at the mall.

15. A ____________ can be a very destructive weapon.

16. I try not to let phone calls ____________ me when I'm studying.

17. The citizens formed a ____________ so they could work together.

18. We take a ____________ stove with us on camping trips.

19. The farmer kept his old ____________ in the barn.

20. Can you name one ____________ that we ship overseas?

Name ______________________________

Underline the six misspelled words in the paragraphs below. Using your knowledge of Latin roots, write the words correctly on the lines.

James was a spektator at all the school basketball games. His mision was to boost the home team's spirits, and he organized a commettee of students to join him in making signs and cheering loudly at each game.

1. ______________ **2.** ______________ **3.** ______________

Soon James's group of cheering students became the main attaction at the games. Did the students distrack the other teams? Some said they did, but their display was always good-natured and done with the greatest respecd for all players.

4. ______________ **5.** ______________ **6.** ______________

Writing Connection

Write a passage for a story about another enthusiastic student. Use at least four spelling words in your writing.

____

____

____

____

____

____

____

____

____

____

____

____

____

Name ______________________________

Remember

Many English words come from the Latin language. Recognizing Latin roots can help you remember a word's spelling and meaning. For example, if you know the root ***tract*** (to pull), you should be able to determine the spelling and meaning of *tractor.*

Read each spelling word aloud. Which words share the same Latin roots?

A. Fill in the missing letters of each word to form a spelling word. Then write the spelling word on the line.

subtraction	export	tractor	inspector	mission
transportation	committee	spectator	distract	import
missile	respect	attraction	spectacle	intermission
portable	transport	dismiss	inspect	suspect

1. re ___ ___ ect ______________
2. transp ___ ___ tation ______________
3. interm ___ ___ sion ______________
4. att ___ ___ ction ______________
5. po ___ ___ able ______________
6. dis ___ ___ ss ______________
7. tr ___ ___ tor ______________
8. spe ___ ___ acle ______________
9. transp ___ ___ t ______________
10. m ___ ___ sile ______________
11. s ___ ___ ctator ______________
12. mi ___ ___ ion ______________
13. ex ___ ___ rt ______________
14. distra ___ ___ ______________
15. insp ___ ___ tor ______________

B. Write these spelling words on the lines in alphabetical order. Alphabetize them to the third letter. ***suspect, import, committee, inspect, subtraction***

16. ______________
17. ______________
18. ______________
19. ______________
20. ______________

Name ______________________________

Literal language says what it means. *Literal* refers to the dictionary definition, or *denotation*. For example: *Storm clouds appeared in the sky.*

Figurative language has a deeper meaning that goes beyond the literal meaning. Writers may include similes, metaphors, personification, hyperbole, or other figures of speech to make the writing more interesting. Figurative language also allows for a deeper connection with the reader due to the *connotation* of the chosen words, or the feelings and ideas associated with them. For example: *The sky suddenly became angry.*

Look at the images below. Then write one sentence about the image using literal language and one sentence about the image using figurative language.

Name ______________________________

Homophones are words that sound the same but are spelled differently and have different meanings. Say the following homophone pairs out loud.

peace, piece	*flower, flour*	*waist, waste*
principle, principal	*sole, soul*	*stationary, stationery*

Read the sentences below and circle the correct word to complete each one. Underline the context clues that help you figure out which word to use. Then use that word in a new sentence.

1. This morning the wind ______ so hard that I nearly fell over. **blew** **blue**

____

____

2. I thought I ______ all the answers to her questions. **knew** **new**

____

____

3. I didn't recognize you when we ______ on the street. **passed** **past**

____

____

4. Call your dog to come ______ now. **hear** **here**

____

____

5. He seems like a nice person and a good friend, ______. **to** **too**

____

____

Name ______________________________

- A **negative** is a word or phrase that means "no."
- Do not use more than one negative in a spoken or written sentence.
- **Negatives** include *no* and *not,* as well as *nobody, nothing, never, no one,* and *nowhere.*
- Positive forms of negative words include words such as *somebody, something, any, ever, anything, anybody, anyone,* and *anywhere.*

Read each sentence. Underline any negative words that you find. Circle any positive forms of negative words that you find.

1. The snack bar will not be open today.
2. No one showed up for work there this morning.
3. Nobody showed up for work in the library, either.
4. Something like this had never happened before.
5. There were no plans in place for a substitute cashier.
6. When I interviewed the principal for our newspaper, he said nothing.
7. I asked if anyone had called the librarian.
8. He told me not to worry about anything.
9. More information about the situation was nowhere to be found.
10. Is there no one else who thinks that this is mysterious?

In your writer's notebook, write instructions explaining good and bad strategies for doing homework. Include at least three negatives. After you finish, read your instructions to a partner. Have your partner restate the instructions. Then ask your partner to read his or her instructions to you. Restate them and remember to follow the good instructions.

Name ____

- A **negative contraction** is made up of a verb and the word *not*. An apostrophe is used in place of the letter *o*: *isn't* (is not), *aren't* (are not).

Read each sentence. Form a contraction using the two words in parentheses. Write the contraction on the line provided.

1. Today (is not) going to be my greatest day ever. ______________
2. For starters, my alarm (did not) go off this morning. ______________
3. After breakfast, I (could not) find my homework. ______________
4. (Has not) anyone seen it lying around somewhere? ______________
5. My sister and brother (were not) very helpful. ______________
6. I (should not) get as upset as I do sometimes. ______________
7. It (does not) help to solve any problems at all. ______________
8. Why (cannot) I ever learn that simple lesson? ______________

Read this paragraph from "Life in the Desert." Then rewrite the underlined sentence to include a negative contraction.

> Dromedaries have a hump on their backs that is made up of fat. They use the fat for energy when food is scarce. <u>These animals sweat very little, which saves water.</u> When they do drink, they can take in as many as thirty gallons of water in a little over ten minutes!

____

Write one fact you know about an animal. Include a negative contraction. Edit and proofread your sentence for grammar and punctuation.

____

Name ____

- Do not use two negatives in the same clause. This is known as a **double negative**: *I didn't do nothing.* (incorrect) *I don't feel like going nowhere.* (incorrect)
- Correct a clause with two negatives by changing one negative to a positive word or eliminating one of the negative words.

  I didn't do anything. (Or: *I did nothing.*)

  I don't feel like going anywhere. (Or: *I feel like going nowhere.*)

Read each sentence. Correct the double negatives and write the new sentence on the line provided.

1. Our car won't never start in rainy weather.

   ____

2. There didn't seem to be nothing we could do.

   ____

3. Our father doesn't want no broken car keeping us stranded at home.

   ____

4. He searched everywhere but couldn't find none of the tools he needed to repair it.

   ____

5. Dad doesn't like no one telling him that something can't be fixed.

   ____

In your writer's notebook, write a short passage about something that bothers you. Include at least five negatives. As you check your work, make sure to avoid double negatives.

Name ______________________________

- A **negative contraction** is made up of a verb and the word *not*. An apostrophe is used in place of the letter *o*.
- Correct a **double negative** in a clause by changing one negative to a positive word or eliminating one of the negative words.

Proofread the paragraph. On the lines below, correct mistakes in contractions and the use of negatives.

The explorers could'nt find no maps that showed the rain forest trails. They didnt want to get lost, so they hired a guide. He wasnot surprised that they needed help. The routes were overgrown, so you couldn't hardly see a thing. There was'nt no trail that looked the same from year to year. The guide had never gotten lost on none of the trails. He didn't expect this trip would be no different.

COMMON ERRORS

Negative adverbs such as *hardly, barely,* and *rarely* mean "almost not" or "not often." Be careful to avoid double negatives when using these adverbs: *The crowd was so loud that I* *<u>could barely</u>* *hear the speaker.*

____

____

____

____

____

____

____

____

____

Name ____

Read the student draft and look for any corrections that need to be made. Then choose the best answer to each question.

(1) My uncle couldn't find his car nowhere in the parking lot. (2) My father told him he shouldn't not wait to report it. (3) The officers weren't surprised to hear about the missing car. (4) They said they hadn't never received so many reports of stolen cars. (5) The officers didnt waste no time gathering information about the case. (6) The police hadn't caught nobody yet, but they had some leads.

1. What change should be made in sentence 1?

A Change ***couldn't*** to **could not**

B Change ***couldn't*** to **couldn't not**

C Change ***nowhere*** to **anywhere**

D Change ***nowhere*** to **anywhere**

2. What change, if any, should be made in sentence 2?

F Change ***shouldn't*** to **should'nt**

G Delete the word ***not***

H Change ***not*** to **no**

J Make no change

3. What change, if any, should be made in sentence 3?

A Change ***weren't*** to **werent**

B Change ***weren't*** to **were no**

C Change ***weren't*** to **weren't not**

D Make no change

4. How does sentence 4 need to be changed?

F Change ***hadn't never*** to **hadn't ever**

G Change ***hadn't never*** to **had ever**

H Change ***hadn't never*** to **hadnt ever**

J Change ***hadn't never*** to **haven't never**

5. What is the correct way to write sentence 5?

A The officers didn't not waste no time gathering information about the case.

B The officers didn't ever waste no time gathering information about the case.

C The officers didn't not waste time gathering information about the case.

D The officers didn't waste any time gathering information about the case.

6. What is the correct way to write sentence 6?

F The police hadn't caught anybody yet, but they had some leads.

G The police hadn't not caught nobody yet, but they had some leads.

H The police had not caught nobody yet, but they had some leads.

J The police hadn't not caught somebody yet, but they had some leads.

Name ______________________________

Fold back the paper along the dotted line. Use the blanks to write each word as it is read aloud. When you finish the test, unfold the paper. Use the list at the right to correct any spelling mistakes.

	1. ________	1. clothes
	2. ________	2. January
	3. ________	3. cereal
	4. ________	4. strength
	5. ________	5. lunar
	6. ________	6. atlas
	7. ________	7. ocean
	8. ________	8. salute
	9. ________	9. fury
	10. ________	10. echo
	11. ________	11. cycle
	12. ________	12. cyclone
	13. ________	13. gigantic
	14. ________	14. Olympics
	15. ________	15. territory
	16. ________	16. terrace
	17. ________	17. parasol
	18. ________	18. fortune
	19. ________	19. furious
	20. ________	20. gracious
Review Words	21. ________	21. suspect
	22. ________	22. inspect
	23. ________	23. mission
Challenge Words	24. ________	24. jovial
	25. ________	25. venerable

Name ______________________________

Many English words have origins in mythology.

- ***Cereal*** has its origin in Roman mythology. Ceres was the goddess of grain and the harvest.
- ***Clothes*** has its origin in Greek mythology. Clotho was a goddess who was responsible for spinning the thread of human life.

Recognizing these relationships can help you determine the meaning of unfamiliar words.

SPELLING TIP

In words of Greek origin, /k/ is often represented by the digraph *ch*. Try saying the words *echo, character, chronology,* and *chaos* out loud.

Write the spelling words that contain the matching number of syllables.

clothes	lunar	fury	gigantic	parasol
January	atlas	echo	Olympics	fortune
cereal	ocean	cycle	territory	furious
strength	salute	cyclone	terrace	gracious

one syllable

1. ____________
2. ____________

two syllables

3. ____________
4. ____________
5. ____________
6. ____________
7. ____________
8. ____________
9. ____________
10. ____________
11. ____________
12. ____________
13. ____________

three syllables

14. ____________
15. ____________
16. ____________
17. ____________
18. ____________

four syllables

19. ____________
20. ____________

Work with a partner to find more words that are connected to Greek or Roman mythology. Use this week's readings and a dictionary. Then create a word sort using the words you found.

Name ______________________________

Many English words have origins in mythology.

- ***Cereal*** has its origin in Roman mythology. Ceres was the goddess of grain and the harvest.
- ***Clothes*** has its origin in Greek mythology. Clotho was a goddess who was responsible for spinning the thread of human life.

Recognizing these relationships can help you determine the meaning of unfamiliar words.

SPELLING TIP

In words of Greek origin, /k/ is often represented by the digraph *ch*. Try saying the words *echo, character, chronology,* and *chaos* out loud.

Write the spelling words that contain the matching number of syllables.

clothes	lunar	fury	gigantic	siren
January	atlas	echo	Olympics	fortune
cereal	ocean	cycle	Titanic	furious
strength	salute	python	terrace	music

one syllable

1. ______________
2. ______________

two syllables

3. ______________
4. ______________
5. ______________
6. ______________
7. ______________
8. ______________
9. ______________
10. ______________
11. ______________
12. ______________
13. ______________
14. ______________

three syllables

15. ______________
16. ______________
17. ______________
18. ______________
19. ______________

four syllables

20. ______________

Work with a partner to find more words that are connected to Greek or Roman mythology. Use this week's readings and a dictionary. Then create a word sort using the words you found.

Name ______________________________

A. Write the spelling words that contain the matching number of syllables.

arachnid	ogre	fury	gigantic	parasol
lethargic	hypnosis	nemesis	Olympics	nocturnal
muse	martial	sphinx	territory	furious
hygiene	salute	cyclone	terrace	gracious

one syllable

1. ______________
2. ______________

two syllables

3. ______________
4. ______________
5. ______________
6. ______________
7. ______________
8. ______________
9. ______________
10. ______________

three syllables

11. ______________
12. ______________
13. ______________
14. ______________
15. ______________
16. ______________
17. ______________
18. ______________
19. ______________

four syllables

20. ______________

B. Read each sentence. Circle the word that has origins in mythology. Then write the meaning of the word on the line. You may use a dictionary.

1. The other team was furious when the referee made an incorrect call.

____

2. When the dentist finished cleaning my teeth, he complimented me on my good hygiene.

____

Work with a partner to find more words that are connected to Greek or Roman mythology. Use this week's readings and a dictionary. Then create a word sort using the words you found.

Name ______________________________

clothes	lunar	fury	gigantic	parasol
January	atlas	echo	Olympics	fortune
cereal	ocean	cycle	territory	furious
strength	salute	cyclone	terrace	gracious

A. Write the spelling word that matches each definition below.

1. rage; great anger ______________
2. repeated sequence ______________
3. book of maps ______________
4. area of land ______________
5. breakfast food ______________
6. garments worn on the body ______________
7. first month of the year ______________
8. give a sign of respect ______________
9. repeated sound ______________
10. international games ______________
11. large body of water ______________
12. having to do with the moon ______________

B. Write the spelling word that best completes each analogy.

13. *Stone* is to *rock* as *tornado* is to ______________.
14. *Mean* is to *kind* as *rude* is to ______________.
15. *Muffler* is to *scarf* as ______________ is to *umbrella*.
16. *Health* is to *well-being* as ______________ is to *riches*.
17. *Porch* is to ______________ as *basement* is to *cellar*.
18. *Power* is to ______________ as *force* is to *might*.
19. ______________ is to *angry* as *relaxed* is to *calm*.
20. ______________ is to *huge* as *tiny* is to *small*.

Name ____

Underline the six misspelled words in the paragraphs below. Write the words correctly on the lines.

The Olympiks began in ancient Greece many centuries ago. Today the games follow a four-year cycal, but the summer and winter games are held in different years. Cities around the world are awarded the honor of being the gracius host for the international competition.

1. ____________ 2. ____________ 3. ____________

Over 200 countries participate in this giantic sporting event. The athletes wear cloths that reflect the colors of their flag. The strength of these great athletes makes them seem to have superhuman abilities!

4. ____________ 5. ____________ 6. ____________

Writing Connection

Write information about a sporting event in your own school or community. Use at least four spelling words in your writing. Edit and proofread your work.

____

____

____

____

____

____

____

____

____

____

____

____

Name ____________________

Remember

Many words in the English language are connected to mythology.

- ***January*** has its origin in Roman mythology. Janus was the Roman god of beginnings.
- ***Panic*** has its origin in Greek mythology. Pan was the Greek god of goatherds and shepherds. He created noise in the woods to scare travelers.

Recognizing an unfamiliar word's origin can help you determine its meaning.

clothes	lunar	fury	gigantic	parasol
January	atlas	echo	Olympics	fortune
cereal	ocean	cycle	territory	furious
strength	salute	cyclone	terrace	gracious

A. Fill in the missing letters of each word to form a spelling word. Then write the spelling word on the line.

1. c __ __ le ____________
2. a __ __ as ____________
3. cl __ th __ s ____________
4. fo __ __ une ____________
5. l __ __ ar ____________
6. f __ __ ious ____________
7. cer __ __ l ____________
8. __ __ ympics ____________
9. ec __ __ ____________
10. c __ __ lone ____________
11. str __ __ gth ____________
12. gr __ __ ious ____________
13. te __ __ ace ____________
14. s __ __ ute ____________
15. terr __ __ ory ____________

B. Write these spelling words on the lines in reverse alphabetical order: *ocean, January, fury, parasol, gigantic.*

16. ____________
17. ____________
18. ____________
19. ____________
20. ____________

Name ______________________________

Content words are words that are specific to a field of study. For example, words like *hypothesis, biology,* and *species* are science content words.

Authors use content words to explain a concept or idea. Sometimes you can figure out what a content word means by using context clues. You can also use a dictionary to help you find the meaning of unfamiliar content words.

Go on a word hunt with a partner. Find as many content words related to survival as you can. Write them in the chart.

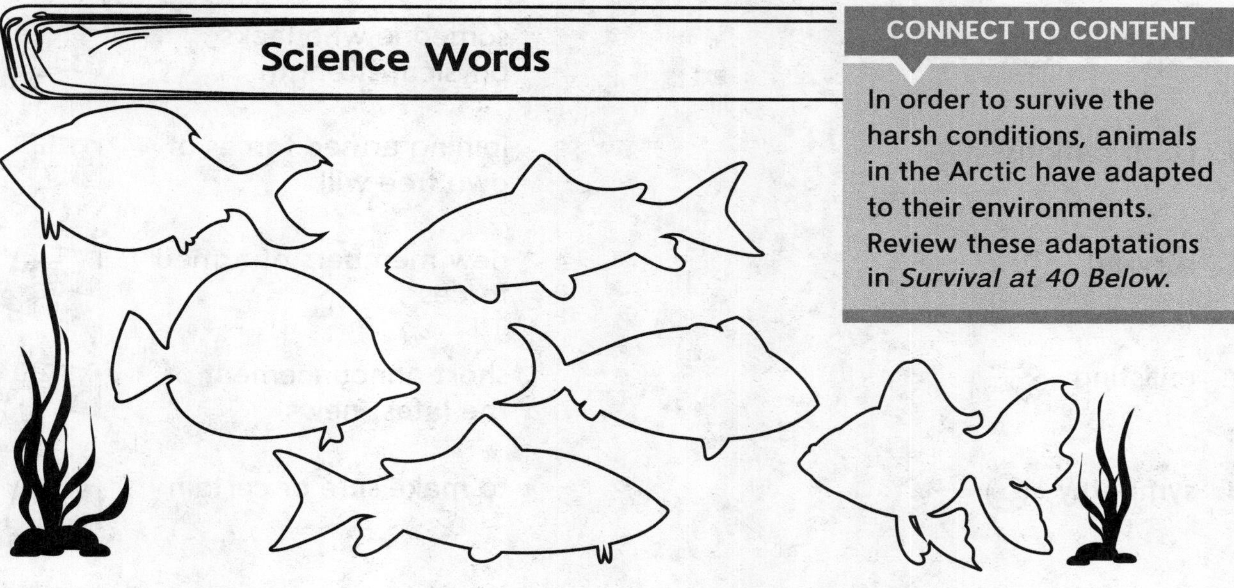

CONNECT TO CONTENT

In order to survive the harsh conditions, animals in the Arctic have adapted to their environments. Review these adaptations in *Survival at 40 Below.*

Circle two words that you were able to figure out the meaning to using context clues. Write the words and what they mean on the lines.

____

____

____

____

____

Name ____________________________

Score! Match the definitions on the left with the vocabulary words on the right. Use a print or electronic dictionary if you get stuck.

1. recruits
2. weakling
3. bulletin
4. diversity
5. contributions
6. survival
7. enlisting
8. sympathy
9. reconsider
10. intercept
11. operations
12. guarantee

a great difference or variety

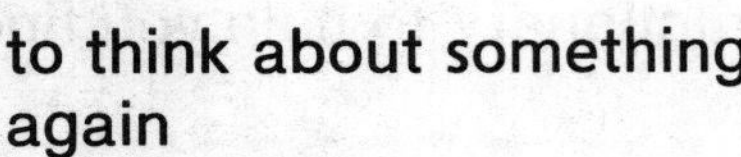

to think about something again

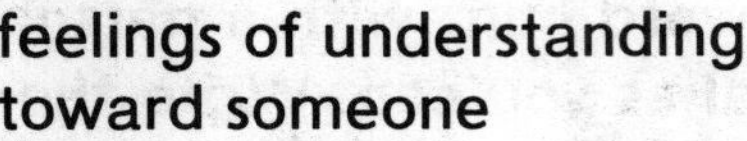

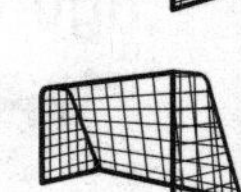

feelings of understanding toward someone

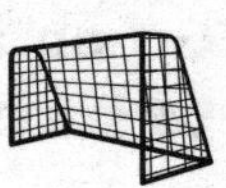

someone who lacks physical strength

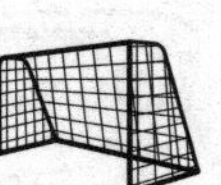

joining armed forces of own free will

new members of armed forces

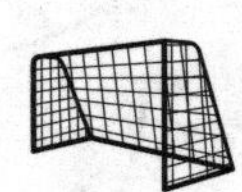

short announcement of the latest news

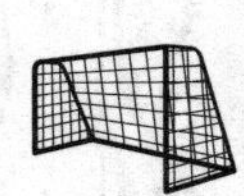

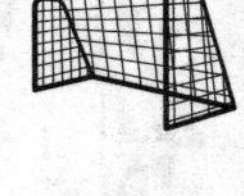

to make sure or certain

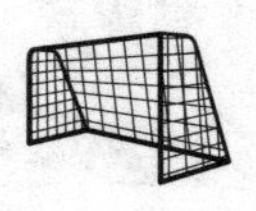

the act of continuing to live

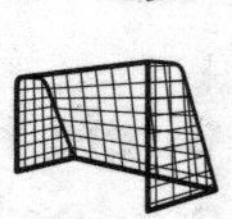

plans or processes for doing something

to stop moving from one place or person to another

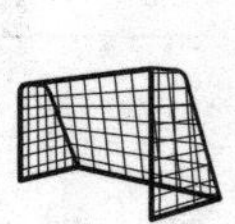

gifts of money, time, or effort given to a cause

Name ____________________

- **Sentence combining** is reducing two or more simple sentences into one sentence.
- Two simple sentences about the same subject can be combined into one **compound sentence**. They can also be combined with a **compound predicate**.
- The paired **conjunctions** *either/or* and *neither/nor* can be used to combine sentences.

Read each of the two sentences. Combine them into one sentence and write it on the lines provided.

1. Our school was having an art contest. I decided to enter.

____

2. My teacher encouraged me to participate. My teacher gave me the entry forms.

____

3. My first painting wasn't very good. I did much better with the next one.

____

Reading/Writing Connection

Read the excerpt from "Life in the Desert." Combine the underlined sentences into one sentence with a compound predicate.

Meerkats are members of the mongoose family that live in Africa. <u>They hunt early in the day to avoid the heat. They live in mobs, or groups, of as many as thirty members.</u> The mob helps keep its members safe. Predators, such as eagles or jackals, are often frightened away by a meerkat mob.

____

____

Name ____

- Adding an **adjective** can combine two sentences that tell about the same noun: *I opened the door. The door was old. I opened the old door.*
- If two sentences tell about the same action, adding an **adverb** can combine them. If two sentences tell about the same time or location, adding a **prepositional phrase** can combine them.

Read each of the two sentences. Combine them into one sentence and write it on the lines provided.

1. The two girls practiced their duet. They practiced it frequently.

____

2. They looked forward to the performance. The performance was in two weeks.

____

3. Their parents bought tickets. They bought them over the phone.

____

4. They planned to meet for dinner before the show. The dinner would be quick.

____

Connect to Community

Talk to a parent or another trusted adult about a performance you could attend in your town. Then write a paragraph describing the event. As you edit your work, combine short sentences using adjectives, adverbs, and prepositional phrases whenever possible.

____

____

____

____

____

____

Name ____

- Use **commas** in the greeting and closing of a friendly letter. Use commas in addresses and dates. Use commas to separate the items in a list.
- Use a **colon** after a salutation or greeting in a business letter. A colon can also separate hours, minutes, and seconds. Use a colon to introduce lists.
- Use a **comma** in direct address with the name of a person. *Jose, what a great idea! Let's go, Shantal!*

Read each group of words. Rewrite the words on the line provided and add the proper punctuation.

1. Dear Superintendent Harriman

____

2. Our school's Activities Club met last Tuesday April 15 2018.

____

3. We changed the starting time of this year's Spring Dance from 630 to 700.

____

____

4. We request funds to purchase the following items decorations snacks beverages and a stereo system.

____

____

5. Sincerely yours

____

In your writer's notebook, write a short letter to a friend requesting information. Make sure to use correct punctuation.

Name ____

- Use **commas** in the greeting and closing of a friendly letter. Use commas in addresses and dates. Use commas to separate the items in a list.
- Use a **colon** after a salutation or greeting in a business letter. A colon can also separate hours, minutes, and seconds. Use a colon to introduce lists.

Proofread the letter. On the lines below, correct mistakes in adverb usage, commas, and colons.

129 Greenwood Lane

Glendale Arizona

May 17 2018

Dear Members of the Chamber of Commerce

Please immediate send the Town Fair committee the following items maps guidebooks and coupon sheets. We'll need them by 700 a.m. on Friday to have them available at the start of the fair at 930.

Very truly yours

____

____

____

____

____

____

____

____

____

____

Name ______________________________

Read the student draft and look for any corrections that need to be made. Then choose the best answer to each question.

(1) I asked the coach if I could play shortstop. (2) I asked him confidently. (3) I had been practicing all year. (4) I was practicing in my yard. (5) He said the position was mine. (6) He said it without hesitation. (7) I dashed home to tell my parents. (8) I went shortly after practice. (9) We went out to our favorite restaurant to celebrate. (10) The restaurant serves Mexican food.

1. How can sentences 1 and 2 be combined?

   A I asked the coach if I could play shortstop, I asked him confidently.

   B I asked the coach if I could play shortstop, confidently.

   C I asked the coach; confidently, if I could play shortstop.

   D I confidently asked the coach if I could play shortstop.

2. What is the most effective way to combine sentences 3 and 4?

   F I had been practicing in my yard all year.

   G I had been in my yard practicing.

   H All year in my yard; I practiced.

   J In my yard I had been all year practicing.

3. How can sentences 5 and 6 be combined?

   A He said the position was mine; without hesitation.

   B He said it without hesitation, he said the position was mine.

   C Without hesitation, he said the position was mine.

   D Hesitation without, he said, the position was mine.

4. What is the **BEST** way to combine sentences 7 and 8?

   F Shortly after practice, I dashed home to tell my parents.

   G I dashed home, shortly after practice; to tell my parents.

   H Shortly after practice, to tell my parents, I dashed home.

   J I dashed home; to tell my parents shortly after practice.

5. What is the **BEST** way to combine sentences 9 and 10?

   A We went out to our Mexican favorite restaurant.

   B We went out to our favorite Mexican restaurant.

   C To our Mexican favorite restaurant we went.

   D To our favorite Mexican restaurant, we went.

Name ______________________________

Fold back the paper along the dotted line. Use the blanks to write each word as it is read aloud. When you finish the test, unfold the paper. Use the list at the right to correct any spelling mistakes.

	1. ______	**1.** tripod
	2. ______	**2.** triplet
	3. ______	**3.** unicorn
	4. ______	**4.** uniform
	5. ______	**5.** unison
	6. ______	**6.** biweekly
	7. ______	**7.** triple
	8. ______	**8.** bicycle
	9. ______	**9.** tricycle
	10. ______	**10.** unicycle
	11. ______	**11.** triangle
	12. ______	**12.** bisect
	13. ______	**13.** trio
	14. ______	**14.** unify
	15. ______	**15.** centipede
	16. ______	**16.** centimeter
	17. ______	**17.** century
	18. ______	**18.** binoculars
	19. ______	**19.** universe
	20. ______	**20.** university
Review Words	**21.** ______	**21.** cereal
	22. ______	**22.** terrace
	23. ______	**23.** atlas
Challenge Words	**24.** ______	**24.** bilingual
	25. ______	**25.** trilogy

Name ______________________________

Some common prefixes stand for numbers.

- ***uni-*** means "one": A *uniform* is an outfit worn by all members of an organization.
- ***bi-*** *means* "two": *Binoculars* have two lenses.
- ***tri-*** means "three": The *triceps* arm muscle has three points of attachment.
- ***cent-*** means "hundred": A *centimeter* equals one hundredth of a meter.

Read each spelling word aloud.

DECODING WORDS

Look at the word part at the beginning of the word *biweekly.* The prefix *bi-* means "two." Use the prefix to read the word and figure out its meaning: *bi/week/ly. Biweekly* means "every two weeks."

Write the spelling words that begin with each prefix.

tripod	unison	tricycle	trio	century
triplet	biweekly	unicycle	unify	binoculars
unicorn	triple	triangle	centipede	universe
uniform	bicycle	bisect	centimeter	university

uni-

1. ______________
2. ______________
3. ______________
4. ______________
5. ______________
6. ______________
7. ______________

bi-

8. ______________
9. ______________
10. ______________
11. ______________

tri-

12. ______________
13. ______________
14. ______________
15. ______________
16. ______________
17. ______________

cent-

18. ______________
19. ______________
20. ______________

Work with a partner to find more words that use the number prefixes *uni-, bi-, tri-,* and *cent-*. Search using a dictionary. Then create a word sort using the words you found.

Name ______________________________

Some common prefixes stand for numbers.

- ***uni-*** means "one": A *uniform* is an outfit worn by all members of an organization.
- ***bi-*** *means* "two": *Binoculars* have two lenses.
- ***tri-*** means "three": The *triceps* arm muscle has three points of attachment.
- ***cent-*** *means* "hundred": A *centimeter* equals one hundredth of a meter.

Read each spelling word aloud.

DECODING WORDS

Look at the word part at the beginning of the word *biweekly.* The prefix *bi-* means "two." Use the prefix to read the word and figure out its meaning: *bi/week/ly. Biweekly* means "every two weeks."

Write the spelling words that begin with each prefix.

tripod	unit	tricycle	trio	century
triplet	biweekly	unicycle	unify	bimonthly
unicorn	triple	tricolor	centipede	unity
uniform	bicycle	bilevel	centimeter	university

uni-

1. ______________
2. ______________
3. ______________
4. ______________
5. ______________
6. ______________
7. ______________

bi-

8. ______________
9. ______________
10. ______________
11. ______________

tri-

12. ______________
13. ______________
14. ______________
15. ______________
16. ______________
17. ______________

cent-

18. ______________
19. ______________
20. ______________

Work with a partner to find more words that use the number prefixes *uni-*, *bi-*, *tri-*, and *cent-*. Search using a dictionary. Then create a word sort using the words you found.

Name ______________________

A. Write the spelling words that begin with each prefix.

triumvirate	unison	tricycle	trio	century
triplet	binary	unicycle	trilogy	binoculars
unicorn	triathlon	triangle	centipede	universe
unilateral	bilingual	bisect	centimeter	university

uni-

1. ______________

2. ______________

3. ______________

4. ______________

5. ______________

6. ______________

bi-

7. ______________

8. ______________

9. ______________

10. ______________

tri-

11. ______________

12. ______________

13. ______________

14. ______________

15. ______________

16. ______________

17. ______________

cent-

18. ______________

19. ______________

20. ______________

B. Compare the words *tricycle* and *unicycle*. How are they alike? How are they different?

____

____

____

Work with a partner to find more words that use the number prefixes *uni-*, *bi-*, *tri-*, and *cent-*. Search using a dictionary. Then create a word sort using the words you found.

Name ______________________________

tripod	unison	tricycle	trio	century
triplet	biweekly	unicycle	unify	binoculars
unicorn	triple	triangle	centipede	universe
uniform	bicycle	bisect	centimeter	university

A. Write the spelling word that matches each definition below.

1. bring together ______________
2. 100 years ______________
3. mythical animal ______________
4. group of three ______________
5. three-legged stand ______________
6. one-wheeled vehicle ______________
7. figure with three sides ______________
8. bug with many legs ______________
9. to divide into two parts ______________
10. school for higher learning ______________

B. Write the spelling word that best completes each sentence.

11. Johnny is too young for a two-wheeler, so he rides a ______________.
12. The students recited the poem together in ______________.
13. One ______________ likes to play sports, while the other two do not.
14. My band ______________ has a white jacket and blue pants.
15. How exciting it would be to explore the ______________ in a spaceship!
16. The huge dog is ______________ the size of my small pet.
17. Grandmother uses ______________ to watch birds in her yard.
18. Instead of taking a bus to school, I ride my ______________.
19. A ______________ is a small unit of measurement.
20. I canceled my subscription to the ______________ newsletter.

Name ______________________________

Underline the six misspelled words in the paragraphs below. Using your knowledge of prefixes, write the words correctly on the lines.

Bikes have been around for more than a sentury. You may have ridden a trycicle when you were young. Your next step might have been a two-wheeler with training wheels. Then the training wheels came off, and you now zoom down the sidewalk like a superhero about to explore the unverse!

1. ______________ **2.** ______________ **3.** ______________

You probably won't get a job riding a unnicycle in a circus, but you may ride your bycycle back and forth to school. It doesn't take a unaversity degree to know that you are much safer on a bike if you wear a helmet.

4. ______________ **5.** ______________ **6.** ______________

Writing Connection

Write information about a recreational activity that you enjoy. Use at least four spelling words in your writing.

____

____

____

____

____

____

____

____

____

____

____

Name ____________________

Remember

Some common prefixes stand for numbers.

- ***uni-*** means "one"
- ***bi-*** means "two"
- ***tri-*** means "three"
- ***cent-*** means "hundred"

Recognizing these prefixes can help you determine the meaning of unfamiliar words.

tripod	unison	tricycle	trio	century
triplet	biweekly	unicycle	unify	binoculars
unicorn	triple	triangle	centipede	universe
uniform	bicycle	bisect	centimeter	university

A. Add the prefix to form a spelling word. Write the spelling word on the line.

1. uni + verse = ____________________
2. tri + angle = ____________________
3. bi + noculars = ____________________
4. cent + imeter = ____________________
5. tri + ple = ____________________
6. uni + corn = ____________________
7. bi + weekly = ____________________
8. uni + versity = ____________________
9. tri + pod = ____________________
10. tri + o = ____________________
11. cent + ipede = ____________________
12. uni + form = ____________________
13. bi + sect = ____________________
14. tri + plet = ____________________
15. uni + son = ____________________

B. Write these spelling words on the lines in reverse alphabetical order: *tricycle, unicycle, century, unify, bicycle.*

16. ____________________
17. ____________________
18. ____________________
19. ____________________
20. ____________________

Name ______________________________

Writers use **figurative language** to create a picture in the reader's mind. **Sound devices** like consonance, assonance, alliteration, and onomatopoeia help them to achieve that purpose.

Consonance is the repetition of the same consonant sounds (*little toads waited for the cricket*), **assonance** is the repetition of the same or similar vowel sounds (*our aunt owns an octopus*), **alliteration** is the repetition of initial letter sounds (*noisy neighbor*), and **onomatopoeia** refers to words that sound like the sound they describe (*buzz*).

Read the poem and circle the sound devices. Then write about how the author's use of the sound devices helped you visualize or understand the poem.

As I stand out on the corner
Waiting for a bus to take,
I feel the cold creep up my legs
Brrrrrr! I shiver and shudder and shake!
The chill that fills me makes me ill
My body begins to cool
And then when I have given in
Screech! The bus shows up for school!

Name ____________________

Read each passage. Underline the context clues that help you figure out the meaning of each word in bold. Then, in your own words, write the definition of the word.

1. One kind of adaptation is **structural**, meaning that the animal's body has changed so that it can survive in the climate.

   ____

2. Another type of adaptation is **behavioral**. Desert animals act in ways that help them survive.

   ____

3. Since it is so hot during the day, many animals are **nocturnal**. They rest under rocks or in other cool places during the day and come out at night to hunt for food.

   ____

4. They come out only at night during the summer. In winter the lizards **hibernate**. During this period of inactivity, they use very little food and energy.

   ____

5. Many different types of snakes live in the desert. Because they are **cold-blooded**, snakes' body temperatures change with that of their surroundings.

   ____

   ____

6. Meerkats are members of the mongoose family that live in Africa. They hunt early in the day to avoid the heat. They live in **mobs**, or groups, of as many as thirty members. The mob helps keep its members safe.

   ____

Name ______________________________

- A **prepositional phrase** is a group of words that contains a **preposition**, an **object**, and possibly a **modifier**. Some common prepositions are *by, from, through, to, of, above, at, behind,* and *with*.
- When a prepositional phrase acts as an **adjective**, it tells *what kind, how many,* or *which one*.

  You can use the plates above the sink. (modifies *plates*)

  I read a long article on endangered animals. (modifies *article*)

Read each sentence. Underline the prepositional phrases used as adjectives. Then write the nouns modified by the prepositional phrases on the lines provided.

1. Our class went to the aquarium in the city. ____________________
2. We counted the sharks in the giant tank. ____________________
3. The one with the torn fin seemed quite mean. ____________________
4. A poster on the wall described their feeding habits. ____________________
5. The students in my class were somewhat frightened. ____________________
6. I have read many books about sharks. ____________________
7. My favorite has a long chapter on their habitats. ____________________
8. Angry encounters with humans are actually not very common. ____________________

In your writer's notebook, write a short description of a museum you have visited. Include at least three prepositional phrases that act as adjectives. Edit and proofread your work.

Name ____

- When a **prepositional phrase** acts as an **adverb**, it tells *how, when,* or *where*: *The woman entered the bus in a hurry.*

Read each sentence. Underline the prepositional phrase used as an adverb in each sentence. Then write the verb that is modified by the prepositional phrase.

1. The storm moved along the coast. ____________
2. We raced around the house gathering emergency supplies. ____________
3. Mom shouted directions in an urgent tone. ____________
4. Swaying power lines made the lights flicker throughout the house. ____________
5. I won't forget that night for the rest of my life! ____________

Reading/Writing Connection

Read the lines from "Big Sky." Underline two prepositional phrases that act as adverbs. Then write four lines of poetry about the weather. Include two prepositional phrases that act as adverbs.

The sun rising from the east
Bounced off soaring clouds
And shot the sky with coral.
I could turn in circles
And see the sky everywhere I looked.
Nothing blocked my view.

____

____

____

____

Name ______________________________

- A **prepositional phrase** begins with a preposition and ends with a noun or a pronoun: *I talked with Paul.*
- When the **object of a preposition** is a pronoun, use the objective case.

  I talked with him.

  I received a letter from her.
- A **gerund** is a verbal ending in *-ing* that is used as a noun. *Swimming is fun.*
- An **infinitive** is the base form of a verb. It is formed by placing *to* in front of the verb. It can also act as a noun, adjective, or adverb. *I plan to write the essay. To bake a cake, read the recipe.*
- A **participial phrase** is a verbal that contains a participle and functions as an adjective. *The dog, barking loudly, woke us up.*

A. Read each sentence. Choose the pronoun in parentheses that best completes the sentence and write it on the line provided.

1. My friends invited me to go camping with (they, them). ______________

2. We hiked along the mountain ridges near (we, us). ______________

3. I brought plenty of food and warm clothing with (me, I). ______________

4. Back home, my mom kept her phone near (she, her). ______________

B. Read the following sentences and circle the gerund, infinitive, or participial phrase. Write on the line whether the sentence contains a gerund, infinitive, or participial phrase.

5. I want to go to the library. ______________

6. The children, walking in a circle, were enjoying the new game.

____

7. Hurrying causes mistakes. ______________

Name ______________________________

- A **prepositional phrase** normally appears close to the word or words that it modifies.
- When the **object of a preposition** is a pronoun, use the objective case.

Proofread the paragraph. On the lines below, correct mistakes in the use of prepositional phrases and pronouns.

My father to the health fair was going. He invited me to attend it with he. Many doctors from our area would be there. I had met some of they when my class visited the local hospital. I received several brochures from their at booths that they had set up. My father also picked up a few for hisself. It is important to have events like this from our town. I will show my friends the materials I got and share my experience with it.

____

____

____

____

____

____

____

____

____

Name ______________________________

Read the student draft and look for any corrections that need to be made. Then choose the best answer to each question.

(1) Our colorful kites above the tall trees soared. (2) With the longest tails, the kites seemed more stable. (3) Strong winds from the south batted them about. (4) My brother photographed the kites and beside me stood. (5) He during the afternoon must have taken a hundred pictures. (6) He will show some best of the photos later today.

1. What is the correct way to write sentence 1?

A The tall trees soared above our colorful kites.

B Colorful our kites, soared above the tall trees.

C Our colorful kites soared above the tall trees.

D The kites soared above the our colorful tall trees.

2. What is the correct way to write sentence 2?

F With the tails longest, the kites seemed more stable.

G The kites with the longest tails seemed more stable.

H The kites with the tails longest seemed more stable.

J The kites seemed with the longest tails more stable.

3. How does the prepositional phrase in sentence 3 function?

A as an adverb

B as a noun

C as a pronoun

D as an adjective

4. What is the correct way to write sentence 4?

F My brother stood beside me and photographed the kites.

G The kites stood beside me and photographed my brother.

H The kites beside I stood and my brother photographed.

J My brother photographed the kites and stood beside I.

5. What is the correct way to write sentence 5?

A One hundred pictures during the afternoon he must have taken.

B He must have taken one hundred pictures during the afternoon.

C He must have taken during the afternoon; one hundred pictures.

D Taken during the afternoon, he must have taken a hundred pictures.

6. What change needs to be made to sentence 6?

F Change ***will show*** to **showed**

G Change ***will show*** to **showing**

H Change ***best of the*** to **of the best**

J Change ***best of the*** to **the best of**

Name ______________________________

Fold back the paper along the dotted line. Use the blanks to write each word as it is read aloud. When you finish the test, unfold the paper. Use the list at the right to correct any spelling mistakes.

1. ____________ 1. enjoyable
2. ____________ 2. breakable
3. ____________ 3. favorable
4. ____________ 4. likable
5. ____________ 5. usable
6. ____________ 6. respectable
7. ____________ 7. affordable
8. ____________ 8. possible
9. ____________ 9. unreasonable
10. ____________ 10. laughable
11. ____________ 11. comfortable
12. ____________ 12. convertible
13. ____________ 13. invisible
14. ____________ 14. honorable
15. ____________ 15. capable
16. ____________ 16. sensible
17. ____________ 17. unbelievable
18. ____________ 18. bearable
19. ____________ 19. collapsible
20. ____________ 20. suitable

Review Words

21. ____________ 21. uniform
22. ____________ 22. bicycle
23. ____________ 23. triangle

Challenge Words

24. ____________ 24. manageable
25. ____________ 25. tangible

Name ______________________________

The suffixes ***-ible*** and ***-able*** mean "can be done."

- *flex* + *ible* = *flexible*: can be flexed
- *enjoy* + *able* = *enjoyable*: can be enjoyed

Read the spelling words aloud. Listen carefully to each syllable.

RULE REVIEW

When *-ible* or *-able* is added to a word that ends in *e*, the *e* is usually dropped before the suffix is added: *believe/believable, sense/sensible, use/usable.* Some exceptions to this rule are *manageable* and *knowledgeable,* which keep the *e.*

Write the spelling words that contain the suffix.

enjoyable	usable	unreasonable	invisible	unbelievable
breakable	respectable	laughable	honorable	bearable
favorable	affordable	comfortable	capable	collapsible
likable	possible	convertible	sensible	suitable

-able

1. ______________
2. ______________
3. ______________
4. ______________
5. ______________
6. ______________
7. ______________
8. ______________
9. ______________
10. ______________
11. ______________
12. ______________
13. ______________
14. ______________
15. ______________

-ible

16. ______________
17. ______________
18. ______________
19. ______________
20. ______________

Work with a partner to find more words that use the suffixes *-able* and *-ible*. Use a dictionary to help you. Then create a word sort using the words you found. How does each suffix change each base word?

Name ______________________________

The suffixes ***-ible*** and ***-able*** mean "can be done."

- *flex* + *ible* = *flexible*: can be flexed
- *enjoy* + *able* = *enjoyable*: can be enjoyed

Read the spelling words aloud. Listen carefully to each syllable.

RULE REVIEW

When *-ible* or *-able* is added to a word that ends in *e*, the *e* is usually dropped before the suffix is added: *believe/believable, sense/sensible, use/usable.* Some exceptions to this rule are *manageable* and *knowledgeable,* which keep the *e.*

Write the spelling words that contain the suffix.

enjoyable	usable	reasonable	invisible	erasable
breakable	respectable	laughable	fixable	bearable
favorable	readable	comfortable	capable	forcible
likable	possible	convertible	sensible	suitable

-able

1. ______________
2. ______________
3. ______________
4. ______________
5. ______________
6. ______________
7. ______________
8. ______________
9. ______________
10. ______________
11. ______________
12. ______________
13. ______________
14. ______________
15. ______________

-ible

16. ______________
17. ______________
18. ______________
19. ______________
20. ______________

Work with a partner to find more words that use the suffixes *-able* and *-ible*. Use a dictionary to help you. Then create a word sort using the words you found.

Name ______________________________

A. Write the spelling words that contain the suffix.

redeemable	observable	unreasonable	reversible	inseparable
transferable	respectable	laughable	honorable	knowledgeable
favorable	affordable	inexcusable	capable	collapsible
likable	gullible	convertible	sensible	suitable

-able

1. ____________
2. ____________
3. ____________
4. ____________
5. ____________
6. ____________
7. ____________
8. ____________
9. ____________
10. ____________
11. ____________
12. ____________
13. ____________
14. ____________
15. ____________

-ible

16. ____________
17. ____________
18. ____________
19. ____________
20. ____________

B. Compare the words *inseparable* and *unreasonable*. How are they alike? How are they different?

____

____

____

____

Work with a partner to find more words that use the suffixes *-able* and *-ible*. Use a dictionary to help you. Then create a word sort using the words you found.

Name ______________________________

enjoyable	usable	unreasonable	invisible	unbelievable
breakable	respectable	laughable	honorable	bearable
favorable	affordable	comfortable	capable	collapsible
likable	possible	convertible	sensible	suitable

A. Write the spelling word that matches each definition below.

1. impossible ________________
2. reasonable ________________
3. unbreakable ________________
4. visible ________________
5. uncomfortable ________________
6. unusable ________________
7. unable ________________
8. believable ________________

B. Write the spelling word that best completes each sentence.

9. My ________________ umbrella is easy to open and close.
10. The club's efforts to raise money for hurricane victims were ________________.
11. My brother is a ________________ person who has many friends.
12. If the weather is ________________, we will have a picnic tomorrow.
13. Mrs. Holden wore ________________ shoes, knowing she would be on her feet all day.
14. We packed our own lunches to keep our outing more ________________.
15. We had an ________________ time at the amusement park.
16. The cloth top of Dad's ________________ matches the color of the car.
17. My light jacket is not ________________ for cold, rainy days.
18. His efforts were ________________, but I doubted his real motives.
19. My small worries are ________________ compared to bigger problems!
20. Running isn't my favorite exercise, but I find it ________________.

Name ______________________________

Underline the six misspelled words in the paragraphs below. Using your knowledge of suffixes and spelling rules, write the words correctly on the lines.

Lana's parents wanted to take an affordible family vacation. They were looking for a lake cottage to rent for a rate that was not unreasonble. If possable, they wanted a place with a large, sunny porch.

1. ____________ **2.** ____________ **3.** ____________

Lana's mother found a tiny cottage that was suitible for the family. It wasn't too expensive, and it had a sunny porch that faced the water. Lana had to sleep on a collapsable cot in her sister's room, but it was bearrable. The cottage had a lot of charm, and the family enjoyed sunny days and starry nights by the lake.

4. ____________ **5.** ____________ **6.** ____________

Writing Connection

Write a passage for a story about another family vacation. Use at least four spelling words in your writing. Edit and proofread your work.

____

____

____

____

____

____

____

____

____

____

____

Name ____________________

Remember

The suffixes ***-ible*** and ***-able*** mean "can be done."

- *collapse* + *ible* = *collapsible* (drop the *e*), which means "can be collapsed"
- *respect* + *able* = *respectable,* which means "can be respected"

As you read each spelling word aloud, think about how the suffix changes the meaning of the base word.

enjoyable	usable	unreasonable	invisible	unbelievable
breakable	respectable	laughable	honorable	bearable
favorable	affordable	comfortable	capable	collapsible
likable	possible	convertible	sensible	suitable

A. Add the suffix to form a spelling word. Write the spelling word on the line.

1. break + able = ____________
2. sens + ible = ____________
3. cap + able = ____________
4. honor + able = ____________
5. convert + ible = ____________
6. afford + able = ____________
7. favor + able = ____________
8. suit + able = ____________
9. comfort + able = ____________
10. poss + ible = ____________
11. respect + able = ____________
12. bear + able = ____________
13. collaps + ible = ____________
14. enjoy + able = ____________
15. invis + ible = ____________

B. Write these spelling words on the lines in alphabetical order. Alphabetize them to the third letter. ***unreasonable, laughable, usable, likable, unbelievable***

16. ____________
17. ____________
18. ____________
19. ____________
20. ____________

Name ______________________________

Expand your vocabulary by generating synonyms.

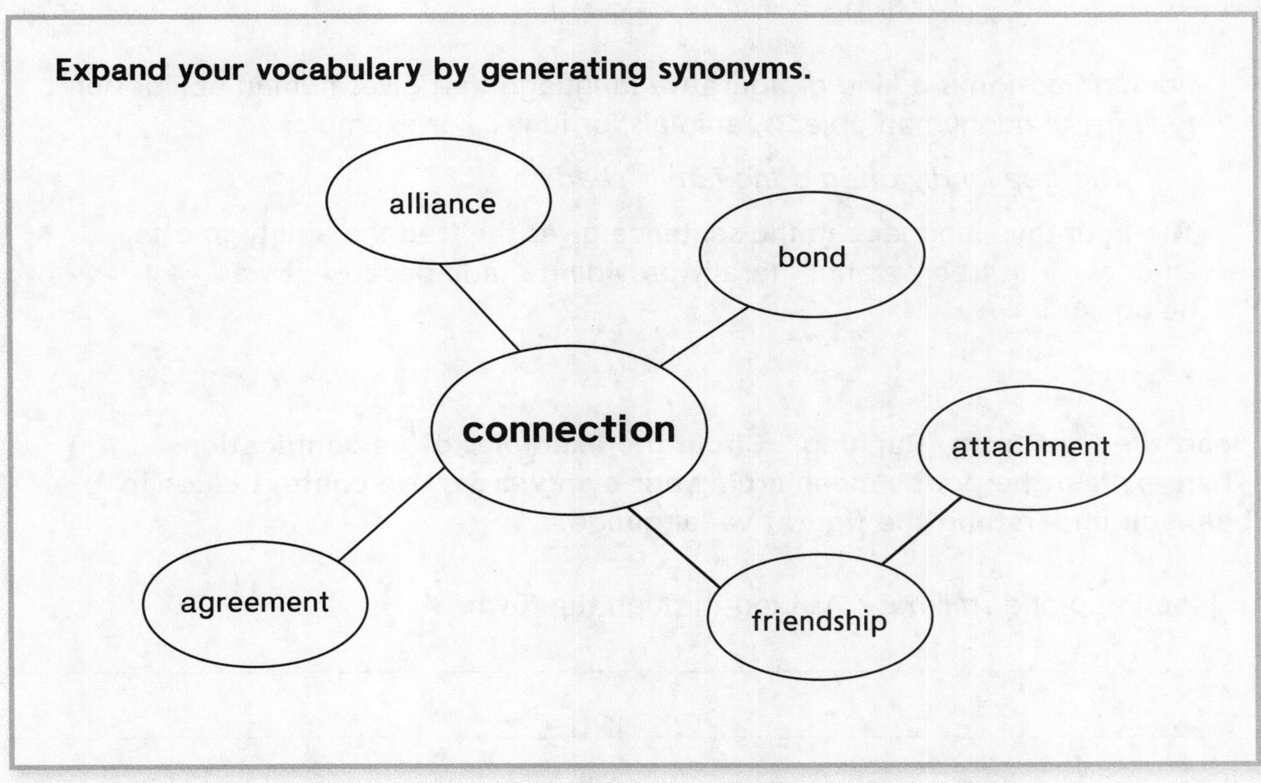

Write as many synonyms for the word *blares* as you can on the lines below. Use a thesaurus to help you.

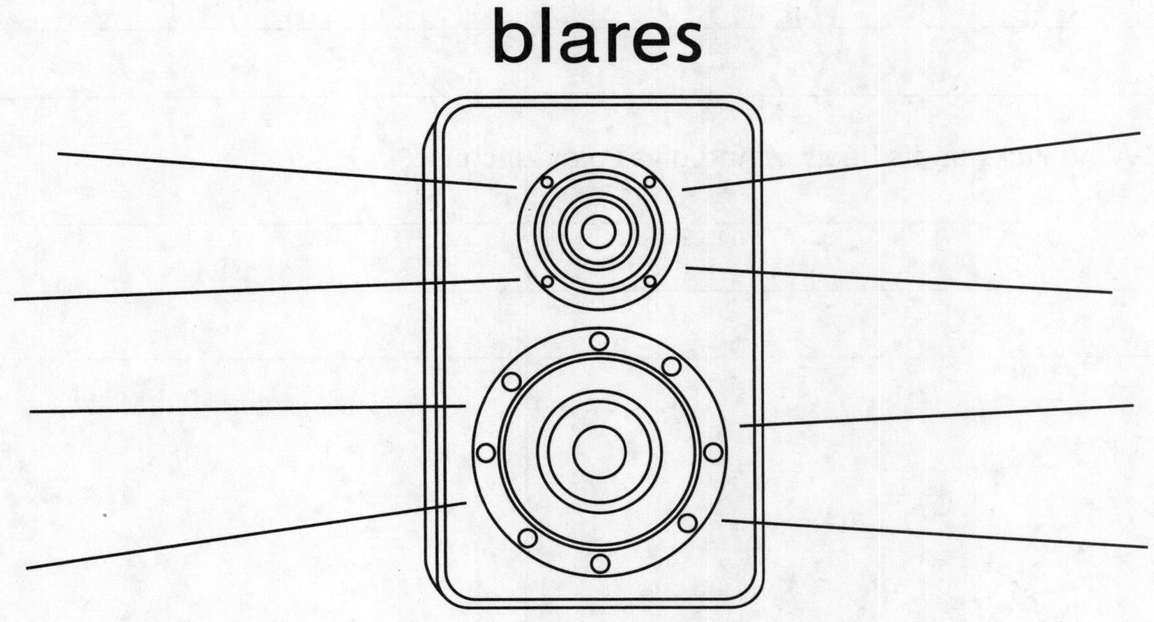

Name ____

Personification is a kind of figurative language that gives human abilities or feelings to nonhuman objects, animals, or ideas. For example:

The tree kindly offered the family shade.

The figurative language in the sentence gives the tree the ability to offer kindness. The tree was not literally providing shade because it was being kind.

Read the lines from "Running." Circle the examples of personification. Then explain the poet's meaning in your own words. Use context clues to help you understand the figurative language.

1. "Sun's up and smiling, / As I jog through the town."

____

____

____

2. "Trees all wave to me, / As I dash on by."

____

____

____

3. "Wind kicks up its heels, / And gives playful chase"

____

____

____

HANDWRITING

Table of Contents

Name ______________________ Date ____________

Cursive Writing Position

Left-Handed Writers

Sit tall. Place both arms on the table.

Keep your feet flat on the floor.

Slant your paper.

Hold your pencil with your first two fingers and your thumb.

Right-Handed Writers

Sit tall. Place both arms on the table.

Keep your feet flat on the floor.

Slant your paper.

Hold your pencil with your first two fingers and your thumb.

Name ______________________ Date ____________

The Cursive Alphabet

Aa Bb Cc Dd
Ee Ff Gg Hh
Ii Jj Kk Ll
Mm Nn Oo Pp
Qq Rr Ss Tt
Uu Vv Ww Xx
Yy Zz

Name ______________________ Date ____________

Size and Shape

Tall letters touch the top line.

Make your writing easy to read.

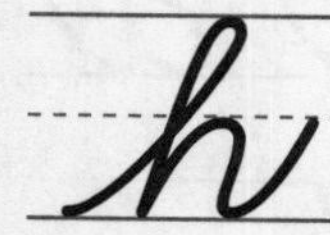

h d l t

Short letters touch the middle line.

o a n m c u w

These letters go below the bottom line.

g f z j p y

Circle the letters that are the right size and shape and sit on the bottom line.

a w h n d

g p e b l

q o f m d

Name ______________________ Date ____________

i t

Trace and write the letters. Then trace and write the word.

i i i i i i i

t t t t t t t

it it it it it

Name ______________________ Date ____________

e l

Trace and write the letters. Then write the words.

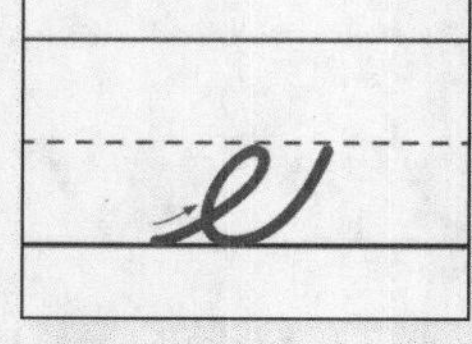

e e e e e e

l l l l l l

ill lit tie tile

Name ______________________ Date ____________

o a

Trace and write the letters. Then write the words.

o o o o o o o

a a a a a a a

toe toll tail ate

tote oil oat lot

Name ______________________ Date ____________

c d

Trace and write the letters. Then write the words and the phrases.

c c c c c c c

d d d d d d d

coat deed code

dime dance time

Name ______________________ Date ____________

n m

Trace and write the letters. Then write the words.

n n n n n n

m m m m m m

name note moat

mitten tame nine

Name ______________________ Date ____________

Connectives

Trace the connectives.

air tie her like

an and end sand

glad just yell

zebra you yarn

gap lazy game

five pick jam

feel plan quite

Name ______________________ Date ____________

u w

Trace and write the letters. Then write the words.

u u u u u u

w w w w w w

wait wit would

undo uncle lute

Name ______________________ Date __________

b f

Trace and write the letters. Then write the words and the phrases.

b b b b b b b

f f f f f f f

boat fall bubble

fine food bat ball

Name ______________________ Date ____________

h k

Trace and write the letters. Then write the words.

h h h h h h

chick hatch hook

kilt luck kite

Name ______________________ Date ______________

g q

Trace and write the letters. Then write the phrases.

g g g g g g g

q q q q q q q

quacked good game

quite a fog

Name ______________________ Date ____________

j p

Trace and write the letters. Then write the phrases.

j j j j j j j

p p p p p p p

jump for joy

picture perfect

Name ______________________ Date ____________

r s

Trace and write the letters. Then write the phrases.

r r r r r r r

s s s s s s s

rose blossom

stars and stripes

Name ______________________ Date ____________

y z

Trace and write the letters. Then write the phrases.

y y y y y y y

z z z z z z z

zip code zoom in

pretty azaleas

Name ______________________ Date ____________

v x

Trace and write the letters. Then write the phrases.

v v v v v v v

x x x x x x x

x marks the spot

vim and vigor

Name ______________________ Date ______________

Size and Shape

All uppercase letters are tall letters.
Tall letters should touch the top line.

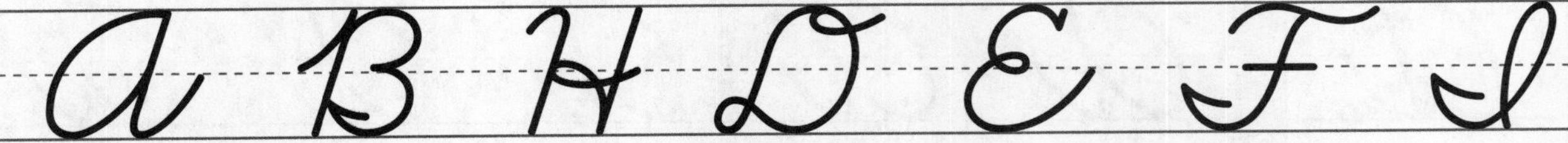

Letters with descenders go below the bottom line.

You can make your writing easy to read.

Look at the letters below. Circle the letters that are the correct size and shape.

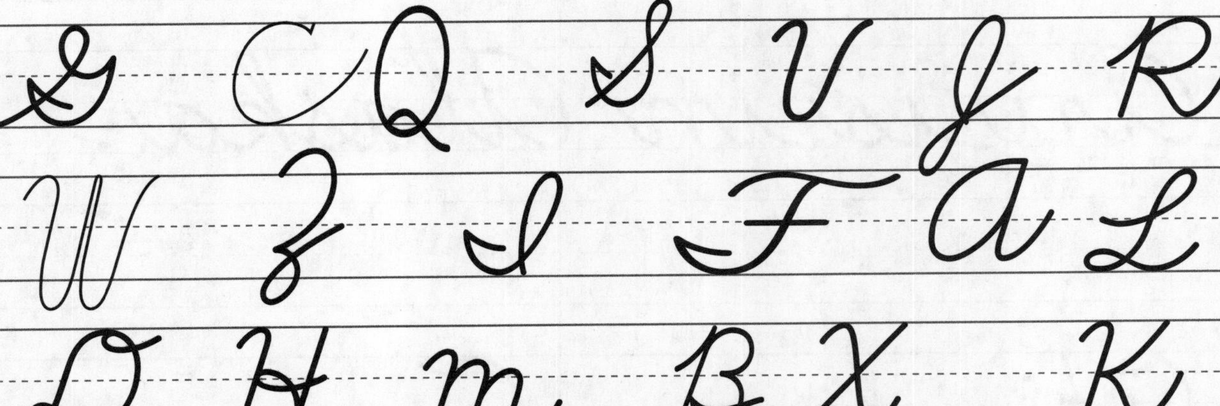

Name ______________________ Date ____________

A O

Trace and write the letters. Then write the sentences.

A A A A A A

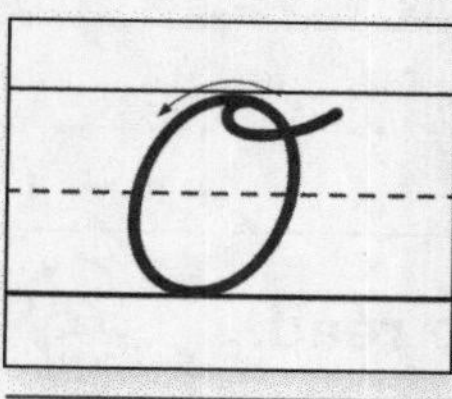

O O O O O O

Ari is in Alaska.

Otis is in Oregon.

Name ______________________ Date ____________

C E

Trace and write the letters. Then write the sentences.

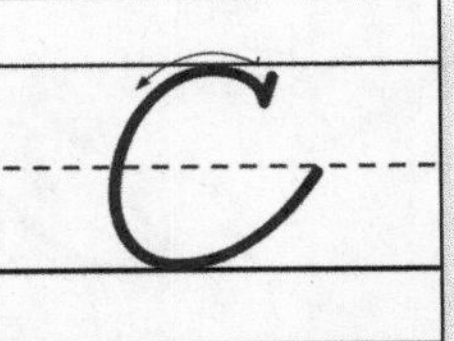
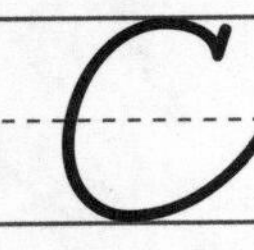
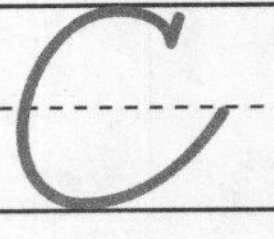
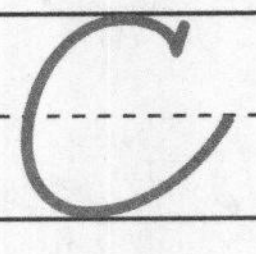
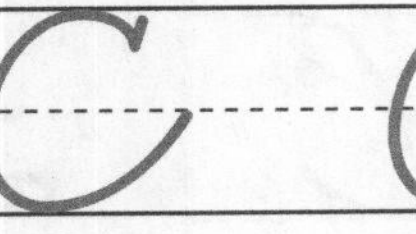

Cece visits China.

Ed is in England.

Name ____________________ Date ____________

L D

Trace and write the letters. Then write the sentences.

L L L L L L

D D D D D D

Dad did a dance.

Leo dined at Del's.

Name ____________________ Date __________

B R

Trace and write the letters. Then write the sentences.

B B B B B B

R R R R R R

Bill is in Brazil.

Rose is in Russia.

Name ______________________ Date ______________

T F

Trace and write the letters. Then write the sentences.

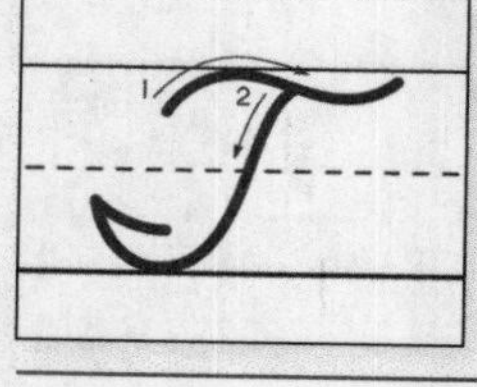

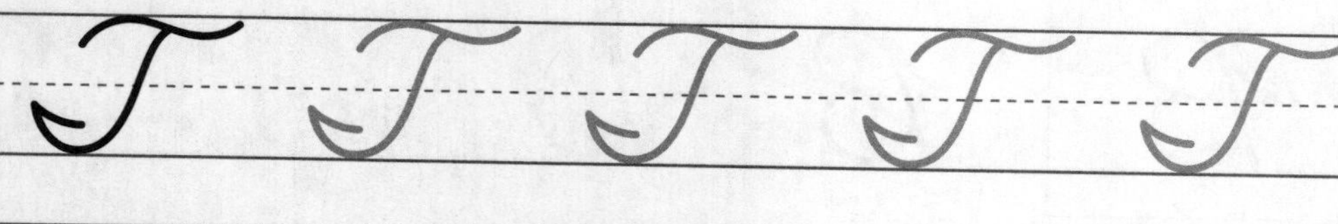

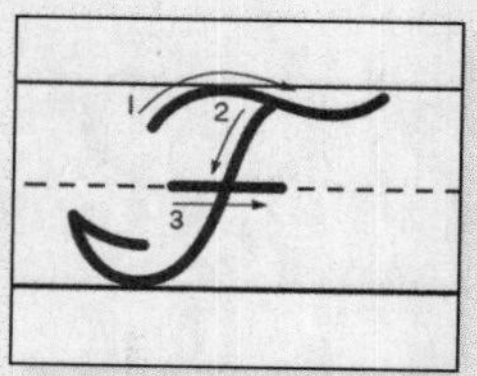

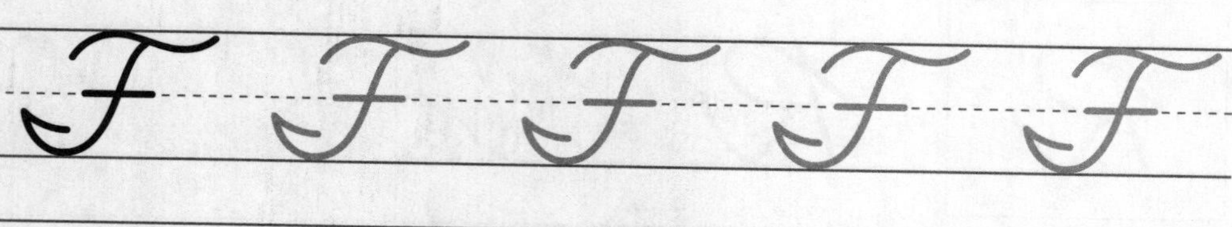

Theodore Roosevelt won. Friends cheer.

Name ______________________ Date ______________

S G

Trace and write the letters. Then write the sentences.

S S S S S S S

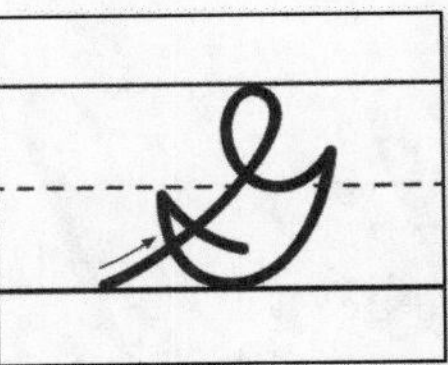

G G G G G G G

Sal Sr. met Gail.

Greg is our guest.

Name ______________________________ Date ______________

I J

Trace and write the letters. Then write the sentences.

I I I I I I I

J J J J J J J

Ida is in India.

Jack is in Japan.

Name ______________________ Date ______________

Spacing Letters and Words

You can make your writing easy to read. Letters should not be too close or too far apart.

These letters are spaced just right.

Draw a slanted line between these words to check that the spacing is as wide as a small o. Then copy the sentences.

The flowers are in bloom.

Smell the flowers!

Name ______________________ Date __________

N M

Trace and write the letters. Then write the sentences.

N N N N N N

M M M M M M

Nebraska Nevada

Minnesota Maine

Name ______________________ Date ______________

H K

Trace and write the letters. Then write the sentences.

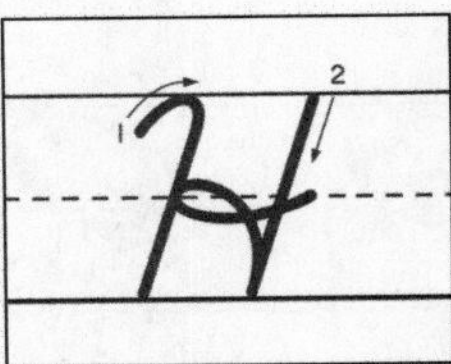

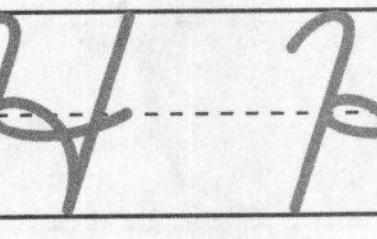

H H H H H H H

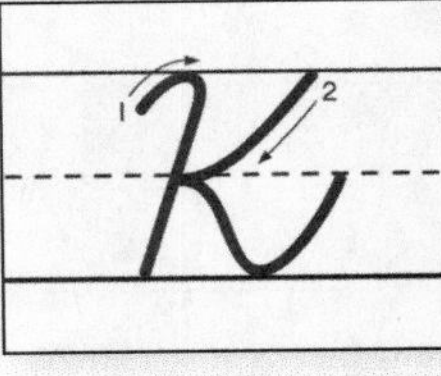

K K K K K K K

Hank likes Haiti.

Kai likes Kansas.

Name ______________________________ Date ________________

P Q

Trace and write the letters. Then write the sentences.

P P P P P P P

Q Q Q Q Q Q Q

Quebec Quin Quito

Pittsburgh Plano

Name ______________________ Date ______________

V U

Trace and write the letters. Then write the sentences.

V V V V V V

U U U U U U

Viv is in Vermont.

Ute lives in Utah.

Name ______________________ Date __________

W X

Trace and write the letters. Then write the words.

W W W W W W

X X X X X X

Will Waco Wales

Xavier Xia X-axis

Name ______________________ Date ____________

Y Z

Trace and write the letters. Then write the words.

Y Y Y Y Y Y

Z Z Z Z Z Z

Yolanda Yukon

Zena Zen Zachary

Name ______________________ Date ____________

Transition to Two Lines

Write the sentences. In the last two rows, write the sentences without the guidelines.

A robin has wings.

Ostriches run fast.

Parrots can talk.

Ducks lay eggs.

Name ______________________ Date ______________

Practice with Small Letters

This is your first complete lesson without a dotted control line. Write your letters and words the same way you have been writing them all year.

e u s r a

i w m n o

see vain mane

Sam was sure

he saw a fox.

Name ______________________ Date ______________

Practice with Tall Letters

Practice writing tall letters and words with tall letters. All tall letters should reach the top line.

t d l k h b f

fit tall doll kit

Tiff is the best.

Jill likes ducks.